WALKING TRACTOR

WALKING TRACTOR

AND OTHER COUNTRY TALES

BRUCE PATTERSON

FOREWORD BY GERALD NICOSIA

HEYDAY BOOKS, BERKELEY, CALIFORNIA
BAYTREE BOOKS

BAYTREE

This book was made possible in part by a generous grant from the BayTree Foundation.

Though everything the author has written is absolutely true in all respects no matter how you look at it, he assumes no responsibility for any inaccuracies, omissions, or inconsistencies herein. Any slights of people, landmarks, or critters, whether furred, feathered, or scaled, are entirely unintentional.

© 2008 by Bruce Patterson
Introduction © 2005 by Gerald Nicosia

Library of Congress Cataloging-in-Publication Data

Patterson, Bruce, 1949-
  [Walking tractor and other tales of Old Anderson Valley]
  Walking tractor and other country tales / Bruce Patterson ; foreword by Gerald Nicosia.
    p. cm.
  Originally published: Walking tractor and other tales of Old Anderson Valley. Boonville, CA : 4Mules Productions, 2006.
  ISBN-13: 978-1-59714-082-9 (pbk. : alk. paper)
  1. Patterson, Bruce, 1949- 2. Agricultural laborers--California--Anderson Valley--Biography. 3. Loggers--California--Anderson Valley--Biography. 4. Mountain life--California--Anderson Valley. 5. Anderson Valley (Calif.)--Biography. I. Title.
  CT275.P418A3 2008
  979.4'15053092--dc22
  [B]

                                    2007047372

Book Design and Cover Photo: Lorraine Rath
Printing and Binding: Thomson-Shore,
Dexter, MI

10 9 8 7 6 5 4 3 2 1

green press INITIATIVE

Heyday Books is committed to preserving ancient forests and natural resources. We elected to print *Walking Tractor* on 50% post consumer recycled paper, processed chlorine free. As a result, for this printing, we have saved:

11 Trees (40' tall and 6-8" diameter)
4,733 Gallons of Wastewater
1,903 Kilowatt Hours of Electricity
522 Pounds of Solid Waste
1,025 Pounds of Greenhouse Gases

Heyday Books made this paper choice because our printer, Thomson-Shore, Inc., is a member of Green Press Initiative, a nonprofit program dedicated to supporting authors, publishers, and suppliers in their efforts to reduce their use of fiber obtained from endangered forests.

For more information, visit www.greenpressinitiative.org

Thanks to my wife, Trisha, my financier, proofreader, and designated driver. Thanks also to my eldest born, Abel, my original editor, and to Lisa K. Manwill, my editor at Heyday. Special thanks to Gerald Nicosia for his encouragement and assistance, and to Bruce Anderson, Mark Scaramella, and the *Anderson Valley Advertiser* for giving me my start.

CONTENTS

A GENTLEMAN OF THE WOODS

Foreword by Gerald Nicosia

Hemingway once said, "You can only write about what you know." And the unspoken corollary of that is, if a writer is writing about himself, the character he creates will only be as authentic as he himself is. Bruce Patterson passes both those tests with flying colors.

When you meet Patterson, you wouldn't immediately take him for a writer. But then a lot of people didn't take Jack Kerouac—with his blue jeans and checkered shirts—for a writer either. Patterson is a big man; unlike a lot of big men, however, he doesn't come across as awkward but rather seems extremely comfortable in his skin. In fact, a lifetime of hard work outdoors has put him on familiar terms with just about every muscle in his body. You can tell he has used every inch of what God gave him, used it again and again, felt the pains and pleasures of it, known its strengths and limitations, and made peace with where it's taking him.

That's a lot for a man to learn, and the sad thing is that a lot of intellectuals, so called, spend a lifetime trying to learn but never actually learning just those very basics. By contrast, a lot of workingmen can't help learning them because it's part of the job—goes with the territory, as they say. The irony, of course, is that most workingmen are not able to articulate what this life in the flesh—and in God's green earth—is all about. They grunt and sigh, smile at their kids, belch after a good meal, and go to bed early to be rested for the next day's labor. But that is where Patterson is the exception.

It's hard to figure where—toting an M-60 light machinegun through the jungles of Vietnam, setting chokers and felling big-tree redwoods, building barns and fences all over Anderson Valley, as well as raising kids and being a reliable partner for his wife of thirty years—Patterson learned to write so well, but he has. His language is simple but intricate as his brain follows out each detail of a day's actions and observations—just like laying tiles in a floor, as Ford Maddox Ford once described good writing. Each word, Ford said, should be as inevitable as where you have to stick that next tile, and that's how Patterson's stories feel. He takes you with him, step by step, through the days of his life—and what is even more remarkable, he makes you feel the beauty of that life in your bones, just as he feels it.

While he's almost always writing about himself, two big themes quickly emerge in Patterson's stories. The first is the dignity of the workingman, of hard, physical labor, the kind that makes you sweat and groan and work up a well-nigh insatiable appetite—the kind that leaves your muscles aching for days, the kind that wears a man (or woman) down, not the bodybuilding of some showman in a gym or the half-hour workout of someone trying to slim their hips and stomach. This is the kind of work you might spend months recovering from. It's rare to read in serious literature accounts of people doing this kind of work that don't patronize or demean them. Steinbeck did it, of course—wrote of ordinary workingmen as if they were to be honored and respected as much as knights and princes. And Bukowski wrote of workingmen as if they are the essential cogs that keep the world turning. Patterson does both.

The second big theme is his love of country—of hills, ravines, creeks, clouds, hawks, ocean winds, and, above all, stands of giant redwoods. Like any lover, he knows the country he lives and works in—every inch of it, every aspect, every hidden secret—as if it were the body of some woman he's loved well and will never forget. I remember walking through Hendy Woods State Park near Boonville with him, and him showing me a thousand things I might otherwise have missed—like "barber chairs," redwoods that split dangerously down the middle as they were falling, and the heartwood of long-fallen redwood trunks that you could carve posts out of that would last a thousand years "if you keep them dry"—pointing all this out as if he were a rich man proudly showing me his million-dollar living room.

First off, he made me appreciate the extraordinary quiet at the base of a group of sky-high redwoods. Almost pinned there by the weight of that hush, as I looked up at the blinding light streaming into the huge cavern of forest darkness, I couldn't help but feel I was inside a cathedral. But Patterson brought me out of that reverie with an immediate laugh, telling me it took two men and a boy to see to the top of those lean, shaggy, still-growing titans. That is the other thing that enriches both his talk and his writing—his love for the native myth of woods and country—the art of local storytelling and, above all, the tall tale that so fascinated Mark Twain. If you're a bit too serious, or you're not prepared to read about coyotes who go joyriding in pickup trucks or herons that give each other the skinny on where to get the best fast-food frogs, you just might find yourself walking off a cliff in one of Patterson's stories.

But Patterson isn't just a humorist, and he isn't just one of what they call the "West Coast bucolic" writers. Like Twain, unquestionably one of his heroes, Patterson's stories show a profound social conscience. That's hardly surprising considering the years he put in with the Vietnam Veterans Against the War as a peace activist or the time he spent in the South doing civil rights work. He also did enough time as a poor kid, a street thug and outcast because of his stutter, on the gang-ridden streets of L.A. to understand that a lot of what a person becomes is determined not by genetics or a democratic form of government but by the money in your pocket and the power—whether in fist or by way of influence—that you can wield over others. In "Stomping Fleeces," as in many of the stories, there is the profound understanding—of one who has been there himself—of how the system conspires to keep poor people poor. "Working the plantation type of agriculture like they've got down there in the San Joaquin, it didn't take me long to figure out that there was no future in it," he writes. "To the contrary, the longer you stayed a farm worker, the poorer you got." It's clear that he writes not just because he wants to document what so many millions in the underclass have to go through every day but also because he believes in the power of the truth to make a difference—to wise people up, to give them the means and, yes, the power, to change their own lives for the better.

For sure, Patterson is an angry man. He's angry at the death and pain that's still happening from the Vietnam War, and he's angry at the new wave of needless death and pain that's currently being inflicted by the American government in Iraq. You'll hear his voice rise, and just about see his hackles raised on the back of his neck, when he talks of such things. Patterson, clearly, is not a man you want to anger too far, but he's not a brawler, and his weapon of choice is the written word. He told me he worries that he comes on "too macho," but the truth is I found him one of the gentlest men I'd ever met—a lot more like Hoss Cartwright than Big Bad Leroy Brown.

This is a man who will delicately fondle a stone pestle he found in his garden one day, and whose voice will crack with emotion when he shows you the stepping-stones that he made by hand with Ensenada rocks he gathered on Baja beaches with his Irish grandmother. He carted those thirty-pound stones by hand all over the country, to wherever he's lived, to preserve them; and if you ask, you'll find there's a story there too—for stories seem to be embedded in everything that surrounds the man. He'll tell you how during his formative years this grandmother was his surrogate mother, and how she died suddenly when he was just back from Vietnam, still recuperating in an army hospital.

This gentle giant is also the man who has wandered the hills of Anderson Valley for thirty-two years listening to every story an old person would tell him, so that he can preserve their words and their lives for posterity. He is the secret planter of four thousand redwood trees in a much-scarred creekside valley near his home, so that generations to come will know the same beauties of a massive redwood forest that he has known—though they will never know the quiet, loving conscience of the man who planted them. And he is the man who once helped lift an entire 1868 Anderson Valley barn several feet off the earth so that they could put a real, lasting concrete foundation under it, making sure it would last at least another century or so.

It's evident that what Patterson is doing in his stories is very much the same kind of effort. He has loved all the places he's been, and all the people he's met—from Lester Seymour, the "catskinner" who taught him how to rig a "straight hook" of logs and "pop them out of the woods" without getting himself killed; even to "old Leon," who got him "accidentally drunk," then ditched him by the side of the road and made him walk home several miles in the middle of the night—so much that he wants to keep them going for at least another century or so, at least in the minds and hearts of those who've been lucky enough to receive his memories, through ink on paper, as their own.

• • •

Gerald Nicosia is the author of the award-winning *Memory Babe: A Critical Biography of Jack Kerouac*. His most recent book is *Home to War: A History of the Vietnam Veterans' Movement*. Nicosia's poetry and literary criticism have been widely published, and he has taught writing, journalism, Beat literature, and Vietnam literature at the University of Illinois at Chicago and UCLA. A native of Chicago, he lives in the San Francisco Bay Area and is currently at work on a biography of Ntozake Shange.

Occasionally a young-buck timber faller, having worked hard while pounding wedges to lift and tip a big redwood tree his way, and having bellowed out his final warning to anyone who might be nearby on the canyonside, whether by hollering/yodeling, "SIDE—AAH-HEE-ILLL!" or "YUP DEE HEE-YI-IILLLL!" (nobody ever hollered "Tim-Burr"), at the last second out at the end of his lay he'd catch sight of a Cat bulldozer crawling up the mountain like a yellow jacket. And instantly the young buck had to decide: Do I wait for the machine to pass out of my way, or should I let her rip and have some fun?

So the young buck lets her rip and the top of his tree comes down like a giant flyswatter. As the treetop shatters in the pulverized dirt of the skid trail just uphill from the Cat, it sends up a billowing white cloud of dust that envelops the tractor and covers it, the front side of the "catskinner," his felt Fedora hat, water jug, and feed bucket with a thick coating of talcum powder.

The young buck leaps aboard his stump and stretches his neck in the direction of the commotion he's caused. As the cloud of dust clears he sees the catskinner, an elderly fellah with a big potbelly and splayed suspenders, standing atop his stalled tractor track and—him knowing full well that young-buck timber fallers ain't above missing a lay by a few degrees to one way or the other—he's violently shaking his fist and furiously spitting and hissing like a barn cat with its tail stuck in the door.

And the young buck lets the old man blow off steam until he's out of steam and then, as the panting old man pauses to catch his breath and to gather in his head more epitaphs to hurl, the young buck hollers back at him, "Calm down, you old mule. I didn't hit yaw."

Or maybe some fellahs on the rigging crew are gathered for lunch next to the creek and, way up on the canyonside and looking not much bigger than a tick on a dog, there's an elderly timber faller swinging his ax-head into his set of wedges stuck in the back-cut of his tree. He's whacking his wedges like piano keys while futilely trying to lift his six-foot-thick, two-hundred-and-fifty-foot-tall, downhill-leaning redwood tree up the hill and into its lay. And, because the old man had underestimated the strength of the tree's downhill lean, all through lunch the fellahs eating next to the creek hear him up there relentlessly pounding his wedges, his sweat stinging his eyes, his body weakening, the palms of his hands bruising and swelling and the loud *cracks* made by his ax-head striking home echoing up and down the canyon like gunshots.

Suddenly booms a thunderous explosion of shattering wood; an ear-splitting, gut-grabbing *bang* that doesn't sound like a bomb going off but something rising from the bowels of the earth. Instantly everybody's eyes are glued to the scene as the big tree topples backward over the tops of the wedges and begins its long fall toward the creek. Simultaneously the old-timer, potbelly, bowed legs, bent back and all, runs for his life with the grace of a scampering deer.

After the tree impacts the forest floor and ends its slide down the canyonside, after the commotion of swinging trees, tumbling rocks, falling limbs, and dust dies down, a dog-faced catskinner in the lunch crowd deadpans to the others gathered around: "I knew that old mule wouldn't let that liddle-biddy pecker pole whip him."

Among big-tree redwood lumberjacks, being called a mule wasn't an insult but a compliment. Mules were stronger, more surefooted and courageous than horses, and they've always played a big part in logging the redwoods. When diesel power replaced the four-legged kind of mule, that left the two-legged kind and, even today, up along California's North Coast, holed up in the nooks and crannies about as far away as they can get from a main road, you'll still find them. You'll find two-legged mules complete with suspenders and felt Fedora hats.

WALKING TRACTOR

STOMPING FLEECES

At last, at the ripe old age of twenty-four, I'd found myself a job I could quit without starving. I wouldn't be starving because for once I'd lined up a job to replace the one I'd be quitting, and this was my last day stomping fleeces, thank God, though nobody on the crew knew it yet. It wasn't just any new job I'd landed, either, but one, what with all of the overtime I'd be working, that would be paying me twice as much money as I was making with this sheep-shearing bunch. Not only that but my new job, "setting choker" (whatever that meant) on a logging operation, was supposed to be fun.

For over a year I'd been kicking around California as a farm worker, and I'd helped plant, tend to, and harvest a bunch of crops. Never once during that time had I ever turned up my nose to any job if it was the best thing going. Down there in the San Joaquin Valley south of Fresno, I'd bucked hay in the pounding heat of August. My partner and I would weave our twenty-four-foot-long White brand flatbed truck through freshly cut and baled fields of alfalfa, snare the bales with our elevator, hook and stack them on the truck seven tier high, and rope them down with butterflies. After getting weighed at a crossroads truck scale, we'd deliver the load to a neighbor, stack it in his barn and, because we didn't own the truck, for it all we'd each get paid eight cents a bale. For doing two truckloads a day, one starting at first light and the other finished by dark (we'd siesta through the worst of the heat), together we made about fifty bucks.

I'd harvested raisin grapes down by Caruthers, onions outside

1

Raisin City, and table grapes over by Dinuba. Under the flinty-eyed San Joaquin sun, I'd hoed row crops eight hours a day. During an onion harvest I worked surrounded by old Mexican gals on a mechanical field sorter so loud it could have been a logging truck tumbling ass over teakettle down a rocky canyonside, what with its gas-powered engine's popping, coughing, and sputtering, its clanking chains, squealing belts, gears, and levers, rattling joints and jiggling wire-mesh floors. It took about ten of us working our arms like an octopus to keep that contraption happy, and the old gals (the young ones were bent over in the fields) had to just about shout to make themselves heard. When they got to gossiping over the racket of that machine, they'd sound like brass-lunged opera singers.

"And lovely Maria the Madonna, that ill-bred floozy, she stole poor Conchita's man away, the no-good vato."

"Maria shall pay, she shall."

"Somewhere along the way, they both shall pay."

All night long I'd switched over flood irrigation in alfalfa fields, sometimes surrounded by swarms of mosquitoes so thick they'd make the stars flicker. So many damned mosquitoes you'd think it was they you were watering and you who'd been set into the dirt as food. Or sometimes a ground squirrel or a badger would burrow through one of your little dirt levees ("checks") and cause a leak that might become a flood unless you spotted it quick enough and managed to plug it with the mud dug up, flung, and smacked into the breach with the backside of your shovel. Racing the eroding, widening hole, your shovel flashing in the moonlight, your sweat glistening, it was like you were calling the mosquitoes home for supper.

Under the sun and down on my knees bent beside a canal filled with Sierra melt water, I'd set so many camel-backed aluminum irrigation pipes—you'd swish them back and forth in the canal to fill them with water to create a siphon before dropping the bottom end down like a high-pressure faucet into a furrow while keeping the top end submerged in the canal—that when I was done and streams of water were pouring down the rows and it was time for me to get back up on my feet, I'd have to be careful not to hurt my back just like I was some kind of old man.

Working the plantation type of agriculture like they've got down there in the San Joaquin, it didn't take me long to figure out that there was no future in it. To the contrary, the longer you stayed a farm worker, the poorer you got. That was because about the only time of year you made out was during harvest season, when the growers, in order to get their crops in quickly and reliably, paid you piecemeal, be it by the pound, the tray, the lug, or the bin. But to take advantage of the piecemeal rate, you'd need to be busting your ass. With winter and the mud coming and jobs about to get scarce, to maybe get up a little nest egg to help to see you through 'til spring, you'd bust your ass seven days a week if they'd let you.

So every harvest season, at least if you were nominally ambitious or had mouths to feed, you'd bust your ass and that took its toll on your body. As you got older your production, and so your income, dropped. Your income dropped even as the price of everything you needed kept going up. And that's what I meant when I said that the longer you stayed a farm worker, the poorer you got.

Naturally I'd worked jobs better than those. In Napa Valley I'd helped tear down a nineteenth-century horse ranch to make way for a vineyard. In Calistoga I'd helped build a trailer park atop some busted old pioneer's worn-out vineyard. Further north in Knights Valley, there in the sunrise shadow of the old volcano called Mount St. Helena, I'd planted wine grapes. Still farther north in Alexander Valley, out by Jimtown, I'd pruned sixty-year-old, free-standing head vines decorating rolling, grassy green hills with the sounds of tumbling creeks and birdsongs filling my ears. Along the Russian River between Chalk Hill Road and River Bend, I worked grapes, plums, and peppers. I'd torn down barns and I'd done the grunt work of installing irrigation systems shaped like underground checkerboards. I'd helped maintain dikes along the water's edge and I'd stood and watched as wood ducks and Canadian geese, herons and ospreys used the river as a highway.

One late autumn afternoon up by Asti, after the last of the year's grapes had been brought in and an autumn chill filled the air, I saw pulsating clouds of starlings flying like silly putty. They were flying like splatters of water, or water balloons getting squeezed and stretched. With tens of thousands of wing-to-wing individuals switching this way and that, pinwheeling with you seeing the undersides of their wings flashing between flickering glimpses of their topsides, the swarm barreling east, west, up and down, back and forth into the distance, it was amazing they never crashed into each other or said a word.

As a young man and recently returned Vietnam veteran, I wanted only the sorts of outdoor jobs I could quit, and farm labor sure fit that bill. If I hired on to operate a shovel and the boss didn't like the way I was doing it, I'd hand him his shovel and allow him to have his own go at it to see if he could do any better. First and foremost, I was after a hobo's freedom, to make it plain; that and cheap entertainment. I wasn't particular about the sorts of jobs I took because, loving novelty, I knew I wouldn't be at them for long.

And more or less that's how, in the spring of 1974, I wound up stuffed into the cab of an old pickup truck rattling down a nameless dirt road in the backlands of the Cooley Ranch, way out there west of Cloverdale along the trackless southern edge of Mendocino County. I was squeezed between two hefty "Port-ah-geeze" (that's what the local ranchers called them) sheep shearers, and the road was so washboarded that our teeth were clattering. The Cooley Ranch had more bumpy dirt roads leading nowhere than a busted and undeveloped "lakeside" subdivision in the Mojave Desert, and over the previous few days it seemed we'd bounced up and down about every one of them.

I'd just moved to a ranch out by Yorkville and so to get to work in the morning I needed to negotiate the narrow, twisty road leading down the mountain to Cloverdale. I'd park my car among the idling big rigs in the beaten dirt field outside Lee's Wheel Café, which was about the only place in town that was open two hours before sunrise. Inside the Wheel—a dozen-seat lunch counter with a couple of small Formica tables stuffed in back for the accidental tourists—I sipped scalding, mud-black coffee and waited for the rest of the crew to assemble.

Since the last man to walk through the door of the Wheel always arrived just when the honcho was itching to go, seeing the lollygagger arrive was the signal for the rest of us to line up at the cash register, pay our tabs, and then, after the straggler had gone to the bathroom, gotten himself a cup of coffee to go, and rejoined us, huddle outside in the murky darkness. After the day's seating had been arranged—two pickups if the crew was six, three if it was seven—we'd continue our journey.

South of town we turned onto a dirt road that took us up and over the scraggly ridge to the west. On the other side we'd meet up with Yorty Creek and meander downstream along beside it until we came to the main canyon at Dry Creek. Next we'd turn either up or downstream, maybe travel some miles, then climb some grazed/grassy ridge and, out in the middle of nowhere, arrive at a redwood sheep-shearing shed. Attached to the shed would be maybe an acre of redwood-plank holding and sorting corrals, and they'd be stuffed with hundreds of loudly bawling sheep.

All and all it might have taken us two hours to arrive at what must have been the noisiest spot in the wilderness. And for all that time we didn't get paid a penny. Nor did we get paid eight or ten hours later when we made our way back out of there, reached blacktop, returned to Lee's Wheel to fetch our rigs, or to drop off our passengers, and then continued on to our homes.

My dad claimed that the most foolish thing a workingman could do was to give away his labor. Having nothing else worth selling, and having only a limited amount of that because there were only so many hours in a day, and only so much one man could do, by giving away your labor you were helping to ensure that'd always be true in your case. If charity didn't begin at home, my dad warned, then chances were I'd see none.

Yet, in spite of my dad's sound advice, there I was putting in some twenty hours a week in travel time squeezed between two hefty Port-ah-geeze fellahs and getting nothing for it. Not only was I not getting paid but, riding with this sheep-shearing bunch, I stood no prospect of them ever so much as standing me an after-work mug of beer.

The honcho of the outfit was the elderly scion of an old pioneering family who rarely uttered a word. Tall and lanky with leathery skin, his straw Stetson hat, sandy gray hair, quiet blue eyes, and pearl white dentures were set against his dark red hillbilly tan. He wore baggy jeans with a big silver belt buckle, a long-sleeved zip-up shirt, and logger's boots—not calks but the kind with rubber soles and super traction; good footing makes wrestling the animals a tad bit easier.

I'd heard the honcho was about the best damned sheep shearer there was in these parts. Then again, I'd heard the same about one of his three Port-ah-geeze sidekicks, though which one it was I couldn't say because they were brothers, they all looked alike, worked the same, and never gabbed much. Riding, working, and sitting down to lunch with those fellahs gave me the feeling that they preferred to allow the sheep to do their talking for them. The sheep that for some reason never seemed to stop their bawling.

The lack of gab inside the pickup truck I came to accept and to not take personally. If they didn't want to talk, fine by me. The silence gave me a chance to sink into the passing scenery, to maybe see things in the landscape I might not have noticed if we'd been yakking all the time.

What was impressive about the Cooley Ranch was that it was Tex-assed sized. Inside this one private estate, which I guess was just one holding inside some family dynasty's portfolio, you saw a bit of everything. In the grassy bottomlands stood valley oaks as wide as they were tall. Up in the shadier nooks and crannies grew lush stands of redwood and Doug fir, tanoak and red madrone. Dry Creek and some of the feeder creeks were running with salmon and steelhead (this was before the building of Warm Springs Dam and the flooding). Here and there were volcanic outcroppings, Indian signs, and rockslides. Pointing like boney fingers were box canyons hiding serpentine cliffs and feathery seasonal waterfalls. Also there were steep, wrinkled scrublands fit only for vermin.

One day while following a road atop a tall ridge I saw, maybe a half mile away and a thousand feet below, a canyon so narrow and steep that even grass couldn't keep a hold of it. The canyon's exposed soils were striped in hues of red, pink, and yellow. And switchbacking along the bottom of the defile like an etched green line were willows just budding out and old redwoods making their own spots of shade. And it occurred to me that in the whole history of the world not many people had ever spread out a bedroll under those trees.

I was tempted to elbow the others and point out the hole to them. But I didn't because I thought all they'd likely do was take a gander and grunt. The brothers took turns with the driving and the one whose turn it was to sit shotgun did his best to sleep, or to at least rest his eyes and neck. To say that they were not interested in the scenery would be about right. Then, on a road like we were bouncing on, in order to take a good safe gander into the canyon the driver would have to stop the rig, and he wasn't about to do that just on general principle.

I'd be lying if I said I learned anything about Port-ah-geeze just by riding with those three. They say, back when about any grassy opening between Santa Rosa and Eureka was dappled with sheep, cattle, or horses, Port-ah-geeze shepherds were about as common as *ki*-oats around here. As for these guys, they were short, barrel-chested, black-haired, and swarthy. Whether their darkness of skin had to do with living out in the hills shepherding sheep or their ethnicity, I couldn't tell. For all I knew, strip them naked and, excepting the reds on their faces, the backs of their necks, and the tops of their hands, they'd be as pale-assed and "olive-skinned" as the rumor said they were.

Actually, I did learn a little bit about those three Port-ah-geeze brothers. For what it's worth, they didn't talk much, they could catch a little shut-eye while sitting beside a green crew working green chain in a highballing lumber mill, they worked like maniacs, they didn't like sheep, and they didn't believe in wasting their wage on after-work treats.

I don't know what it was about sheepmen, though I suspect it had to do with how they were portrayed in Hollywood movies. In the movies you saw these ruff-tuff cattlemen who'd single-handedly conquered the West. The cattlemen were king and they laid claim to all they could see in all directions. Out of the Wilderness and with their own hands they'd scraped out their little Empires, and from the high ground on their spreads you could see their herds stretched out to the horizon, their hand-hewn barns and sheds, bunkhouses and main houses, and all was peaceful on the land.

Then came these docile little central European peasant immigrants with their round wives and herds of towheaded little children. These "nesters" showed you papers that proved they'd bought your land from the railroad, or from the railroad's government, and so they had free and clear title to all you'd worked for. And, if that weren't bad enough, they also brought along their wooly little four-legged locusts and, once their sheep were through with your pastures, the land was no longer fit for cattle, horses, or anything else.

In the name of first come, first served, you went to war against them to drive them and their locusts from your land. But during your war you discovered that the invaders had brought with them things far worse than sheep, barbed wire, clapboard churches, and loathsome fields of corn and soybeans.

They brought The Law. They brought Civilization.

About every Western movie I ever saw, while pretending to sympathize with the cowering, weak-kneed "squatters," always glorified the wealth, ruthlessness, and machismo of the Cattle Barons. Even if, as usual, they were depicted as cads, still you wanted to be a cattleman and not a sheepman, a baron and not a squatter, a cowboy and not a shepherd.

The sheepmen I came to know over the years (they didn't used to be so scarce in these hills) were, putting aside the particulars to their way of life, the same as anybody else and in the same combinations. Yet almost to a man they were quieter than most. It was like they thought words, like their stores of physical energy during shearing season, weren't to be wasted on trifles. Which helped explain why when a sheepman did speak to you, you could do worse than to listen.

Take the honcho. Everything about him said "integrity," and if you questioned it, then you'd have a fight on your hands. Question the honcho's integrity and you may as well question his love for his family, or his dedication to his great-grandpa's land. The honcho was running a sheep-shearing outfit to help get up the money to hold on to his family's homestead, and that's about all you needed to know about him. Ranching was never easy and seldom profitable, but the honcho didn't give a damn about easy and he was used to unprofitable. The way he saw things, he had something far more valuable than creature comforts or money. He had his land, and with it came a heritage that was a way of life that allowed him to be his own man.

So in a sense the honcho was in the same predicament I was in. As the price of lamb, mutton, and wool kept dropping, the price of everything else kept going up. As the years went on, more and more he'd need to farm himself out, and the more he did that, the less time he had on his own spread and the less he was his own man.

Folks like the honcho were called "land rich." Among other things, that meant they could run as many sheep, cattle, or zebras as they wanted and still not make out on the homesteads they saw as their birthrights. The blood, sweat, and worry that went into providing food and clothing for people—why, they saw that as a part of their lot and they didn't complain much about it. They just worked harder is all. And still they couldn't make it.

Yet, when they were home and the chores were done and they went off to be alone at a favorite spot on their ranch, be it a Worry Log beside a creek, or a Thinking Rock up on a canyonside, they passed by the relics left by their kin. They might go and sit next to where their family erected their first lean-to back in 1855. Or they might go and sit next to their favorite grandpa's grave in the family cemetery. While eating lunch, they might rest their backs against the stump of the redwood tree that provided the lumber to build their homestead's first main house. Among the hand-dug wells, nurtured springs, split-rail pasture fences and shake-shingled barns and sheds, redwood windmills and water tanks, they might pass by the place where they themselves first got thrown from a horse, or first got kissed.

But, wherever they went to get alone, it wasn't like they were turning on a TV to escape the world. Alone in their special places, they reconnected with it.

• • •

A sheep-shearing operation was simple enough. Out in the corrals might be one or three guys whose job it was to sort and manhandle the sheep into this box or that box to await their haircuts. Inside the shed was a long wood-floored hallway where the shearing got done. At one end of the hallway was a blanket-covered chute stuffed with bawling "woolies" (so scared and out of sorts were the sheep that they'd never get close enough to touch that spooky, hanging blanket). Also, next to each of the shearers was a blanket-covered open stall that served as an exit door for the shell-shocked sheep that'd just gotten the treatment.

After a shearer was finished with one sheep, he'd walk down the hallway, throw aside the blanket, and grab ahold of the critter that was most handy. He wouldn't do it like he was picking up a kitten, either. He'd grab the sheep by the scruff of its neck, drag it down the hallway, knock its feet out from under it, pin it to the floor with a Vulcan death grip, and proceed to give it a nose-to-ass haircut. Next, without even allowing the poor scalped and nicked-up creature to regain its feet, he'd half-yank and half-toss it into the exit. Then he'd go and fetch his next victim.

The whole process seemed sort of cruel to me. At first I thought it might have to do with the Port-ah-geeze "national character" or something. But watching the honcho work the sheep cured me of that illusion. When the honcho threw aside the blanket to fetch his next victim, a big wooly buck would take one look at him and want to drop his fleece right there.

I was told that sheep didn't feel pain, terror, or humiliation the way us people do. That was on account of sheep having simple minds. A sheep's whole universe was divided into Food and Unfood, and his whole philosophy of life consisted of, "When in Unfood, go to Food. When in Food, stay."

Or, as the old bandit's saw went, "If God hadn't wanted them to get fleeced, He wouldn't have made them sheep."

The four shearers averaged over one hundred head per day per man. That meant that on a good day close to five hundred head got run through the process and left their fleeces on the floor. From there the fleeces would get wadded up into a ball by the "tyer." The tyer would pin a fleece with a knee, wrap a length of twine around it, and tie it off like he was in a rodeo roping steer. Then he'd grab it and toss it up into the loft that was suspended above the end of the hallway opposite the sheep's entry.

Since I was the greenhorn on the crew, my work station was up in the loft. In the middle of the loft's floor was a circular hole, and clamped open inside of it was a burlap cotton bag that hung nearly down to the floor. Maybe thirty-six inches in diameter and eight feet long, each bag held anywhere from far too few to never too many fleeces. When the tyer threw a balled fleece up into the loft, I'd catch it and drop it into the bag. When I judged the time was right, I'd jump into the bag and start stomping the fleeces with my feet, flattening them into the corners and along the edges of the bag. Then I'd look up to see what I'd have to do to get myself back up into the loft. If I'd judged right, I'd be able to reach up and grab ahold of the edges of the hole and, using the fleeces as a floor to leap from, get myself up to where my upper body was propped up in the loft on my braced arms. From there it was a simple matter of squeezing either one or the other of my knees up through the hole, propping it on the floor and, using it as a lever, freeing the rest of my body from the bag.

But if I'd judged wrong, then I'd have to do a chin-up. Once I had my head and fingertips peeking through the hole, I'd prop myself up on one elbow, my feet kicking, then the other, one hand, then the other, and so on until I was again free of the bag and ready to start over.

Or—sometimes this happened, but never to me, thank God—if you couldn't escape the bag using your own power, you'd have to holler for help.

One valuable thing I did learn while stomping fleeces was where lanolin comes from. Being a child of the 1950s, I'd grown up watching soap commercials on TV that glorified the cleansing and beautifying and life-enhancing powers of lanolin. To hear the TV tell it, store-bought soap was the fountain of youth and lanolin was the essence of its precious, purifying waters. Never in a million years would I have guessed that lanolin was nothing more than sheep sweat.

Come my last lunchtime, we spread out in the nearest shady oak grove as usual. We rested our backs against tree trunks, except for the tyer, who lay down propped up on one elbow. With the bawling sheep so close by, we didn't talk much. I suppose we could have moved farther away and found a sound break to get us some peace and quiet, but the others never seemed to think it'd be worth it.

When about halfway through lunch I loudly announced that this day was my last, I gathered everybody's attention. Judging by their shocked expressions, you'd have thought none of them had ever before heard of anybody up and quitting a sheep-shearing outfit. They looked at me like I'd just announced I was gay or, while they'd been distracted by the contents of their lunch boxes, I'd up and grown myself two heads.

They all looked to the honcho to see what he thought. Which, at first, didn't seem like much. The honcho carefully poured himself a cup of steaming coffee, replaced the cap on his thermos, leaned back against the trunk of his big wide oak tree, and sighed. For maybe three minutes he sipped his coffee and seemed to gaze at nothing in particular. Finally he looked me in the eye and quietly said, "We've only got a few days to go. When you hired on, you said you'd finish the job. Now you've changed your mind."

Until that moment I'd found it convenient to believe the honcho would have no trouble replacing me. I mean, how hard could it be to find somebody able to stomp fleeces? It wasn't like you needed any special training or equipment. But now, given the honcho's words and tone of voice, it seemed I'd miscalculated.

I began to apologize, but the honcho cut me short. He said he'd stomp fleeces his own self if he had to. Hell, he'd shear, tie, toss, and stomp fleeces to boot if he took a mind. So it wasn't about how they were going to do without me. They'd do just fine and I needn't worry about that. Instead it was about my word and what it was worth, which couldn't be much unless I gave it with utmost seriousness.

I meekly explained that I hadn't been looking for a job and how I'd never have taken this one if it hadn't've fallen into my lap and if it didn't pay me twice as much money.

And then the honcho said something I'll never forget. He said, "Chokersetting jobs are a dime a dozen."

• • •

About a decade later I happened upon the honcho in Cloverdale's old Penny Faire market. I remember being surprised by how much the honcho had aged. Going from sixty to seventy years old, I saw, was different than going from twenty-four to thirty-four. The honcho didn't recognize me until I bashfully reminded him that I was the greenhorn who'd quit him out there on the Cooley Ranch all those years before.

The honcho's eyes lit with recognition and he smiled. How were the woods, by golly? Was I still a lumberjack?

Impulsively, as if he hadn't gotten the message first time around, I again apologized for having quit him like I had.

At first he didn't understand. Then he slowly shook his head and said dismissively, "Don't you go and sweat it now. If I'd have been a young man in your boots, I'd have done the same thing."

He touched the rim of his Stetson hat with a finger, wished me luck, and went back to his grocery shopping.

I stood there and watched the honcho shrink down the aisle and I knew the old geezer had just told me one bald-faced lie.

SLINGING STEEL

It wasn't like I was a stranger to adventure. When I was six or seven years old, running ahead of my family down the trail from the top of Yosemite Falls, I almost got eaten by a bear. I was about the same age when, walking home from school, I got attacked by a flock of geese. When I was eight, while vacationing with my family down in Rosarito Beach in Baja, I got kicked in the nose by a horse (it just nicked me). That same summer I ran out into the street and got hit by a car. Luckily for me, the woman behind the wheel slammed on her brakes, I bounced backward off her hood, and I was only slightly hurt. At least, I was only slightly hurt until my dad found out what I'd done and he laid his belt across my ass for being so heedless and irresponsible.

In the sixth grade, on a dare, I got stuck forty feet up a fifty-foot cliff and had to be rescued by the fire department. Crazy drunk on Red Mountain wine, I totaled-out my first car when I was sixteen.

During my three years in the army infantry, I experienced even more hair-raising adventures. As punishment, I ladled out a mess hall's grease pit using a teaspoon. I did thousands of pushups and I ran hundreds of miles. I got clocked while bouncing through obstacle courses; I did forced marches, live fire exercises, extreme camping, and escape and evasion drills.

In Vietnam I flew in open Huey helicopters with my feet dangling into empty space. Back in The World, I'd buckle on a parachute, get up "a big case of the ass," and jump out of a chopper, too. I also made parachute jumps out of C-119s and C-130s. Yet the biggest "blast" of all was the time I jumped out of a C-141 Starlifter, at the time the largest cargo jet in the world. When they flung open the doors on that rig and I heard the insane siren screaming its four back-thrusting, draft-horse jet engines, it was like they'd opened a portal to Hell.

So you wouldn't think hopping aboard an old cable-bladed D-7 Caterpillar bulldozer would have provided me with much of an adrenaline rush. And if you were thinking about nowadays, you'd be right. It's been over thirty years since Cat tractors were allowed to go the sorts of places they used to go, or do the sorts of things they used to do, back when I first started logging. Back then a Cat could go about anyplace provided the "catskinner" (operator) was willing to cut enough trail, push enough dirt, and pop enough stumps out of his way. A catskinner would punch a skid trail across the bald face of a landslide if that's what it took to get at the logs laid out on the other side. But nowadays, for the obvious environmental reasons, once the ground starts turning steep, Cats are usually banned altogether.

But when I showed up for my first chokersetting job in May of 1974, it was still the Wild West. Back then you logged redwoods the way you strip-mined coal. Only two rules counted: Get the product out quick and don't get killed or mangled while doing it. The American consumers wanted redwood lumber and they wanted it cheap. And so we gave them what they wanted and we let the devil take the hindmost.

I'll never forget my first trip up a mountainside riding that old cable-bladed bulldozer (nowadays everything is hydraulics). It was out at Spooner Creek, which runs just west of Bailey Summit out on the old Masonite Road. Spooner Canyon was deep and V-shaped and all along its bottom snaked a watered-dirt truck road just wide enough to allow two logging trucks—one empty and incoming and the other full and racing out of there—to speed past each other without clipping mirrors.

At intervals along the truck road were "landings," which were carved, dusty flats beside, or sometimes on top of, the creek. The landings were big enough to hold between two and four "decks" of logs, that word being the fancy one for piles.

Beside and behind the landings were "slash piles" sometimes as big as houses. Landings were where the logs were gathered, cleaned up, sorted, and then loaded aboard the trucks that'd take them to the lumber mill. Because redwood timber fallers were a generally greedy bunch, lots of their logs that got skidded down to the landings were not really logs but limby, busted tree parts or "long logs" with the remains of worthless treetops attached to them. So the slash piles were made up of shattered treetops, hitchhiking limbs, forty-foot-long strips of "busted" redwood bark, shorter flaps of bark, "bucked-off" (sawed-off) chunks of broken trunk, bucked-off "stobs" (the spear-like remains of busted or torn-off limbs extending from logs that were also called "gut gougers"), little sucker trees, and lots and lots of pulverized dirt. Whenever the loader man got a chance (on this show he was running a giant rubber-tired forklift that articulated in the middle), he'd "sweep" the surface of his landing of debris by dropping his lift and using its rear base plate as a broom.

The landings were lined up like the vertebrae of a snake because both sides of Spooner Canyon had been "clear-cut." The remains of the forest made quite a sight. Every redwood and Doug fir tree over eighteen inches in diameter "at breast height" had been felled, somewhat de-limbed, and bucked into logs. Because so many trees were felled all at once in so small an area, about every skinny little baby tree in the old understory had had its top knocked out of it, or had been smashed flat, or had been partially knocked over and was leaning at a grotesque angle. It was the first time I'd ever laid eyes on a clear-cut logging operation and, beyond the devastation, what was most striking was the amount of light that had been let into the canyon. Virtually nowhere was there any shade left, and the blond dirt was glaring.

Think of a mountain as a human hand propped up on its thumb and fingertips. The fingertips reach to the creek and they are called sub-ridges. The spaces between the fingers also reach to the creek and they are called side canyons. Spooner Creek, which runs for a couple of miles, had dozens of fingers, and down the tops of each of them ran the main skid trails that were called "trunk trails." Forking off from them and running more or less level into the side canyons were more trails called "branches." Because "bull-lines" were only one hundred feet long, the branch trails couldn't be much more than one hundred feet apart, one above the next going up the mountain. Together the trunk and branch trails made a "Christmas tree" that covered every finger.

I was introduced to the catskinner I'd spend the next few months working behind. He was a very old and a very rotund, brown-skinned, blue-eyed, self-described half-breed Pomo Indian by the name of Lester Seymour. Without much more than a ritual handshake and a hearty "howdy-do," Lester climbed back aboard his loudly idling, knocking, popping Cat, took his seat behind the controls, made himself comfortable, and then invited me to climb on up and to sit on down on the lid of the big metal toolbox that was bolted to the deck beside him. The Cat had a solid steel canopy (a "headache bar") strong enough to function as a roll bar in case the machine tumbled down a canyon, and as the roof of a bunker in the case of falling trees, limbs, and tumbling boulders.

Over the racket of his diesel engine Lester hollered for me to hold on tight to the middle support beam of the canopy that was welded and bolted into place directly in front of me. I was to keep my feet planted flat on the deck and my eyeballs glued straight up ahead watching out for overhanging limbs. Lester had to be watching the corners of his blade and other things besides, so he might forget about me there on his toolbox, a limb might get caught on the front beam of the canopy and, as we pulled ahead, get loaded like a rock in a catapult and then slap me upside the head and maybe knock me clean off the ass end of the tractor.

The instant Lester was satisfied I'd digested all that, he yanked on his Johnson Bar, which engaged the clutch, and off we went, lurching forward on clanking and squealing tracks. We "crawled"— bulldozers are sometimes called "crawlers"—up the truck road a ways and then we pivoted abruptly and joined a trunk trail leading up a canyonside so steep that, to stay aboard the lid of the toolbox, I had to throw my weight forward as if I was aboard a rearing horse. With me holding on to the beam with both hands, the floor with my feet, and the toolbox with my ass, we'd nearly made it to the top of the mountain when, the tracks of the bulldozer unable to keep purchase in the pulverized dirt, we started sliding backward.

To keep the machine from sliding backward out of control, Lester let out with a yip, simultaneously dropped his blade with a thump, and revved his already screaming engine, making the bulldozer's tracks race faster forward even as we kept sliding backward.

Finally, after Lester had managed to get us stopped by building a big mound of churning dirt under the backside of his dropped blade, he gawked at me all wide-eyed and breathless and grinned like we'd just gotten away with something.

"Gotta get the grease monkey to loosen these tracks so we can get some traction," Lester hollered as he nonchalantly started us back up the grade. We made it up to just about exactly where we'd gotten before when again the Cat broke loose, we slid backward down the hill, and Lester yipped and got us stopped again.

"I need you to climb up front and set yourself atop the middle of the blade," Lester hollered at me out of the side of his mouth. "We need more weight up front if we're ever gonna make it up this damned little hill."

And when my jaw dropped and the color drained from my face, Lester laughed lustily and advised me to pay him no mind.

That was one thing about Lester. He was tickled pink to have in his old age the golden opportunity to cut the teeth of a genuine greenhorn like me, and that was partly because of all of the bald-faced lies he'd get to tell me, and all of the tricks he'd get to play (the sliding Cat had been one of Lester's tricks). Before the logging season was over, Lester would tell me about the collection of pioneer scalps his grandpa had collected, and about his Pit River woman who could conjure up some weird scary shit and, among other things, about the old days when the redwoods stood so tall it took two men and a boy to see to the top of one of them.

Beyond telling me lies and pulling tricks on me, Lester also got to work me to death. Back then on steep ground among the big trees, most everybody was a "highballer," which meant they busted ass. Redwood logging was a seasonal form of employment, and with the big trees going the way of the buffalo, the whole idea was to get while the getting was good. Chokersetters in those days worked six ten-hour days per week, and that didn't count travel time. Often, especially if the skinner was a "gyppo" (slang for an independent contractor, which was a fancy title for a catskinner who owned the Cat he was abusing), he'd work even more hours than that while punching in skid trails to fresh lays of logs, or working on improving, or extending, the truck road.

Then just the day-to-day dangers that went along with the job proved that big-tree lumberjacks weren't exactly the forward-looking kind. Deep into autumn when the cookie jar was full, the rains were overdue, and his worn-out body was dog-ragged, a logger might look forward to getting laid off for the winter. Maybe he'd look forward to collecting some "rockingchair money" from the State and, between time spent licking his paws and scratching his private parts, cutting a bit of firewood to sell "under the table" to help put some salt in the bacon.

Next, with spring coming, the cookie jar empty, and the wife starting to get used to him lying around like a spoiled fireside dog, he'd look forward to getting back to the redwoods and back to work again. Naturally he might also look forward to the birth of a child, or the marriage of a child, and that sort of thing. But when it came to logging and his chosen way of life, winter and spring were about the only things he'd ever have to look forward to. He'd look forward to winter and spring, plus the occasional fat paycheck.

Another thing about Lester was he never took his jokes too far. He never used his position as my protector and mentor as an excuse to torment me or to take chances with my life. Since it'd been left to Lester to cut my teeth in the redwoods, he was going to do it right, and that meant, front and center, keeping me alive and kicking and showing up for work the next morning. Lester was going to keep me safe by teaching me to watch out for myself (something I was already fairly good at). Lester was going to show me how to "highball," too, which he reckoned was the only way to stay alive in the woods long-term—long-term meaning for any real length of time. When it came to logging, the stupider you were about the woods, the quicker you'd get squished, run over, or driven into the dirt like a spike. To survive in the woods you needed to know the woods, and Lester wasn't at all bashful about sharing with a greenhorn the lessons he'd learned during his lifetime. And since Lester was bound to do that then, just naturally along the way, he'd want to have himself a little fun to boot.

Out at Spooner Creek some of the skid trails were too steep to get the tractor up. Like the trail we'd been sliding backward on. Ordinarily Lester would head only down that trail, and then only providing he was dragging a full skid of logs as ballast and a big churning mound of dirt in front of his blade acting as his accelerator/de-accelerator (drop the blade and build a bigger mound of dirt to go slower, or raise it to go faster). On a trail as steep as that one, each time you went down you took maybe an inch of dirt so that, before you were done and you'd cleared the finger of logs, the trail might be cut into the high spots of the mountain as much as five foot deep. You also wanted your trunk trail to become a "straight shot" without high or low points, something your skidded bundles of logs tended to do on their own. Not much wider than the width of the bulldozer's blade, with use the skid trails got to be like chutes, flumes, or slides with vertical cutbanks a person on foot couldn't easily escape over. That's why, my first ride up the mountain, Lester had shown me how that twenty-five-ton Cat could slide backward like an ice skater. If ever I got into the habit of following the Cat up steep hills like that one, Lester wanted to show me, then I was asking to get squished.

By the way, to get a Cat tractor to slide backward, just put it to climbing up its maximum grade. With the blade of the Cat held just an inch above the ground, the machine's center of gravity is kept low and the Cat climbs. But raise the blade and the machine's center of gravity shifts backward, the Cat breaks free, and there you go.

If going up on the steep stuff you never wanted to be following close behind a Cat, there was nothing to say you couldn't follow it down the mountain if you wanted to. If you were feeling lazy or extra worn out, you could even hitch a ride sitting on the toolbox of the Cat. But I never liked riding down on the toolbox because, if somehow my hands lost their grip on the beam and I landed on the moving tracks then, if I bounced wrong, I'd get crushed under them. So, fearing the prospect of a gruesome death, I always followed the bulldozer down the mountain.

And since I was following along, I figured I may as well save myself some steps by riding the logs (Lester had first suggested it). I'd plant my spiked boots into the ends of two forty-footers and keep my body balanced and plumb like I was surfing. It was especially fun when the trail was a straight shot and carved deep like a toboggan run and, having six fat logs trailing as ballast and it getting on to the start of lunchtime, Lester would lift his blade, let go of his dirt, shift the Cat's tranny into neutral, and "freewheel" us down to the landing. We'd get up such a head of steam that we'd arrive in a massive cloud of dust that rose and billowed upward into the sky above the canyon like a giant smoke signal.

Another interesting thing was when logs broke loose. Ordinarily you'd drag logs behind the Cat with them "sucked up" to the winch. That kept their noses from digging into the dirt so much and made them come that much easier. But heading down steep ground, to keep a hold of the trail, you'd let the logs out some; give them longer rein because you wanted their noses digging into the dirt to act as brakes.

But still occasionally one or more logs would break loose and slam into the back of the Cat. Because of the friction in the middle of the skid, it was nearly always one of the outside logs that broke loose, and sometimes they'd clatter up the tracks of the bulldozer and bang and lurch forward as if they were on a conveyor belt. Almost instantaneously, a log might get up so much speed that it's like an arrow out to beat you to the landing. When that happened, the chokersetter didn't want to be riding the toolbox, and the catskinner had to act fast. He needed to act fast because, if the "choker" (steel rope) lassoed around the runaway log's nose broke like a thread, then one of its flying ends might slice him in half. And so the instant Lester heard a log slam into the back of the Cat, he'd immediately drop his blade, stand up on his brakes, and slap his winch into neutral to let the spool freewheel and allow the log to go free.

A choker was typically a fifteen-foot-long steel rope that was three-quarters of an inch thick and weighed about twenty pounds (we usually worked with a set of six). On one end was a snub-nosed, bullet-shaped steel "nubbin," and on the other end was a loop that was called an "eye." Between the eye and the nubbin was a sliding "bell" with a slot in it that fit the nubbin like a buttonhole fits a button. When the nubbin was fitted inside the sliding bell it made a noose that cinched down and "choked" the log when someone pulled on the eye.

It terms of its operating parts, a choker was no more complicated than, say, a wheelbarrow.

Behind the Cat hung a forty-ton Hyster winch, and rolled up in the spool of that was a one-hundred-foot-long, inch-and-an-eighth-thick steel cable called a "bull-line." Knotted on the end of the bull-line was a heavy steel hook big enough to fit the eyes of eight chokers at once. To get the eyes of his "set" chokers wrapped around the hook on the bull-line was a major part of a chokersetter's job, and that usually meant pulling bull-line because, as a practical matter up on a canyonside, a Cat couldn't always get up close to the logs.

When it came to pulling bull-line, you wanted to be pulling down the hill. Because of the steepness of the ground, the roundness of the logs and the pull of gravity, for safety reasons you never wanted to be spending much time downhill from logs. Or, when you were, then you absolutely wanted them anchored to the slope so that, unless you were awfully unlucky, they flat out couldn't roll down on you and squish you like you were a spot of dough for a cookie.

So, to stay above the logs, you cleared them off the mountain beginning at the ridge top and working your way down the fingers to the creek. Ideally, whenever you were working the logs below any branch trail in the side canyons, you hooked them all so that, when you dropped down to the next trail, not a single log was left above you.

Even putting aside considerations of safety, again because of the steepness of the ground and the pull of gravity, you wanted to be pulling your bull-line straight down the hill. In fact, the steeper the mountain, the easier the pull. The hook must have weighed at least twenty pounds, and even a one-foot length of bull-line was Pittsburgh-blue-steel-heavy, especially when working against the winch to keep the cable tight in the spool (bull-lines had a way of going "haywire" and getting tangled in the spool if you didn't pull against them to keep them taut).

Because of the need to keep the bull-line taut, even on flat ground in deep shade you wouldn't want to be pulling out one hundred foot of bull-line more than a few times running. And when it comes to pulling bull-line up the hill, if you do even a small bit of that you're going to get tuckered out real quick. Pull enough bull-line up the hill and you are going to get to panting, wheezing, and seeing spots. If you're bulldog strong you'll get far enough up the hill so that, when the bent coils in the cable finally overpower you and the bull-line retracts like an over-stretched slinky, you're going to get dragged headfirst right back down the hill unless you let loose of the hook.

Anyway, when things were going smooth you'd hook one or more of your logs, escape to somewhere safe, and then signal the catskinner to engage his winch. Once he'd engaged his winch, the spool had started turning, and the bull-line had lifted off the ground and snapped tight, only one of three things could happen. Either your logs could "pop" out of the woods and get sucked toward the Cat, or the Cat could rear up and slide backward or, if the catskinner didn't stop pulling quick enough, the rigging could break (usually a choker below the collar binding the eye, but sometimes the bull-line).

Because the woods were full of obstructions, a choker could be set that would roll the nose of a log up and over a stump, or make it back up and go around a "stander" (standing tree). Other hitches could be used to tie one log to another, nose to tail or side by side. The various hitches had names like "kicks," "rolls," "Swedes," "bridles," "jackpots," and "bar-buckles." So knowing how and where to set a choker to get a log to smoothly pop out of the woods could get slightly complicated. Then to rig the ultimate smooth set—the "straight hook" that was six logs popped out of the woods all at once with no holdups—took a fair bit of practice and a reasonable amount of know-how. Also, I should mention, sometimes just getting one single choker under and around one single log could seem near-on impossible.

Most any chokersetter, but especially a highballing greenhorn like me, was going to reach the limit of his physical endurance. A fellah would hit bottom usually two or three weeks into the logging season. His legs shredded by all of the climbing up and down, the pulling, lifting, and dragging, his backbone turned to jelly, his grip weak, his gaze dim, he couldn't eat enough food to make him feel strong, or get enough sleep to make himself stop feeling drowsy, or enough rest and relaxation to make him feel refreshed. A fair percentage of greenhorns, along with some others who'd allowed themselves to get lazy and out of shape during the winter, fell out before the new logging season was a month old. One morning their alarm clocks would go off and they'd be unwilling to set their feet on the floor.

That's how I'd gotten my job slinging steel behind Lester. The fellah I replaced could no longer pull himself out of bed. And then, about three weeks into my own season, I started wondering if the same thing would happen to me. Weaker day by day, sore, cut up and bruised, I started looking back nostalgically at stomping fleeces. And that had to be a sure sign that I was in the wrong line of work. I still remember the exact moment when I hit bottom. It was an extraordinarily hot afternoon, I was working the sunny side of the canyon, and for maybe ten minutes I'd been struggling to punch a choker under a four-foot-thick log that was bedded atop a mishmash of broken, bastard limbs. I'd finally found a place where my nubbin could almost break free to the other side—there was a glorious hole that was just a teensy bit too skinny and a weensy bit too short—but using stubbornness, rage, and brute strength I'd tried to force my nubbin through. Now defeated in my aim and utterly exhausted, my hands shaking, my knees knocking, half-blind because of the salty sweat in my eyes, and frustrated nearly to the point of tears, I felt a gentle tap on my shoulder. I looked up and, beyond the smudges and smears on my eyeballs, I saw Lester. Without saying a word, he took the choker out of my hands and moved down the log a couple of feet. Kneeling on one knee, he stuck the nubbin under the log, probed with it, moved farther down the hill a few inches, probed again, and the nubbin slid through to the other side like a spoon through ice cream.

"Don't ever let these logs outsmart you," he advised me as he climbed back up toward his Cat.

After you've hit bottom, naturally you've got nowhere to go but up—or out. If you chose to stick with it, as I did, then your blisters started getting calluses on them, you started getting your "woods legs" and, no longer so newborn clumsy, you stopped constantly adding to your collection of bumps and bruises. As time went on, you even started getting a little bit graceful. Your torn-down muscles slowly rebuilt and, as your skill level increased, you stopped wasting so many moves and so got much more out of burning the same number of calories. The logs popped out of the woods easier, the bull-line felt lighter and, by mid-season, you started feeling like Paul Bunyan. Back home admiring such a fine physical specimen as yourself in the mirror, you might trick yourself into thinking that you could chase down and bulldog a steer without using a horse.

And then, just when your head started swelling to the size of a county fair pumpkin, the grind of the months got to you and you started getting weaker again, more torn-down and weary. Come October or November, with you again dragging ass, in your mind you'd start doing a little rain dance and praying for mud.

• • •

"Why pull bull-line when you ain't got to?" Lester asked me one day after lunch. We were standing at the end of a branch trail about halfway up the mountain, and down below us was a side canyon with a wide bottom that was covered with a thick lay of fat logs. There were so many logs down there that the ground was just barely visible. Such a thick lay of logs was called a "jackpot" or a "pumpkin patch" because, especially if you were a gyppo and were getting paid "bushel rate" (by volume as measured by board feet of lumber), they represented easy money.

When Lester got excited, he rubbed his hands together. And now, overlooking the veritable bonanza of logs, he was rubbing his hands together and grinning like a Cheshire Cat. I was pretty well broken in by then—in fact I was entering my Paul Bunyan stage—and Lester, fairly well pleased with my progress, decided I was ready to learn how to "dive off."

He asked me if I saw the truck road down there in the distance. Had I noticed how there was no cutbank between us; how the wide mouth of the canyon just sort of blended into the road? What was to keep us from taking the logs out from there? Had I noticed how, with virtually all of the logs laying side-hill, nearly all of them were pointing at the road and so were easy pickings? And look at the steep ground on the canyonside just below us. Did I see how the Cat could just dive off the embankment, slide to the bottom and onward to the truck road from there?

Seeing me nodding vaguely—it seemed to me there were a lot of stumps and logs between us and the truck road—was enough to make Lester decide to dive off. He fetched his Cat, brought it to the end of the trail, squared it up to the grade and, grabbing a mound of dirt as a brake, flopped onto the slope and slid to the bottom and right into the middle of the pumpkin patch.

After that, we dove off about any chance we got. Though the technique played hell with the terrain and was outrageously dangerous (at least if you didn't know what you were doing), there was simply no easier and quicker way to move logs. When we were diving off, most of the time I wouldn't even have to unhook my chokers because, as Lester punched ahead on the Cat, he would pivot the logs in his way with his blade and lay them out parallel with the tracks. So when the winch of the Cat cleared the nose of a log, Lester would stop moving and I'd get in there and choke it. Then Lester would pull ahead, lay out more logs, stop, and I'd go in and rig some more until we had six logs skidding and he was on his way to the landing.

About the only problem with diving off and rigging logs like that was that after you had two or three logs skidding, the loose ends of your empty chokers would get buried beneath them. The easiest solution was to ride the logs, which I did. Once we had two or three logs skidding, I'd jump aboard them, plant my spikes, grab up the ends of the empty chokers, and pull back on them like they were the long reins on a stagecoach. The Cat would pull ahead and stop, I'd jump down, rig a log or two, and then jump back up and away we'd go.

All and all, logging that way was easier than barking a shin.

• • •

One more thing about riding logs. A couple of seasons later I was slinging steel for a much larger and more reputable outfit, working behind a catskinner named Bryce. We were bringing a skid down the truck road and I was riding the tail of a fat forty-footer. Without me noticing, my new woods boss snuck up behind me in his company pickup truck and he blasted his horn at me. The sudden blaring about scared me to death, and I nearly tumbled off the log.

Yet, before I could get mad, my new boss was out of his truck and in my face. Did I know what would happen to him if OSHA came out and saw me riding logs? Did I have any idea what would happen to him if the insurance inspector caught me doing that? My God, man, could I even conceive of the amount of money I'd cost him if ever I fell off a log and broke an arm or a leg?

He went on some, but that was the gist of it. And after he'd laid down the law and he was back in his pickup truck and was charging away in reverse gear and throwing up a big rooster tail of dust—my new boss was sort of speedy—it finally dawned on me what had just happened and why. While stung by the tongue-lashing, I had to laugh and shake my head because old Lester had gotten me again. Teaching me how to ride logs had been another one of Lester's tricks.

HIGHBALLING

Old Lester had seen the world from the seat of a D-7 Caterpillar tractor. Born on the Mendocino coast in Caspar, California, around 1905, Lester used to brag that he'd been too young to get shot up in World War One and too old to get shot up in World War Two. Since between the wars folks saw no sense in paying the upkeep on a peacetime army, never once in his life did Lester ever stand the chance of getting drafted, thrown into uniform, and shipped off to God knows where. Also, Lester not being too bashful to earn an honest living, and him quickly having himself a Pit River woman and a small herd of kids, he had no time to be biding, be it by spit-shining boots, polishing brass, or going to town and getting hammered every weekend. So even when Lester was a fresh young buck just getting started in the world, it never occurred to him to up and join the army.

No Siree. As a young boy, Lester joined his dad in the big-tree redwoods. The way, once the boy's got his feet under him, a city fellah might take his son to see the monkeys in the zoo, Lester's dad took him out into the woods to watch the lumberjacks. When Lester was old enough to hump an ax without hurting himself or making himself into a pest, then he was out in the woods humping ax for his dad. Later on, once he'd gotten a little meat on his bones and a bit of head about him, working after school, on weekends, and during the summer, Lester grew into a first-class lumber camp "go-fer" ("go-fer" being the lazy way of saying "errand boy"). Part water boy, messenger, delivery boy, signalman, mule, rabbit, and mountain goat, Lester did fairly well as a go-fer. For a full day's work he'd sometimes earn a dollar, by golly, which weren't half bad for a boy in the lumber camps in those days.

Both of Lester's parents were pure half-breeds, meaning half settler and half Pomo. "Half and half," the white school boys used to call Lester until his dad taught him how to smack a white boy in the nose. Once Lester started smacking the kids who talked bad about him, or bad about any of his kin right down to his second cousins living way out there in Covelo, the white boys learned to call him Lester and they stopped having trouble.

Because his Indian blood supposedly gave him a special way with animals, they started Lester's dad off in the woods as a stable boy. He mucked stalls and, as he got older, he started feeding, tending to, and doctoring the livestock. By the time Lester was born his dad had graduated to "bull-whacking," which was skidding logs by manhandling teams of oxen, mules, or horses. When steam-driven yarders reared their ugly heads and started belching out of their smokestacks half-burnt water popping skyward as smoke rings, Lester's dad switched over to "donkey punching," which was a lumberjack's way of saying that he operated one of the contraptions.

To hear old Lester tell it, his dad could do most anything he set his mind to. By the time Lester was old enough to remember, his dad was already working on Union Lumber Company's old logging railroad that used to run between Fort Bragg and Willits (today's Skunk Train). Out there in the lumber camps set along the tracks next to the Noyo River in what is now Jackson State Forest was where Lester had done most of his growing up. Over the years his dad did it all on the railroad, including some rip-roaring engineering. The trains were always running, Lester's dad was always working and, any chance he got, Lester was out there beside him in the locomotive. With young Lester at his elbow and his dad at the controls and searching ahead, they'd run people and supplies into the camps and logs out of them, never going either way empty and never slowing down or stopping for anybody waving from beside the tracks.

They were some original, genuine "highballers," Lester didn't mind saying. Out along that old logging spur, when a gully-washing

North Pacific rainstorm or a wild, roaring gale—or a rainstorm *and* a roaring gale—blew in off the ocean and got squeezed up against the mountains, those were the only times the trains didn't run. But immediately after the storm had blown over, they'd send out crews of men on handcarts to inspect and repair the tracks. After the crews had cleared away the windfalls, landslides, and the like, and after they had inspected or repaired the trestles and tunnels and were sure the way was clear, they'd set the road's signal arms pointing skyward in the "highballing" position. Rounding a bend in that old locomotive and seeing the highballing sign meant the engineer could open up his throttle and go as fast as the tracks could take them.

• • •

Because Lester didn't much like hanging out on noisy, dusty landings, come lunchtime we'd usually picnic up on the mountain. After finding a shady stander on a branch trail to park under, Lester would drop his blade and kill his engine. Next he'd slowly remove his cotton gloves a finger at a time, neatly set them side by side atop his dashboard, push back his dust-caked felt Fedora hat, kick up his feet, and proceed to roll himself a cigarette. Which was funny because Lester had once told me that no woods boss worth his sawdust ever hired a man who wore work gloves and rolled his own cigarettes.

While I made myself comfortable in the soft berm on the downhill side of the Cat and started eating (the Cat sheltered me from tumbling rocks and rolling logs), Lester would sit in his seat and savor his cigarette in silence. When he was finished, he'd spit a little puddle into the palm of his hand and douse his stub before tossing it overboard. Then he'd wipe his hand on his pants leg and open the lid of his lunch box. After inspecting its contents, he'd set the individual items where they were most handy and begin eating and talking.

With his big blue eyes, dark, sorrel skin, and white-toothed grin, Lester had a sort of "golly gee" expression about him. As if simple things like gravity and inertia were the source of endless puzzlement to him. The way country people sometimes do, Lester would look off into the distance as if something had caught his eye. As if, just through those bushes or up and over that liddle-biddy rise, there was something that was seriously worth looking at; something strange and mysterious but in no way threatening. And you'd look to try to see what he was staring at, but there was nothing there so far as you could tell. Which made you think he was actually looking inward and his eyes seemed fixed just because they needed something to rest on.

When it came to working in the woods, Lester believed that any man who wasn't a highballer would get killed or crippled sooner rather than later. That's the way it was in the woods and Lester let me know right off that anybody who didn't like it was just plain in the wrong line of work as far as he was concerned. Take a lazy chokersetter. Lester claimed any chokersetter looking for an easy way of slinging steel may as well go and throw a saddle on a house cat. He may as well throw rocks at the moon.

The sooner the catskinner was heading down the mountain, Lester claimed, the sooner a lazy chokersetter was sitting down panting in a spot of shade. He'd nestle his back into a stump and guzzle some water, or smoke a cigarette, or eat a candy bar. While he was lollygagging he might get around to thinking about his wife or girlfriend or all of the great things he was going to do when he got off work. Being worn out, bumped and bruised, he might get to brooding over his general all-around weariness. He might even get to stewing over the fact that he either should be making twice the money or be working half as hard. If the mountain was tall and the skid long, the boy might take himself a little nap.

And all the time he's sitting there twiddling his thumbs, Lester declared, his voice indignant, he wasn't up and scouting his next lay of logs. He wasn't sniffing out the dangers: the widowmakers hanging above his head, the logs that might roll for no reason, the broken limbs like spears that he didn't want to be belly-flopping on, the rocks that might get kicked loose by his bull-line and what all.

So when the Cat returned and his next skid of logs started moving, the ground shaking, the limbs falling, the "Jill-pokes" swinging, and the little trees popping and snapping, the poor boy had no idea of where he should be.

I should pause here to explain what Jill-pokes are since they mangled as many big-tree loggers as anything else. In a pristine forest, during a windstorm, a big redwood might drop limbs a foot thick on the butt and forty-foot long. Since windstorms are common in the redwoods, in its natural state the forest floor is littered with a mishmash of fallen limbs. Although, because of the year-round dampness (redwoods generate their own summer precipitation), the limbs quickly get buried in duff and rot into the soil.

But now here you come with your chainsaw out to knock the forest down. Redwoods grow close together and their roots are intertwined—one tree stands because they all stand. Their canopies are also intertwined, woven into a thick mat that waves and ripples but doesn't rip apart in a gale. So to fell your first tree you'd need to make a hole in the canopy. As your tree "washed" by a stander on its way to the earth, limbs snapped off the trunks of both trees and showered the forest floor. Limbs growing up on big redwoods snapped off like carrots, often clean and flush with the trunk, and sometimes a highballing timber faller would deliberately fell a tree close past a stander to "wash" both of them of some limbs to save him the trouble (he'd be knocking all of the big trees down anyway). Also, once his trees were down, he'd "bump" (cut off) all of the limbs he could reasonably get to.

So when the timber faller had finished clear-cutting his strip, had moved on, and the chokersetter arrived to fetch his logs, the canyonside might be littered with thousands of loose-lying limbs. The ones washed down from the standers laid every which way like a jumble of giant, bowed fiddle sticks, while the limbs bumped off the felled trees laid parallel to each other like the bleached ribs of beached whales—beached whales laying crisscrossed atop each other.

I don't think anybody knows why the limbs are called Jill-pokes. One time Lester tried to tell me that they were named after a particularly ugly-looking logging-camp whore named Jill, but the twinkle in his eyes told me he was lying. Besides, Jill-pokes were named for what they did and not for what they were or what they looked like. A loose limb laying there is just a limb, in other words. But a limb that breaks out of the dirt and comes down like a flyswatter is called a Jill-poke. By way of example, take a round, bowed stick of wood and set it on a table with the ends facing away from you. Now, using the palm of your hand, roll the stick toward you. See how the two ends rise up, flip, and smack the table? That's one kind of Jill-poke. If the limb is stout enough, is being flipped by the moving tracks of the Cat, and you're standing in the way, the limb is going to smack the earth just as if you weren't there. It'll either pick you up and throw you out of its way or, if it lands on you, it'll crush any part of you it catches.

Or sometimes the pearling nose of a log getting sucked up to the Cat will catch a long, skinny, young, and limber limb, twist one end of it down into an old stump hole and make the other end fly into the air. If you are foolish or unlucky enough to be standing on the limb with your spiked boots then you too are going flying—and that was another kind of Jill-poke. One of the worst sorts of Jill-poke was a young, skinny, limber one still attached to the trunk of a log getting sucked up the hill on the end of a stretched out bull-line. When the limb gets caught under something, gets pulled back like the string of a bow and then, after its top snaps off, fires up the hill as it reassumes its natural shape, you didn't want to be standing in its way. Again, the Jill-poke is going to act just as if you weren't there.

When you fell a tree into a bed of loose limbs and some shattered chunks of them explode into the air and tumble end over end in long arcs—those too are Jill-pokes. Or say you were felling timber and you had an eighty-foot-long length of felled tree laying side-hill on a steep canyonside that you needed to buck into two forty-foot-long logs. If there's nothing holding the middle section of the tree on the hill, then when the two sides of your cut separate, the logs are going to swing down the hill and keep on swinging until a stump or a stander stops them. If what stops a log leaves it pointing straight up and down the hill, and if it rammed the obstruction hard enough, then the log might "break" (separate) from its sopping-wet, banana-peel-slippery inner bark, slide out of it like a pig out of a blanket, and disappear on its way to the creek (when the log's nose pierces the water and plunges into the gravels, you can bet that it scares the hell out of the fish).

So knowing that something like that might happen meant that, before you bucked your tree, you'd cut any limbs aiming up and down the hill that you might be standing on, or over, or nearby. If you didn't and your log stirred up a limb underfoot that rose and smacked you between the legs and sent you airborne—that too was a Jill-poke.

Another sort of Jill-poke was a limb buried in the powder pointing straight up and down a steep branch trail. With all of the dust and the big blade in the way, if the catskinner doesn't see it and one of his tracks rolls atop it, that track will slide, pivot the Cat, and maybe jam the corner of the blade into a cutbank, causing the Cat to come to a halt in mid-screech and the catskinner to exit his seat by way of the top of his hood (because of rollovers, catskinners in those days rarely wore safety belts). That limb was also called a Jill-poke.

Given an interlocked mesh of limbs and the powers of mass, velocity, and leverage, one Jill-poke might cause another to lift a log over a stump and get it rolling down the hill, which might cause more logs to break free of their anchors, roll, and cause even more Jill-pokes to spring to life. If chaos was unpredictability, then what logging caused was called a commotion.

"I quartered a big pumpkin up the hill this morning," a timber faller might tell his buddies while sitting on his tailgate and swilling a windblown can of beer. Once the afternoon winds kicked up and the trees started swaying, most timber fallers called it a day. They'd climb or drop out of their canyons, gather around their pickup trucks, pop open some beers out of their ice chests, and commence to bragging to each other.

"And when that big pumpkin hit the dirt," the fellah might continue, savoring the memory, "you should have seen the commotion."

And so, to get back to what Lester was telling me about his philosophy of work and his high regard for lazy chokersetters—what with all of the hazards to watch out for, a lazy chokersetter was his own worst enemy. He didn't know up from down, or sideways from backward. And that's why, if a catskinner got stuck working with a lazy chokersetter, he'd always have to be extra careful not to get him killed. And having to be extra careful all the time took the fun out of the job and so working with a lazy chokersetter wasn't the sort of thing any self-respecting highballer ever looked forward to.

In fact, Lester let me know, he himself was too old to be fooling with one. If he got stuck working with a lazy chokersetter, why, he'd run him off by working him to death. He'd get to highballing and be back from the landing so quick the poor boy couldn't finish his cigarette or even his ration of water. Lester would jump off the Cat, grab up a choker, and set it himself to try to shame the boy into working harder. And if a couple of skids of that didn't work, then he'd just keep highballing to keep the poor boy from ever getting the chance to rest his weary bones.

If the poor boy wasn't too bright, Lester didn't mind telling me with a bit of pride in his voice that he might last for a couple of weeks after Lester got to highballing. And all that time Lester got to watch him wither like a leaf. Come lunchtime, the poor boy might devour two pounds of food and a quart of water but still he couldn't keep himself from shrinking. It'd get so Lester could hardly bring himself to look at him, the boy dragging his raggedy ass up and down the mountain like some wounded porcupine. Finally the Lord would have mercy and the poor boy would never be seen again.

• • •

Because Lester never wanted to be anything but a lumberjack, he never did get much in the way of formal schooling. Book learning was worthless in the woods—worst than that if you thought otherwise. In the woods you needed woods sense. You needed balance and sure-footedness, smooth moves and an ability to see ahead. Using all of your senses plus whatever spirit allies you could muster, you needed to keep a firm grip on your situation at all times. You wanted the strength of an ox and, because falling down with a bundle of shouldered chokers was the most common way of getting broken up, you wanted to have the grace of a deer. You needed relentlessness and even fierceness, and sometimes a single choker got slung around a single log only because you refused to take "no" for an answer. At times in the woods a bit of rage didn't hurt you, and you'd try sweet-talking a problem away before you attacked it head-on, jumping on it with both feet. The minimum amount of force necessary might mean all of the strength you've got, and getting riled helped make you stronger. Like with shearing sheep or bringing in a harvest, logging brought out a certain brutality and, of course, a hot-blooded strain of All-American Machismo. First and foremost, a lumberjack was a fighter living out his woodsmen's dreams by grabbing life by the ass and never giving an inch.

And none of those qualities could be taught properly from inside the walls of a schoolroom.

Also, I think, those qualities helped explain why loggers spent so much time in watering holes recounting all of the trees they'd felled that morning, or all of the logs they'd choked or skidded that day. Their way of life was so raw, elemental, and physical; so hard, dangerous, and low-paying that they were a wonderment even to themselves.

Not only did Lester rarely set foot in a schoolhouse, only twice in his life had he set foot in a big city. And judging by what he'd seen and heard, he didn't think he'd missed much. Growing up he'd been warned about what happened to Indians when they moved into the white man's metropolis. As a matter of tribal lore and just plain common sense, cities were the pits people fell into after they'd lost their ability to take their living from the land. Lester considered Indians living in the city to be refugees, and he felt sorry for them because they had no land, no heritage, and no tribe.

As a young buck feeling his oats, Lester did get out of the redwoods enough times to see at least a bit of the outside world. When he was young and spry and had mouths to feed, he took up timber felling because that's where the money was. If local jobs dried up or weren't paying right, then he'd leave his family behind and go where the pickings were good. During parts of the 1920s and '30s, Lester had chased after pumpkin patches all through the Rockies. He'd chopped lodgepole up in Wyoming, and pine, fir, and spruce in Colorado and New Mexico. One time, somewhere or another, he'd even hired on to knock down some giant granddaddy cottonwoods growing along a rimrocked arroyo. If he found himself out of money—he sent nearly his entire paycheck home—he'd even saw firewood if he had to.

During those years Lester slept outside of bunkhouses crawling with fleas that still wouldn't allow admittance to a half-breed, and he'd slept in barns smelling of horse piss. During the worst times he'd gone a working day on just a loaf of French bread hollowed out and filled with a cold can of beans.

If all that weren't bad enough, the Rockies hid their own peculiar kinds of dangers. Up along the high points, more than one logger got bit by a rattlesnake, or crushed by a rockfall, struck by lightning, or overrun by wildfire. And even if you didn't mind that, there was still the fact that the boomers had been drawn from all over the country and so there was no end to the constant fussing and fighting, the feuding and name-calling, drunkenness, and other sorts of rude and loutish behavior.

No, Lester couldn't say he missed his old booming days. In the Rockies the summers were god-awful hot, the winters bitter cold, and about the only real pumpkins standing anywhere were the ponderosas, and they grew few and far between. Back home in the redwoods Lester might spend his whole day felling trees in an area not much bigger than a football field. But to get the same scale out of a stand of ponderosas, he'd have to hump his gear for three miles. And even if the money had been good and the living easy, still he'd rather have been home with his family. The truth was, Lester admitted, he'd only boomed because he'd had to.

• • •

I'd been setting choker behind Lester for two or three weeks before I found out who he really was. I'd hit the bottom of my endurance, I got drunk after work, and I arrived at the show the next morning about an hour late and six cards shy of a full deck. Thinking I might be able to sneak past the "bullbuck" (the woods boss), I drove in real slow trying not to raise any dust. But the bullbuck caught me and he stopped my car by jumping into the road in front of me with an outstretched hand. I'd never seen him mad before, but I was about to.

An elderly, bent-over, red-necked, one-eyed horse logger down from Idaho, he lit into me even before I could get my car's window rolled down.

"Do you know you've got that fat old man up there on the mountain setting his own chokers?" the bullbuck hollered in my ear. "Do you know who you're messing with? You got any idea?

When the first goddamned Cat tractor crawled out into these woods, Lester came aboard it, you miserable son-ah-bitch! You're messing with a legend, now—you hear me? If that fat old bastard gets a heart attack and croaks up there you'd best beat it out of here the back way because if I lay my eyes on you, I'm gonna grab my rifle and shoot your ass! Now you get your sorry ass up the mountain and don't you ever show up here late again."

And, I swear, all I could think to do was to step on my gas pedal and start hurrying.

One more thing I should mention about my first woods boss. He was down from Idaho to do his wheeler-dealer kid brother a favor, and that's what he intended to do. While tougher than stale jerky, still he prided himself on being fair-minded and understanding (like you wanted to be with horses). I found that out about him after I'd been working about a week and his wheeler-dealer kid brother showed up to inspect his diggings. He saw me pulling bull-line up on the canyonside, spotted my long ponytail sticking out from under my hardhat and fluttering in the breeze, and he couldn't believe his eyes. He pointed at me, turned to his brother and sputtered, "Fire the hippy."

But that old horse logger was having none of it. He told his brother that Lester liked me and that he liked Lester, and that's all there was to it. They had more important things to talk about.

• • •

Lester had come down from where he was living in the pine country out by the Pit River, and he'd brought along a little bubble trailer to sleep in. He'd made himself a nice little camp on a flat spot under some standers next to the creek and, with his permission, I made my own camp a respectable distance downstream. I had a pup tent, a camp stove, and an ice chest, and when I was too tired to want to drive the two hours home, I'd wash off in the creek and sleep in the tent.

Because Lester's camp was better than mine, and since I was young and spry and he was old and fat, whenever I saw that he had one of his illegal campfires going, I'd make my way upstream and join him around his soundless and smokeless flames. We'd sit and smoke cigarettes, maybe toast some hot dogs, and generally relax (except for an occasional single can of beer, Lester never drank alcohol).

Around the campfire, we didn't talk shop. During the workday Lester was teaching me the ways of the woods, but around the campfire, if Lester wasn't into one of his long quiet spells, I mostly just listened to his stories.

According to Lester, the big-tree redwoods had been all but played out by 1960. Him having been breathing redwood dust his whole life, by then he was well on his way to getting emphysema. To live to a ripe old age, his doctor had warned him in no uncertain terms, he'd need to get out of the dust and find himself a civilized way of making a living. And that was news enough to allow his Pit River woman and his kids to get him to listen to the more prudent side of his nature and to follow the doctor's advice.

So they packed up and they moved into the northern shadow of Mt. Shasta. Up there the ground was smooth and rolling instead of steep and creased, and the sugar pine and Shasta fir sometimes grew to eight foot on the butt and two hundred foot tall. The pumpkins carpeted the hills for as far as you could see, and the frequent summer lightning storms helped keep the dust down.

Lester spent fifteen years in the pines, and all that while he'd run loader instead of a Cat. The hours running loader were longer and so the job paid better, and the machine didn't kick up near so much dust. And it wasn't redwood dust anyway.

Moreover, his wife was tickled pink to be back home with her kin—she was very much into the tribal thing—and Lester, although himself half-breed Pomo and not Pit River, went along with it because he liked seeing her happy. She had kin all up through that country, and when Lester wasn't working she kept him busy visiting her relatives. They'd sit around lollygagging, or maybe do a barbeque or some sort of ceremony, though he only did what he had to in order to show proper respect.

All and all, Lester reckoned, life in the pines was mighty good.

When I asked Lester why he'd returned to the redwoods, at first he claimed it was to do an old friend—the bullbuck—a favor. Later Lester amended that by adding that he'd also come for the big trees and the wage that went with them. Also he himself had kin all up and down the coast, and while the white side of the family wanted next to nothing to do with him, the Pomo side wouldn't leave him alone. He'd go out to pay a little visit and, the next thing he knew, they'd have him out hunting or fishing. Finally, when the season was about done and there was a nip in the morning air, Lester admitted that the real reason why he'd come was to catskin the redwoods one more time before he died.

In late November when the show wrapped, I helped Lester hitch up his trailer. After we had meticulously erased all signs of his camp, he took one final look around at the devastation we were leaving behind, and the white man within him seemed to smile. We shook hands and he told me if ever I wanted to come and make some easy money up in the pines then all I needed to do was to get in touch with him. I thanked him for all he'd done for me—the whole season I'd barely scuffed a knuckle—and I took my own final look around. Then I told him I figured I'd stay in the redwoods for a while. He smiled again like he understood, and that was how we parted company.

CHRISTMAS IN CLOVERDALE

Before Cloverdale became a bedroom community it was a mill town. Some of the biggest trees ever milled anywhere on earth were sawed in Cloverdale, and during the logging boom of the 1970s (it turned out to be a liquidation sale) there must have been a half dozen lumber mills of various sizes and kinds operating thereabouts. On the south end of town, next to the railroad tracks back when the railroad was running, there used to be a burl factory that had a giant chainsaw mounted on rollers. The saw's bar was eight foot long and it could slice through a redwood root wad as big and gnarly as a lowboy trailer could haul or a 977 loader could lift and swing.

Back during the logging boom Cloverdale had more saloons than churches, and a young boomer could get about anything he wanted so long as he had the money. Or, if an unfortunate lumberjack or mill hand was about broke, then he could always belly up to one of Cloverdale's bars and sit there and drink himself silly, telling tall tales, bragging, snorting, spitting, and maybe, once his nose got numb and his spirit rambunctious, picking a fight with somebody, or at the least throwing something, or knocking something over.

Nowadays most folks living in Cloverdale are either from Back East or Down South, or from Really Down South, or from Even Farther Down South Than That. So I don't think many of them know just how much the ground under their feet has been desecrated. Even a partial listing of the kinds of sinning that took place regularly and on schedule in Cloverdale has no place in a proper family-friendly publication. Why, just the Friday night debauchery and fornications, the taking of the Lord's name in vain (the only thing more foul-mouthed than a lumberjack is one with a broken leg), the senseless fistfights and barroom brawls, overflowing barroom brawls, sidewalk and parking lot drunken riots, mischief and mayhem, noise and disorder, lawlessness, irreverence, and downright blasphemy was enough to keep the respectable citizens of Cloverdale off the streets, locked in their homes and peeking through the cracks in their curtains.

Speaking of the streets and highways, after the bars closed in Cloverdale you'd have to be crazy to be out driving unless you were drunk yourself. Being drunk yourself was about the only way you'd feel safe enough to get behind the wheel anywhere in these hills after the bars closed in those days. Close beside Highway 128 there was hardly a tree standing between Cloverdale and the Navarro River's mouth that hadn't had its bark knocked off it by some car or pickup truck careening off the highway. Local ranchers didn't know what was costing them the most money: was it the *ki*-oats feasting on their lambs or was it the drunken yahoos plowing through their fences, banging into their barns and barking up their trees?

But that's another story. This here is a Christmas story and so I won't mention the wild goings-on inside Dante's Saloon, or Elmer's Bar and Pool Hall, the lover's row up in the old Oat Valley Drive-In Movie Theater, the hanky-panky that went on up at the old Kelly Bridge, or the lewd dancing on display inside of the Depot. Also I won't mention the old cowgirl, Eva, whose husband had up and died on her and bequeathed her sole title to the Lockhorn Saloon. Old Eva talked so much while she was tending bar that her place was nicknamed the Lockjaw because you couldn't get a word in edgewise. Nor will I mention the silver-haired, dignified, and kindly old gentleman who single-handedly ran the Park Walker liquor store, joyfully selling whiskey, beer, guns, and ammunition; or sweet Cleo, the Wheel's overnight waitress, who knew the stories of about every long-haul trucker who'd ever stopped by to see her for a thermos of scalding hot coffee and a plate of biscuits and bulldog. I won't mention the old lumbering dogface who ran Tony's Pizza there on the north edge of town below Self's Market, even though once in Tony's while camped behind slices of pizza and frosted pitchers of beer, on the TV hanging above the bar some friends and myself watched as Ken Norton threw the punch that broke Muhammad Ali's jaw.

No, this story takes place in broad daylight inside the old Bank of America and so it's fit for children and prudes. Back then I was a logger and the previous season I'd felled timber out along Dry Creek where the land would soon be flooded by Lake Sonoma. I'd never had any bank accounts in my own name, but my girlfriend and some of her friends had bought the old Schoenahl place up on Shady Grade using a mortgage from Cloverdale's branch of the Bank of America. The various ranch and orchard accounts were also there and, after my girlfriend had introduced me to the senior teller, a famously friendly and handsome old gal with a nearly perpetual smile, she'd cash my paychecks anytime, no problem.

Back then the banks didn't herd their customers through a chute like they do nowadays, and you could wait for the teller you wanted to see if you wanted to. It was customary for teller and customer to exchange a bit of chitchat while doing business, and that was the activity that the banks wanted to stamp out. Anyway, it 's three days before Christmas and I walk into the bank and—whoa!—the place is mobbed. Not only that but my teller has gone on Christmas vacation. I look behind the counter for somebody I know, but there are only two tellers working and they are both strangers.

Since I'd never had any bank accounts in my own name, to cash a check I was used to being asked for two picture IDs, and for that purpose I carried my driver's license plus my old passport. But now I didn't want to cash a paycheck but just an unemployment check, it being winter and me being laid off because of the rainstorms and the mud. Moreover, it wasn't even a full-sized unemployment check because I was at the end of one "claim" and before the start of the next one.

For anyone who has never collected unemployment before, I should explain that the State draws lines in the sand and uses bogus accounting practices that are designed to screw you, the unemployed worker. Take this notion of a "claim": While you were collecting unemployment you'd have a set amount of money provided for you on a biweekly basis. Except, that is, if you'd gone through all of the money set aside in your claim. If that was the case, then, even though you were no less unemployed, you'd get no check for a week while you completed your "Waiting Period" before the start of your next claim. And if that weren't cold-blooded enough, they'd always find a "surplus" in your original claim so that the last check you got was for only a part of, or sometimes just a fraction of, the amount you usually received every two weeks.

So there I am three days before Christmas waiting in a crowded lobby to cash my thirteen-dollar unemployment check and looking forward to more beans and rice, bread and tortillas. When my turn comes, I step forward, cheerfully greet the teller, and place my check and my identification on the counter in front of her. She's a young woman about my age but, perhaps reacting somewhat to my unclean and unshaven appearance (I'd been out cutting firewood), or maybe just curious because she's never seen one before, she looks extra careful at my passport. Noticing that it has recently expired, she lifts her eyebrows, takes the measure of me with a discerning eye, and then pushes my check back at me.

"I'm sorry, sir. An expired passport is not valid identification."

Not wanting to quibble, I smile and patiently open my passport and show her all of the elaborate visa stamps in the back of the book, and the tooled picture of me and how it compares to the mug shot decorating my brand-new driver's license. Has she noticed how the dates of birth match, the brown hair, brown eyes, weight and height?

Well, the teller looks at me like I'm some kind of idiot because I'm not programmed to know in my bones that bank rules are unquestionably bank rules and I flip. I'd gone and taken my living straight from the hills mostly because I wasn't a child or a GI anymore, and because I didn't want to be treated like one. I liked having jobs I could quit, and I liked having people I could talk back to.

Speaking loud enough so everyone into the crowd stops and listens, I ask the teller if she thinks I'd go and forge a U.S. passport and all of those foreign visas just so I could walk into her bank and have her cash me a thirteen-dollar unemployment check three days before Christmas. She must think me some kind of mastermind crook who's just happened to have fallen upon hard times and so thinks he has some kind of an excuse for breaking the rules—the holy rules. But I was here to tell her that the only rule that counts is the one requiring us to say to hell with the rules when they fly in the face of common sense and common decency. The laws against breaking and entering, I haughtily pointed out to her, didn't prevent a person from rescuing somebody whose house is on fire.

I push my check back in front of her and, somewhat surprised by the passion I'd put into my outburst, I look into her eyes and smile meekly. Even if I'd stolen the passport, I confide to her as if I could appreciate her point of view, the amount of money is so tiny that even a hippy wouldn't miss it. And how is the check going to bounce when it's been issued by the Great State of California not but a few days before? If my little unemployment check bounces, why by springtime we're all going to be either cannibals or cannibees anyway—so where's the risk in just going ahead and cashing my check? How big of a gamble is that for the Bank of America? Moreover, I urge her while sweeping my arm at the assembled hoard, she should consider all of the people behind me in line and waiting for service. And to this from the crowd comes some encouraging, if mumbled, "hear hear"s and "lets get on with it"s.

Still, the teller isn't convinced. Not only that, but now I've gone and wounded her pride, and from here on out she ain't budging just out of redneck spite. She pushes my check away a second time and I push it back at her and she pushes it right back at me.

"Cash the damned check," the other teller orders under her breath. "Cash his check and get him the hell out of here."

Being younger and so on the short end of the totem pole lashed between them, my teller grudgingly does as she is told even though I can tell she wants to stick her tongue out at me or, even better, come out from behind the counter to stomp on my foot. But she contains herself and does everything right except, when she counts out my money, it's only eight dollars instead of thirteen. When I ask her what that's about, she tells me it's the fee they charge to cash the checks of rank strangers like myself.

"What?" I roar. "It's three days before Christmas, I hand you a thirteen-dollar unemployment check, and you want to keep five bucks of it? Why not keep the whole damned thing if you're that hard up for money? You want my shoes, too? How about my coat? You want my coat?"

"What's the problem here?" the branch manager asks as quietly as he can. Somehow he's appeared over the young woman's shoulder. He was addressing her, but I beat her to the punch.

"I live on sixty acres," I assert loud enough so all can hear, "and your bank holds the mortgage. I fell timber for Bud You-Know-Who and sometimes I cash his paychecks in here. Your senior teller is my friend, I sometimes eat lunch at Picks, and about every respectable drunk in every bar in Cloverdale can vouch that they've seen me behaving like a gentleman at least once in their lives. And here it's three days before Christmas and I've got me a thirteen-dollar unemployment check that this stubborn young woman at first refuses to..."

After patiently hearing me out while discreetly giving me the "keep it down" signal with his hand, and taking into account the mood of the waiting crowd, the branch manager settles the matter by quietly apologizing to me and telling the teller to pay me what my check is worth and to be more sensitive with the customers in the future.

And the crowd, like at last it's able to let out its breath, bursts into cheers and applause. I turn around and look and everybody in the joint is grinning at me, clapping or giving me an enthusiastic two thumbs up. So I start grinning, too, and the manager grins and even the teller who'd started all the trouble starts fighting off the urge to grin and, just like that, it feels like Christmas in Cloverdale.

When I left the bank flush with my fresh cash, I had some glide in my stride.

WALKING TRACTOR

For fifteen years I walked farm tractors up and down State Highway 128 between Philo and Navarro. Not often, mind you. Mostly just during spring and fall, and then I'd only make four or six round-trips per year. All told, I got in more than five hundred miles worth of rolling through the northern half of Anderson Valley at fifteen miles per hour.

Walking tractor was a seasonal chore I looked forward to. Ranch work paid by the hour, and most hours required me to engage in a bit of aerobic exercise. Working a horse ranch in Anderson Valley meant pounding fence posts and stretching pasture wire, bucking hay and hauling feed bags, digging up busted waterlines and clearing away windfall trees from atop downed power lines. Horse ranching around here meant nailing together redwood corrals and hanging steel cattle gates, mixing concrete in wheelbarrows, making firewood, and chopping and burning brush. Since horses are destructive critters—one horse kicking up its heels and double-barreling the top of one split-redwood fence post could create a day's work for you—whatever time you had for maintenance came after you'd caught up on your repairs. And you caught up on your repairs only after you'd gotten ahead of your daily chores, plus—if possible—whatever construction or cultivation project you happened to be in the middle of.

But walking tractor was ghost time. It was the sort of chore that, at worst, gave you a flat ass and a round potbelly. While fighting a powerful headwind blowing between Navarro and Philo, a fellah might burn all of the calories contained in one lunch box Twinkie. And what was a ranch hand but a lazy farm hand? I suppose if I'd have walked enough tractor on a daily basis, and if the tractor's steering was as sloppy as mine was, then all of that constant swinging of my little round Brodie Knob between ten and two o'clock might have taken something out of me. If I put in enough hours working my steering wheel like that, my arm might get repetitive motion syndrome or who knows what else. Then again, had the road still been washboarded dirt instead of a paved, modern thruway, the whole experience would have been different.

But, for me, walking tractor was nearly always a pleasure.

I used to love the feel of the wind in my face. I loved the wind rippling my clothing, the foliage in the trees, and the seed heads of the spring grass. Under a slowly drifting pinto sky, with puffs of white clouds sliding across the ceiling of the valley, occasionally a dab of shadow passed over and slowly overtook me as if we were racing. And if I was traveling a straightaway and the direction of the wind was aligned with it, then race we would, at least for one wild moment, my imaginary companion and me side by side and going for the gold.

Canyons breathe in and out with the arc of the sun and creeks always radiate cool air. The highway bridge over Mill Creek, sunk down in its deep swale, always feels cooler than the road on either side of it. "The deeper the shade, the cooler the breeze," the loggers say, and even during the hottest summer afternoon, passing through the deep shadows cast by the tall redwoods of Christine Woods was always refreshing. Even a small and gentle side canyon like the one carved by Floodgate Creek usually threw me a kiss of wind as I rolled by. A little no-name, peek-a-boo feeder creek channeling through a twenty-four-inch-wide highway culvert, a sunny grass knuckle, a low-lying meadow, a solitary, broad-branched valley oak—every wrinkle in the terrain seemed home to its own temperature and wind, its own smell and feeling.

Naturally, on the down side, I couldn't hear anything, what with the whining diesel engine in front of me and the over-sized, rumbling, wobbly tires at my elbows.

Mingled with the local breezes was the Pacific Ocean wind that pushed up the throat of the valley most every afternoon no matter what time of year. If I was heading toward Philo in the afternoon, the ocean wind pushed me along, at times powerfully enough to save me diesel. If I was heading toward Navarro and the wind was against me, it'd take back the diesel I'd saved during the opposite run. Yet, no matter which way the ocean wind was blowing—most building rainstorms blew down the valley instead of up it—I always saw it as a great blessing. The ocean wind was not just a natural air conditioner but an air clearer, since it had birthed somewhere in Manchuria or Kamchatka before sailing over the wide North Pacific and making landfall at the Navarro River mouth. With the ocean wind came some of the purest air anywhere in the northern hemisphere, and I always appreciated that.

Not so pleasant were the manmade winds: the *swooshes* of oncoming vehicles. As with the landscape, each type of oncoming rig made its own kind of wind. The slap of air thrown aside by a little four-banging Honda sports car was like the air pushed ahead by a swinging ping-pong paddle; the blast of air made by a loaded logging truck, however, would send my baseball hat flying if I didn't watch out. I'm proud to say that during all of my years walking tractors in Anderson Valley, never once did I lose my hat. A few times I had my hat blown off my head, sure enough, but only back when I was first learning the winds of the highway. But even then each time my hat got blown off I was able to pull off the road and hike back to rescue it.

In fact, once I became a seasoned tractor walker, I stopped worrying about my hat altogether. A loaded logging truck bearing down on me at sixty-five miles per hour wasn't enough to get me to raise an eyebrow. Before impact I'd screw down my hat, drop my chin to my breastbone, keep my hands on my steering wheel, and let her rip. With the top of my head pointing like it was, the blast of the logging truck just screwed my hat down tighter.

At the same time I never did figure out a way to keep my hat on my head while facing an oncoming lumber-mill chip truck. Spotting one of those towering metal boxes rushing at me made me abandon the idea altogether. I'd stuff my hat under my right thigh, weigh it down with my leg, and get a death grip on my steering wheel with both hands. For if a chip truck was aiming for me and I was looking off into the landscape stone deaf and daydreaming, nonchalantly working my steering wheel with the tips of a thumb and two fingers resting on my Brodie Knob, half-sitting my seat with my clutch leg kicked up, and I didn't notice a flying chip truck bearing down on me, then when its humongous blast of air hit me it might throw me clean off the ass end of my tractor.

Or, if it didn't do that, it'd damn sure snap me back out of my daydreams.

The only kind of rig that struck terror in me was an oncoming or passing gravel truck. Usually on the gravy train contracting by the load to Caltrans, gravel trucks were always speeding, and watching one of those massive high-tech wheelbarrows barreling down on me from either way sent me to my battle stations. I'd pin my hat under my leg, scrunch down in my seat, drop my chin, grit my teeth, narrow my shoulders, squint my eyes, tuck in my knees, and hold on to my steering wheel for dear life knowing that, if a flying rock beaned me, it wouldn't be because I was offering it a large target or I hadn't been watching out.

Yet, because I usually only walked tractor during mid-morning or mid-afternoon, most of the time I had Highway 128 all to myself and I could indulge in some leisurely sightseeing.

Anderson Valley looks a whole lot different moseying along atop a tractor than it does while encased in a speeding bullet. Every trip between Philo and Navarro my eye caught on something new. I might spot the remains of a leaning split-rail pasture fence overtaken by forest, or an old buckled-over ranch house tucked into a shady cranny. I might catch sight of an abandoned, hand-hewn redwood water trough hiding under a patch of blackberries, somebody's vegetable garden, berry patch, or flower bed. It got so I tried to lay my eyes on something new each trip, and I always did. Because I couldn't sightsee when I had traffic backed up behind me, passing me, or coming at me, there were stretches of roadside scenery that it took me years to fully eyeball. I must have made a dozen trips back and forth before discovering the supple young apple orchard growing up in the bowl opposite Greenwood Ridge Road. Then, not long ago, while stopped in my truck beside the highway at Reilly Heights Ranch, I noticed a broken old wooden wagon wheel lying in the barnyard that I'd never spotted from the seat of my tractor.

A walking tractor moved at the speed of a trotting horse. My tractor's speed was of another era and, letting my imagination play, it moved at the speed of a Pomo hunter on foot racing the setting sun to get back home to his wife and children before dark. A newlywed Pomo girl running for joy at daybreak might have paced me. It wasn't hard to imagine getting passed by a drunken, love-struck, young-buck homesteader aboard his lathered, heaving horse, whipping his hat in the wind and raising dust to high heaven. Or maybe, next to that heap of collapsed pioneer cabin, there in the sheltered opening beneath the redwoods, beside that bubbling finger of earth-filtered rainwater and with his or her worn-out back to a tree, somebody had sat down to die.

Woven into the rest was the living human landscape. Friends flicked their headlights in greeting as we passed each other. Or, if they came up behind me, they'd wait patiently a respectable distance away until, when the time was right, surging forward to momentarily pause beside me, glance sideways, and wave before again stepping on their gas pedals, accelerating, and shrinking into the highway. Once or twice rowdy hillbilly friends snuck up behind me in the rolling country there by Lazy Creek and, when I least expected it, they shot past me like bats out of hell overdue for some malicious hillbilly fun. They'd scare me about half out of my seat—which was precisely what they'd been after.

Boy I used to hate it when they did that. I'd imagine them up in the Boonville Lodge wetting their lips and bragging about the great thing they'd just done, and I'd be plotting my revenge.

Somewhere along the way I might pass a lonesome, stranded ex-con hitchhiker in rags who, for the moment at least, has given up the ghost and is napping in dappled shade atop a soft carpet of redwood duff. I might pass a weathered campesino in a clean straw village hat stepping it out along the shoulder of the highway with his back straight, his eyes forward, and his legs moving with purpose. Once I saw a young road gypsy woman rising out of the morning grass. Another time, while passing a clapboard house, I watched as young lovers battled it out on their rickety front porch, she with a baby tucked under her arm and he shaking a long-necked quart of beer at her. Occasionally as I passed, folks would rise from working in their gardens frowning and impatient and, seeing me, smile slightly as if they forgave me for my untimely intrusion of racket. As I passed by Gowan's apples, old compadres sometimes waved their pruning saws at me from the tops of orchard ladders. I might spot a pair of old partners building a fence, stop the tractor to go and jaw with them, making sure to mention at some point during our conversation that I envied them mightily for being able to stretch out all of that nasty, ugly-assed barbed wire all over hill and dale while I was stuck walking a tractor.

Chugging along Highway 128 at fifteen miles per hour, it seemed I'd encounter people everywhere. And woven into the winds, landscape, history, and people were the animals. In the thick brush in a canyon passing below the highway, out of the corner of my eye, I might catch the twitch of a cougar's tail, knowing the sight by the flash of buckskin brown in the interwoven greenery. Across a grassy opening, I might catch the glimpse of a coyote prancing/slinking into a tree line. Up ahead, hovering stationary like a helicopter directly above the painted double yellow line, I might see a snowy white kite hawk eyeballing me like I was some giant and noisy new kind of roadkill. Because I was into the woodsman's habit of knowing what was hanging above me, every trip I'd spot perched in roadside trees watching me buzzards and raptors, ravens, jays, and crows.

Once a yearling doe, perhaps playing chicken with me, at the very last second darted in front of the tractor and made it past my front tires by inches. Another time a jackrabbit, no doubt playing chicken, jumped out in front of me and, engaging its afterburners, raced ahead before stopping in the middle of my lane, turning and staring at me, its ears erect as if it was wondering what I could possibly do to match that. And once he realized I wasn't going to slam on my brakes, jerk on my steering wheel, or make any other sort of rash move for one crazy rabbit, just before I ran it over it leaped into a roadside thicket of poison oak.

Once, while minding my own business and tooling along in the breeze, I got attacked by a furious blue jay. Thinking she might be guarding her hatchlings, I tried to tell her that I meant her and hers no harm. But it wasn't until I'd gotten out of range of her nest that she left me alone.

Another time, just like I was standing still, a shot glass–sized hummingbird checked me out from all angles before streaking away like a bumblebee. Another time, shooting from the tall grass, a skunk tried to spray me.

Once a mama quail, just like I was moseying along some back country ranch road, jumped out in front of me with her half dozen egg-sized offspring and, stealing glances over this shoulder and that, zigging and zagging and bobbing and weaving in mock panic, tried to pace me up the center of my lane.

And, knowing the rascality of quail, when I accelerated and tried to run them over to get them to show their hand, in an explosion of wings they scattered sideways out of my way in weird, wobbly trajectories, half kind of following their mother leftward, and the other half going the opposite way.

Once, I brought my tractor to a complete halt to allow a lumbering porcupine to cross the road. Another time a wood rat scampered under my tires and got squished, leaving in my tracks a furry red flat spot as a meal for anyone who was interested or who got there first.

But perhaps my most memorable experience was the time a huge barn owl stirred from a tree and, in broad daylight, its creamy white wings outstretched and stone steady, soared by my face so close I felt the wind.

TRESPASSING

If you were kids and you wanted to trespass, it was usually left up to the wife of the rancher to decide what to do with you. Eyeballing the bunch of you standing expectantly on her porch, your canteens, lunch bags, and walking sticks at the ready, the wife might rub her chin a good long while before deciding whether or not to grant you the permission to pass. And, if she did, then she'd tell you no fires, no litter, no harassing the livestock, and no pasture gate left any way but how you found it. Finally—she might even wag her finger at this point—there'd be no getting hurt and no getting lost.

Naturally there were a certain number of ranchers who were ornery. While they weren't silly enough to truly believe that they could own a mountain, they very well could lay legal claim to the exclusive use of one, and some of them surely did. And if the rancher was good and ornery in that way, then you could bet your ass that his wife was, too. Sharing qualities like orneriness helped husbands and wives to get along with each other. And if it was a wife like that standing between the bunch of you kids and your right to pass, then there could be no child on earth capable of sweet-talking her into going against her instincts and her better judgment. She'd make up any kind of an excuse to keep you off their land and, having no more time for small talk, she'd shoo you off her porch.

If the rejected, dejected, and ejected kids were anything like my two boys and their headstrong friends, they'd go and trespass anyway. If a particular old coot's place was standing in the way of them getting to where they wanted to get, well, they were leaving behind some discreet footprints. And because they'd be doing no harm, where was the foul? The waterfall or swimming hole they'd be hiking to had been welcoming herds of kids like them for centuries. First native kids, then pioneer kids, then their kids and those that came after them. And just in case they needed any more justification than that, breaking the rules was good for the soul. The Golden Rule was the only one that counted, anyway. All of the rest had been negotiated.

At one time about every ranching community in America had at least one elderly, reclusive couple who hated kids of all shapes and sizes. Anderson Valley was no exception. And for every one of those old battleaxes and bastards, there might be three more who liked pretending that they too were heartless old battleaxes and stingy old bastards. For what could be easier and more fun than fooling with the minds of some snot-nosed little kids?

"You kids don't be wandering up into that top canyon, now. My husband saw a big old mountain lion up in there not three days ago. The way the big cat was stalking around and stopping every few steps to sniff the breeze and search in the distance, he looked to be mighty hungry, too. But by the time my husband got out his rifle, the lion was gone and so you'd best be watching out now."

That's how it was back when people knew each other and day-to-day business was conducted with a promise and a handshake. But once ranchland gets taken out of production and subdivided and filled with newcomers, community life, such as it is, becomes a whole lot more complicated. For starters, now a landowner is surrounded by landowning strangers and so he feels like he's camped out in alien if not hostile territory. A landowner in such circumstances needs liability insurance and, once you start paying protection money, there's no end to it. You start off by building walls around you to protect yourself and your own and you wind up rattling the bars of your cage. No Trespassing goes for you, too, and you'd best watch where you step. And even if nothing untoward ever happens, your insurance payments keep going up year after year, and heaven help you if ever somebody does trespass on your land and gets hurt in any way. If a little kid ignores your posted warning signs, climbs over your fence and gets eaten by a mountain lion—don't even think about how much money it's going to cost you.

Nowadays, if the horror stories are true, by allowing some kids on your land you risk losing everything you own. To do such a thing would be totally irresponsible from an estate planner's point of view, not to mention a bean counter's. By taking such a huge, reckless risk, what conceivably could be gained by it?

• • •

The first time I noticed the pyramid mountain on the skyline, I was a young man pruning grapes in the hills southeast of Geyserville. Looking north from the vineyard I could see the long, broad, shadowy ridge that rises like a wall above Cloverdale and then meanders all the way to Willits. And along that waving skyline, somewhere in the high mountains above Yorkville, I spotted this little pyramid that seemed to be higher than everyplace else (nowadays you can also see the pyramid on the skyline from the "new" 101 freeway as it bypasses Geyserville).

Driving up out of Ukiah on the Boonville road, starting at the Eye of the Needle and then from most of the way along the flat, snaking ridge-top stretch of highway that connects you to the headwaters of Soda Creek and the eastern rim of Anderson Valley, off to the left on the skyline you'll see the same pyramid. It's the opposite face, of course, but it's unmistakably the same peak. Except from this perspective it no longer appears to be the high point on the ridge (it isn't).

Above the pyramid is the crown of Snow Mountain. From up there on a clear day, looking eastward, in the foreground almost straight below you sits the thumbnail summit of Duncan Peak. Looking southward you see a barren, banded area of colored rocks and churned-up soils that used to be the site of a mining camp. Farther east are the mountains that form the divide between Mendocino and Lake Counties. Peeking above them are the caps of Cobb Mountain, Mt. Konocti, Sanhedrin, and others.

Returning your gaze to the bottomlands you see a wide swath of the flat Sanel Valley and the trees lining the Russian River and you know that, were the landscape covered with enough snow, you could ski downhill from here and not stop until you reached downtown Hopland.

Turning westward, straight below you see the main fork of Rancheria Creek with its uncharted archaeological treasures (back in the 1700s, Spanish horsemen supposedly camped down there). You see Bloomfield's Roost with its hangman's tree still vigorous, sprawling, sturdy and alone. You see the Ornbaum Opening and Kristell's Peak edging the badlands and, resting on the horizon like a hairy tarantula, Pardaloe Mountain.

Not far from Snow Mountain is a twenty-foot-tall waterfall. During winter when the land is saturated and just after a gully-washing overnight downpour, the water plunging over the fall makes a continuous thunder that can be heard a mile away.

Within a thousand feet of the waterfall is a pigmy forest made up of stunted juniper trees. Some of the junipers are one foot thick at the butt and only five or six feet tall. Time has taken ancient volcanic rocks and pulverized them into gravels, and their roan and pink pastels, especially set against the verdant green foliage and the frosty blue clusters of juniper berries, reminds you that great beauty also resides in small places.

Farther along the ridge, capping a nearby high point, is a stand of giant sugar pines. Like a palm oasis in the desert, or a solitary ship at sea, the circle of sugar pines looks nothing like anything else that can be seen in any direction. Their stout buttery trunks are tall and straight like the masts of clipper ships, and their feathery canopies, alive with millions of needles, fill, sway, and sing in the mountaintop wind. Close your eyes and the pine's wind songs sound like placid shore breaks rippling and receding on a sandy beach, like a waterfall, a cascade, or a storm at sea.

As seeds did the sugar pines sail in on the wind? Why are they growing only here and nowhere else nearby? Maybe, like redwoods or Joshua trees, the sugar pines are the remnants of a ghost forest that is gone. Or maybe, just maybe, they are the outpost of a colony soon to come.

Walking beneath the pine's waving crowns, you notice that the duff is so thick that your footsteps feel springy.

• • •

Maybe twenty years ago an old Vietnam vet partner and me hiked through the mountains from the Page Malliard Ranch to Leo Marcott's old roadhouse in Yorkville. My partner was the ranch's caretaker and, using a map and compass, we took off from his place not much past sunrise and we made a beeline. Still, since the ridges were running against us, we had to force march ourselves the final three hours to get out of that chaos of terrain and onto our bar stools at Leo's before dark.

At one point, in order to play it safe and keep to our azimuth, we dove off a towering canyonside consisting of crumbling shale outcrops and landslides. Wary of the possibility of a cliff standing hidden in the brush below us, we climbed down slowly, our footing not much different than what we'd get while climbing down the face of a sand dune. The ground leveled some, redwoods grew thick, and we came into the sound of a cascade. The cascade sounded real close, which was strange because we were only about halfway down the slope. We spotted some ferns growing here and there under the trees, and before long we were surrounded by a forest of sword ferns standing eight foot tall. The ground underfoot turned to shale and out of every crack and fissure—oozing like from pores—was running water. The deeper down we climbed, the more water we saw until we were standing in the middle of a rocky, fern-covered amphitheater of rushing, splashing, bubbling, cascading rivulets and streams. The shale was a giant filter, a saturated, oozing sponge. And we realized that here, exactly here, began a river.

We spotted a whitewashed elk horn nestled in among the overarching, giant ferns. My partner, suddenly feeling superstitious, warned me not to touch the horn. But I picked it up anyway. The horn felt hard, cold, and heavy in my hand; heavy as if while laying in the wet rocks over the seasons it had absorbed minerals and had become petrified. With so much breadth, and so many forks, it had to be an elk horn, we knew, because no coastal deer ever grew so big. So the horn was a trophy to be taken home, a true relic, a veritable conversation piece. Who could possibly object if I took the horn and made human use of it?

Somebody who climbs a lot of mountains will occasionally, after a hard day's scramble, stop short of a particular summit. He'll stop short to honor the gods. Now you or he might claim to believe in just One True God and One True God only, or even to believe in no gods at all. But that doesn't mean you can't be superstitious. There is no line between Creator and Creation, and Creation shows a million faces.

After a couple of minutes of what must have been one crazy bush bunny conversation, we wound up leaving the elk horn where we'd found it.

HILLBILLY CAPITALISM

As much as I enjoyed setting choker, even before the end of my first season working behind Lester I saw the job as a stepping-stone. Not all catskinners were as fun to work with as Lester—not to mention "handy" (skillful)—and over my seasons spent rigging logs I'd work behind a couple of catskinners who, being beginners with neither the aptitude nor the temperament for the job, were not only not fun to work with but were downright dangerous to be around. Take a greenhorn catskinner and get him in a big hurry and he's going to get frustrated and, if he's prone to tantrums and you're on foot, you don't want to be anywhere around him once he flips out and starts violently horsing his bulldozer back and forth, huffing and puffing and punching and banging things out of his way.

If you were like me and your partner was having a tantrum, then to get your relationship back on a professional footing you'd find yourself a four-by-heavy length of broken redwood limb, pick it up, and hurl it as hard and as accurately as you could into the side of his cage, aiming for his head and hoping to put a ding into the heavy-duty wire mesh protecting it. Get off a good enough shot and that'd halt him in his tracks and refocus his attention.

Once I hurled a limb at a greenhorn catskinner who, in the middle of his tantrum, carelessly backed his Cat into a stump on the bottom lip of the trail and broke loose a tall, skinny redwood stump shoot that came down like a flyswatter. If I hadn't've been watching and leaped out of its way, the knockdown would have killed me or at least

61

ended my logging career. In retaliation I climbed up the hill above him, flung my limb at his cage, smacked it, and got him stopped, all right. In fact, I'm proud to say, I scared the shit out of him.

Yet, instead of calming down, he decided to come after me. Spotting me standing up the hill with my hands on my hips, he flew out of his seat, leaped from his track, hit the dirt running like a spider, and started scrambling up the hill at me on all fours, claws scratching and him snarling even though, given his fit of temper and the steepness and looseness of the ground, he wasn't making too much headway.

Figuring I'd better do something, I made a quick search of the ground at my feet, found a broken length of limb about the size of a caveman's club, and picked it up and shook it at him threateningly. Since he kept on coming, acting like I was in the batter's box, I held my limb like it was a baseball bat and I was getting set to hit a home run. The sight of that finally got him stopped and, halting a respectable distance away, he settled for tongue-lashing me up one side and, out of breath, halfway down the other.

When it was my turn to talk, I told him simply that if he didn't want me to be using his cage for target practice then he'd best stop nearly getting me killed.

That's how it was with us chokersetters, whether homegrown or imported like me. Even while working behind Lester during my first season, once he knew I knew what I was doing, I became not just his eyes and ears, hands and feet, but also his ringmaster. If Lester saw I was making an obvious mistake, he'd call a halt so he could point it out to me and instruct me in the right way of getting what I wanted done. As the season wore on and I made fewer and fewer mistakes, Lester had less and less to say.

Once I was completely broken-in Lester and his bulldozer became my giant circus elephant and, using an elaborate system of hand signals, facial expressions, and body language, I put my elephant through its routines. Skidding logs to the landing and coming back for more was Lester's job, but getting logs to pop out of the woods and organizing skids was mine. And while I was doing my job Lester didn't make a move without my say so. That was the way it was done, and that's how logs got moved.

Anyway, even before Lester and I broke camp and said our

goodbyes, I already knew what I wanted to be when I grew up. I wanted to become a rip-roaring big-tree redwood timber faller. I wanted to be out single-jacking, booming, busheling, and never returning to the same spot twice. I'd wound up working nearly alone in some of the most rugged and remote mountain headwaters on the West Coast because, chased by war demons, I figured that point zero three people per acre was about the right population density for me. And now, with my dream of felling timber taking shape in my mind, I figured I had a way to stay in the hills forever while making something beyond beans-and-rice money. Not only that but as a timber faller I'd be working according to the weather and seasons and not according to a punch clock or somebody's instructions.

If I was felling timber and a contrary wind came up early in the afternoon (you can't fell a strip of timber against the wind), then I'd call it a day no matter what the clock said. Though I carried a pocketwatch I rarely looked at it since the sun and my belly told me roughly what time it was. If I got blown out early, the next morning I'd be back in my strip at the first light of day. I'd be out early to make up for lost production and hoping to get a jump on that day's afternoon winds. Or, if we were in a heat wave, I'd show up at dawn just to beat the heat. If the morning was ocean-foggy and neither wind nor heat was in the "forecast," I might not show up until ten in the morning and still I'd get a full day in, the only difference being a late ride home while feeling a powerful hunger for food. While working my strip of timber I not only wouldn't have a boss, I wouldn't even have anybody to consult with.

On top of all that—this was the best part—the work was seasonal and, once the winter rains set in, I'd get laid off and then paid for sitting around in my cabin and tending to the fire in my woodstove. I'd get paid not just for staying dry and warm but also for doing the other things I wanted to do, like spending some time with my wife and babies and writing a little bit. Also, because nobody can live off an unemployment check, I'd get to spend the off-season cutting firewood and doing ranch jobs, raking in the very best kind of working money: hillbilly bootleg money. If the household grub was getting low, I'd take a cash-on-the-barrelhead "odd job" and, unless the grub was really low, if I didn't like the boss or his attitude, or if

I thought his project, or the way he wanted me to go about it, was foolish, or if I found something else intolerable, I'd quit.

If I contracted to take on a strip of hardwoods to make firewood, whether as a part of a reforestation project or to clear the land for something else or just to "thin the yield," before I cranked up my saw and made my first cut in my first tree, already I'd figured the angles. Having done my head-scratching I felt confident that, when the deal I'd made with the rancher was done, I'd make out. And if I got into the middle of a strip and I realized I'd underbid the job, then I'd speed up to get it done so I could move on to a better job. The reason I did that was plain enough. In these hills in matters of trade a man is only as good as his word and, given the hillbilly grapevine, to break your word to one rancher means you won't ever get the chance to break it to another.

Throw every aspect of living as a timber faller/woodcutter/ranch hand together and, as an ex-GI wanting to put as much distance as possible between myself and The Military Way, I could think of nothing better. Other than going off to sea (I was a mountain person and not an ocean person), becoming a woodsman put me as far away as I could get from my past, and that in and of itself was enough to make me fall in love with it. In the woods was a future free of my past.

So, reaching for the stars, I used the last paycheck of my first season setting choker behind Lester to *Capitalize*. Since I already owned the pickup truck, tin hat, lunch box, water jug, spiked boots, and suspenders, to get me on the road to success all I needed was a chainsaw and some accessories. I needed a chainsaw to build up the right muscles and so I bought me a used heavy-duty faller's saw equipped with a hotrod engine and a thirty-six-inch-long cutting bar. I also bought a short-handled faller's ax, a set of red-headed plastic wedges, a pair of steel wedges, a splitting maul, a peeve, a tourniquet (bandana), and (kept in a second lunch box) a few miniature chainsaw tools, bandages, antiseptic, tweezers, and needle-nose pliers for pulling out wood splinters. Add a gas can, oil can, Buck knife, and a baseball cap (I only wore my tin hat while I was felling trees) and that was the full extent of my capital investment. Thus equipped and raring to go, I began my career as a gyppo firewood cutter.

My first job was chopping black oak and madrone for Wayne

McGimsey way up above Yorkville on a bench of land set on the sunny side of Ward Mountain. Boy was I sorry. Since I didn't know the first thing about how to safely and efficiently operate a chainsaw, watching me wielding that long-nosed, wood-eating hotrod must have made quite some sight. It made the kind of sight you peeked at through the crack between your fingers covering your eyes. Because getting paid by the number of cords you produced was a huge disadvantage if you didn't know how to run chainsaw, my first few days I worked myself ragged and hardly made a dime. If I wasn't trying to free my pinched bar from the trunk of a tree or learning how to swing my ax and actually hit a wedge, then I was sitting down trying to reset my thrown chain or down on my knees half-assed filing my chain because I'd accidentally run it through the rocks again (when you see sparks flying off the nose of your bar, that's God's way of telling you to shut down and re-sharpen). I spent even more time tearing down my saw to free my bent bar so I could take it to a likely stump and, like a blacksmith swinging sledge into an anvil, pound it back into shape with my ax-head. I got my truck stuck in the mud, pinched my fingers, dropped a round of firewood on my foot, barked my shins, and got my thigh charley-horsed by my kicking-back, rearing-up, and pissed-off chainsaw.

I was doing about everything up on Ward Mountain except making firewood and money, and even without considering my fear of accidentally slicing off my own head, after a week I'd have quit in embarrassment and frustration if Wayne, along with my partner, a seasoned logger out bootlegging with me, hadn't've taken me under their wings. They took the time to show me how it was done and to instruct me in the dos and don'ts, the nature and way of things and, especially so with my partner, they also took the time to help me out of the trouble I was constantly getting myself into and to teach me how to avoid that particular type of trouble in the future.

Over the years it got so I was fairly decent working the hardwoods. Sometimes during the off-season I'd hire on just felling and bucking and getting paid by the cord once the wood got shipped off the mountain. Other times I'd hire on to do that plus stack the brush for burning. But mostly I worked gyppo. I'd pay a rancher "stumpage," back then usually about 15 percent of retail value, and do everything myself without him having to lift a finger. That arrangement suited the rancher fine because if he had the time for worrying over firewood, he'd be out cutting it himself.

For safety reasons I always worked with a partner, although, aside from sharing transportation and production costs, we always kept our books separate. Only once did I take on a real partner, working fifty-fifty, and that was because we were good friends, the show was on the ranch he was caretaking, the stumpage was sweet, we worked well together, and—not the least—we had fun together, both in the woods and afterward in town lollygagging in saloons.

Though I never liked it much and tried to avoid it, occasionally, under the pressure of a project deadline, I hired "employees." While most businessmen are mighty proud of the number of people held in their employ, I saw my own success in independence and self-reliance, simplicity and harmony. About the only people I could hire and trust to not hurt themselves or somebody else were laid-off young-buck loggers like me, and they were a contentious and unreliable bunch capable of causing all kinds of disharmony. They showed up for work when they wanted and they left work when they damn well pleased. Also, since they knew in their muscles and bones that virtually the entire value of a cord of firewood was in the human labor that went into it and not in the wood, they were shrewd about prices and wise to the sometimes crooked ways of "jobbers" (wheeler-dealers) like me.

Once, starting up a major land-clearing operation on Chalk Hill Road down in Sonoma County, after drawing straws I tried assigning four woodcutters their individual strips and they made me feel like I was dealing them a crooked hand of poker. I showed the first fellah his assigned strip and, instead of eyeballing it, with an eagle's eye he got to inspecting the strips flanking it, taking a mental inventory to see if he'd gotten a raw deal. Determining he had, he wondered aloud just how much money it was going to cost him and suggested how I might want to adjust his boundaries some, or raise his bushel rate or—what would be really fair—go back and start all over by drawing straws again. Add in the three fellahs who'd gotten the other short sticks and, before we'd even cranked up our chainsaws, already we were raising a commotion. By the time we were finished negotiating, the sun was a hand above the horizon.

Beyond a bootlegging hillbilly's contentiousness was his principled unreliability. They worked hard so they could party hard, and they were used to doing things their own way. They weren't above blowing a big chunk of a day's wage while "tying one on" in a saloon and, if one of them woke up the next morning hungover, then you'd as soon bag a mountain lion as get him to show up for work if you were a small-time gyppo like me. The very same fellah who twenty times during the course of the official logging season arrived in the redwoods not just hungover but still sloppy drunk (the rules for drunks were: Don't puke on the Cat, the rigging, the logs, or on the ground where you'd be needing to lay down to set a choker, and never puke on your partner) would, if he was bootlegging firewood for me, coldcock his alarm clock, fluff his pillow, pull up his covers, roll over, and go back to blowing big, happy Zs.

Or, if he is feeling responsible, or if he just happens to be the sort of fellah who wants to do the right thing, he'll show up for work so woozy that when he opens his door he falls out of his pickup truck. If that's the case then it might take me a half hour of vigorous gab to convince him that I cannot in good conscience allow him to start work and, no, I didn't want to join him on his day off so the two of us could go and sit in a bar and get to know each other better.

Finally, with hillbillies you had to deal with hillbilly pride. The ghetto bloods I'd holed up with in the infantry called the act/feeling "getting up a big case of the ass." Loggers had a whole slew of phrases to describe the phenomenon, most of which are unfit to repeat in proper company. What it boiled down to was individual freedom as an act and an attitude of rebellion. Whether you rebelled against your own fears, guilt, regrets, place in life, or the whole wide, crazy world itself, that was the only freedom you'd ever know. And since woodsmen—like all mountain people everywhere—loved to experience freedom, they'd rebel any chance they got. Throw in the fact that they all knew that their way of life was being destroyed (some blamed the environmentalists, others the rape-and-run corporate timber pirates, and everyone blamed the government), and that just made them all the more stubborn, contentious, and rebellious. Losing the economic basis of their way of life meant they held on all the more tenaciously to their hillbilly ways and values.

As a practical matter, if ever you uttered a cross word, or demanded some extra work from them, or even demanded an explanation from them, they'd up and quit you. On the spot they'd shut her down, pull the plug, get down the road, head out of there, cash it in, move on, and shit-can it. They'd call it a day, a week, a year, and jolly-good-riddance with one short phrase and one sharp and happy glint in their eye. If you want them to walk, tell them to run.

Occasionally, without me saying a word or interfering in any way, a fellah would still quit. He'd quit because he took a great notion and, if his notion was great enough and his thirst for change powerful enough, he'd quit even as a tree he'd just felled was still suspended in midair. Once a fellah up and walked off and disappeared so that I couldn't even pay him the money I owed him. I later heard that he'd gone to log the Sierra and, expecting his eventual return, I held on to his money until, years later, I figured I'd never see him again.

Beyond the disharmony, I avoided hiring employees because of the ethics involved. I never much cared for air-conditioned, company pickup–driving straw bosses, labor contractors, and sharpers, and it was one thing to join in the hillbilly economy and another to try to profit from it. I didn't want to model my enterprise on a Kentucky coal combine or a redwood timber baron, and I knew that choosing hillbilly capitalism meant living close to the bone with the wolf of poverty sometimes on my front porch and scratching at my door. That part of the deal didn't bother me much because I didn't want a luxurious office so much as a magnificent front yard. More than anything else, as the years passed it got so I wanted to spend my life with my people, my adopted family. Push come to shove, whatever was good enough for them was good enough for me.

Also, I didn't like the illegality of hiring employees. Three years spent living under the tender mercies of the Uniform Code of Military Justice had made me an outlaw (yank on the bit, get thrown from the horse). As an outlaw, my first duty, aside from trying to practice the Golden Rule, was to keep myself from getting tangled up with the law and its enforcers. I'd rather get attacked by a bear or bit by a rattlesnake than get into the gun sights of the IRS, and to say I was scared of getting busted wouldn't be too harsh a judgment.

So as a gyppo woodcutter I kept my dealings simple and fair, my appetites in check, and my crews small. Over the years I rarely worked with more than one or two partners, and each of us single-jacked and none of us took a cut from anybody. Our partnerships were always verbal and temporary, and our arrangements were always made on the basis of equality.

· · ·

When it came to wholesaling, retailing, and customer relations, I developed my own peculiar ways of doing things. For instance, I charged local people living in shanties less money than I charged other locals who I thought could afford to pay the full mountain price. I didn't offer deals to friends (most all of them made their own firewood anyway), but if a friend or a neighbor felt they were entitled to a discount then, to avoid hurting their feelings, I'd give them 10 percent off—no more, no less. At the same time, if I was delivering firewood to a city weekender visiting his or her mothballed vacation home, then I'd charge the full flatland price (using the Cloverdale market as my measure) and never give them an inch.

So I guess you might say I was a crook. I know if I was a landlord and I got caught charging my Anglo tenants more rent than my Mexican tenants, or vice versa, I'd be thrown before a court bound in chains. But since I wasn't selling a political relationship but just a product with no strings attached, I don't know if the same rules apply.

I do know that I got a big kick out of some of my customers. Some of the hills folk instinctively mistrusted me because I was an outsider, and some of my social betters assumed I was an oaf. Since I was an independent businessman living the real American Dream, it was fascinating how little respect I got from some of my customers. As a woodcutter I was afforded so little social status that over the years I'd occasionally meet people who thought it was their noble birthright to try to take advantage of me. Claiming a bad back, bum knees, or the need to attend to more pressing business, all pathetic-like a customer would ask me if I'd be so kind as to neatly stack my firewood in their woodshed for them. And when I replied that I'd be glad to for an extra 20 percent (time is money), he or she would look all hurt and disappointed and decide, come to think of it, they could manage to do it for themselves (or hire somebody else to do for it a few bucks cheaper).

I especially enjoyed my customers who, in deliberate violation of our explicit agreement, tried to pay me with a personal check instead of cash. My cure for them was to never throw a stick of firewood off my tailgate before I had my money in hand. Unused to such raw treatment from an oaf, the would-be check writer, checkbook and pen held pensively in hand, would bite his or her lip and pretend to be at a loss as to what to do next. I'd tell him or her to drive into town their own self to cash their own damned check while I, being a patient man on a loose schedule, sat under a likely shade tree, sipped ice water from my jug, soaked in the view, and awaited their return.

Once I delivered a cord of firewood to an elderly widow living alone in a shanty full of cats. Locally famous for her large herd, her cats weren't the ordinary kind of felines, either. Living on the pittance provided by her dead husband's Social Security plus some food stamps, and having with age lost the sharpness of her mind, the widow would adopt a feral cat and invite it into her home while making space for it by throwing a house cat out into the wilds. Her herd of cats having their paws in two worlds at the same time and not quite fitting in either, they developed a sort of group-think and acted as the widow's watchdogs. They'd gather together and spit and hiss at strangers, especially strangers who had the audacity to drive a truck into her yard. And the poor old widow would have to expend a good deal of energy scolding the cats and shooing them away so that I could safely set foot outside. Then she'd expend even more energy while profusely apologizing to me for her cats' inhospitality, insolence, and insubordination while confiding that, underneath their hackles, above their claws, and behind their bared fangs, they were just purring little pussycats.

Anyway, winter was hard coming, I'd had a good season logging, I had a large stockpile of seasoned firewood, and the widow was spending as much of her income on cat food as she was on feeding herself. Seeing her threadbare clothes and taking account of the skinniness of her cats, on impulse I decided I'd "donate" my product. I charged her for my expenses plus not much more than minimum wage. As always when I was dealing with the elderly or infirm, I also stacked her firewood for free.

Afterward we sat a spell on her porch drinking glasses of tepid water and talking, and I even got to stroke one, then two, then a whole bunch of her circling, arching cats. And while we talked I could see the widow's muddled mind worrying over how she was going to fit this latest expense into her budget.

And, you know what? A couple of days later that old widow called me on the phone and ordered two more cord to be delivered and stacked at her house. Lacking the heart to refuse or to raise my price, I went ahead and delivered the wood. In fact, for as long as I was in the business, I always sold dirt-cheap firewood to her or to others like her in similar circumstances.

Another time I delivered a high-priced, beautifully manufactured, and bone-dry cord of "gentleman's wood" to a hilltop estate. The master of the domain was a big-city multimillionaire whose hobby was weaseling bargains out of people. When I passed through his wrought iron electric gate swinging between granite rock pillars in my 1968 Dodge three-quarter-ton Camper Special with its woods dents, rust, battered wood sideboards, and 16.5-inch split rims spinning muddy, worn-out mud tires, the fellah was standing at the head of his paved black cul-de-sac eyeballing me like I was Jed Clampett and he was the Beverly Hills banker.

The fellah had two Mexican immigrants as groundskeepers, and as they carried inside of his four-car garage the wood I was tossing off my tailgate, the fellah stood in the shade sipping a martini and questioning me about all aspects of my business as if, seeking fresh opportunity, he was considering taking up my profession for himself. I answered all of his questions honestly and respectfully, even though I knew what he was building up to was an offer to buy more cordage from me but at a lower, renegotiated price.

When my truck was off-loaded and the fellah tried to open negotiations, I ended them by stating flatly that the agreed-upon price was right and fair for the both of us and so we had nothing to talk about when it came to that. And, used to having the last word and being treated with the deference to which a man of his social position was entitled, even though he shrugged his shoulders as if he didn't care, I could tell my uppity attitude had pissed him off. I left his place feeling a chill but, like him, I tried not to care.

As soon as I got home the fellah called me on the phone and, barely able to contain his anger, accused me of cheating him. He'd carefully measured my stack and, according to his calculations, it consisted of only 121 cubic feet instead of 128 cubic feet like it was supposed to. Therefore—this wasn't a negotiation or a discussion as far as he was concerned—he wanted a full and immediate refund for the amount of missing wood.

When he allowed me to respond, I told him his story sounded funny because when I had loaded the wood in my pickup it was a measured 130 cubic feet because I always threw in an extra few sticks to avoid such misunderstandings. I told him to go back and remeasure and, if the stack still came out short, then he'd have to tear it apart, throw it into a random pile, and then restack and remeasure it. If he did that and it still didn't come out right, then he could call me back and, I guessed, in that case I'd have to return up there to his place to see if I could figure out what he was doing wrong.

As you might have guessed, I never did sell any more cords of firewood to that fellah.

I'd be lying if I said I never got my feelings hurt. That fool on the hill wasn't the only customer to greet me with a suspicious eye or a haughty, superior attitude. Having lowly social status means enduring all kinds of slights and slanders but, instead of taking insult, I usually tried to school my suspicious customers on just how the firewood game was played.

Like, were there crooked woodcutters? "Yabetcha," I'd confirm. But I'd assure my wary customers that a crooked woodcutter wasn't going to cheat them by "short-cording" them. Or, if one did, then all he'd get out of them was pocket change. By far the most common and easiest way to cheat a customer was to sell green wood as half-seasoned, or half-seasoned wood as bone dry and "guaranteed not to sizzle."

And the surefire way to avoid ever getting burned like that, I'd generously advise my customers, was to buy green firewood from me and to season it themselves. Most of the wood I produced I wholesaled sopping wet to jobbers (nearly always I was in need of a payday), and

I could deliver to my customers the same wood for wholesale price plus 20 percent. After they stacked the wood in full sun and let it season over the course of two summers then, without them having to lift another finger, their stockpile would have nearly doubled in value. Not only that but, by seasoning their own firewood, never again would they get stuck during some frigid-frosty December sunrise trying to squeeze some heat out of firewood that only wants to hiss, steam, and blow bubbles.

Now do you think I made many sales that way? What was I, a financial advisor? I and woodcutters like me exported from Anderson Valley enough green cordage to cover the floor of the Rose Bowl, but none of us ever had much luck retailing green wood to the locals. The fact was that few people bought firewood before they had to and, come spring, after the mud had dried, the woods opened up, and green firewood became available and cheap, the local market died.

• • •

If woodcutters were burdened with less than enviable reputations, jobbers were downright infamous. Jobbers were legendary for cutting corners, sharp practices, larceny, grand larceny, and worse. Yet every year for thirty years, either as a gyppo or as a ranch foreman, I sold firewood to at least one jobber and only once did I ever get burnt.

It was back when I was working fifty-fifty with my partner up near Yorkville. Engaged in a beautification/reforestation project covering some acres beneath towering, residual redwoods, we were wholesaling most of our wood to one jobber operating out of Petaluma and another living just outside of Cloverdale. Having between us four little kids with voracious appetites, whatever we could stockpile and season for the local market wasn't much.

So I get a phone call from a jobber I've never heard of before. Based in Santa Rosa, fast-talking and offering a long list of references, he tells me he has a quick deal for us. He wants to buy from us five cord of three-tier firewood, special order for prompt delivery. How green the wood is or what type of hardwood it is doesn't matter to him because he already has the load sold to a customer who doesn't care. What the jobber wants special is the length. Instead of cutting sixteen-inch-long pieces, he wants us to cut them a half-inch short. That way, he explains, his customer will be able to comfortably fit the pieces into his woodstove. Also, the short wood will allow him to fit an extra tier across his tailgate, and that extra tier, he points out with emphasis, will pay for his diesel. Because he is getting top price, and because he wants quick service, the jobber further informs me, he can afford to pay us 10 percent more per cord than we were getting from the other jobbers. Did that sound good? Did we have a deal?

After talking it over with my partner, we decided to take the deal. We had two big tanoak pumpkins standing handy and big enough to fill the order, and we figured we'd make some quick and easy money. So I called the jobber back and told him we'd cut the "short cord" for him, but only if we got paid for that extra tier we'd be producing. And, sealing the deal, the jobber assured me that'd be no problem.

So at the appointed time (always a good sign) the jobber arrives on the ranch and at our landing in a white cab-over dump truck with a twenty-four-foot-long flatbed. The flatbed is holding erect, spotless black plywood sideboards anchored so securely that they don't rattle on the way in. His truck is new, its ten tires are packing plenty of tread, and his whole rig is so immaculately clean that I'm surprised he's brought it in on a dirt road, especially one as narrow, twisty, and brushy as ours.

As he climbs down from his idling cab my first impression is of a crew-cut Aryan weightlifter; an ex-jarhead, ex-cop, ex-nightclub bouncer who has been reborn as a pure mercenary, in his mind money in pocket being like territory seized. When we shake hands he crushes mine and, while I was used to that from old-time loggers and so never offered my hand to one of them without being prepared to "palm rassle," I wasn't expecting it from this guy and he hurt my hand.

Seeing the surprised and injured expression on my face seemed to please the jobber and right away I pegged him for the type of fellah I didn't want to be doing business with.

The three of us loaded his truck, my partner and me tossing and him aboard the flatbed stacking. When we were finished loading and he handed me a wad of money, I counted it out and realized it was pay for only fifteen truck tiers instead of the sixteen tiers as we'd agreed. I reminded the jobber of our deal but, acting shocked, he pretended that he'd never heard of such a thing. Firewood always got wholesaled truck scale—didn't we know the rules?

"Dump the load," my partner ordered in a disgusted tone, his Cajun blood heating up. "If he don't want to pay us right then he can dump the damned load and go back out of here empty."

My partner's outburst caused the jobber to react like now we wanted to burn him. I called a time out so that my partner and me could powwow. We walked off under the redwoods and, once we were out of earshot (to avoid further trouble I was hoping the jobber would take the opportunity to drive away), I mentioned to my partner that we both needed the payday and that we didn't have to be battling over a few percentage points, especially since we'd put aside our reservations about cutting the short cord in the first place. We'd lain down with a dog and we'd gotten some fleas was all.

"It's the greedy bloodsucking ticks I can't stand," my partner declared, which was a point we both agreed on. But getting cheated on payday wasn't exactly a novel experience for either of us and, all things considered, this load had been easy money and—principle be damned—we should just take this fellah's cash and be done with him. Finally, my partner agreed.

The jobber was still waiting for us when we returned. He was pacing and I could tell his wicked imagination had taken ahold of him, though I doubt it ever occurred to him to pay us the money he owed us. My partner refused to look at him but I smiled broadly and told the jobber that everything was fine. We'd call it being paid in full and he could get on with his business and not have to worry about us. And, by the way, as he was leaving the ranch, could he please drive slowly and not raise any dust?

Without saying a word, the jobber climbed up behind his steering wheel and, as I watched him go, he drove plenty fast and raised lots of dust. And seeing him do that made me wonder what he'd be telling his wife when he got home to the suburbs, or whether he'd tell her anything. And, not wanting to open that can of worms, I took the lesson I'd learned about short-cording as a tip for the future, and I put him and his kind out of my mind.

• • •

Beyond the mountain workshops, the company of the weather, the challenges, the training for redwood timber felling, the fun, freedom, bootleg money, friendships, and the wholesome ballet of hard physical labor, there was one other aspect of woodcutting that I thoroughly enjoyed. Plainly put, never in my life in all of my various occupations would I ever be so productive. Once, while I was in my thirties and in my woodcutting prime, I fell and worked up a tanoak pumpkin that was clear-grained and without a limb for the bottom forty feet. In less than seven hours I bucked four cord out of it and, over the coming four days, after I'd finished with my morning's felling and bucking and the pumpkin was lying in the shade, I'd return with my maul and hand-split a cord out of it, which took me less than two hours each day. So, all told, and throwing in the hauling, stacking, and delivering, in less than two workdays I made enough firewood to keep two local families warm through one full winter. Not only that but my wood would heat my customers twice because, when it was time for them to put on their rubber boots and raincoats and go outside to fetch more wood to bring inside for their fireplace, just that little bit of exercise would take the chill off their bones even before they'd struck a match. As a bonus they'd also get fine clean ashes for their summer gardens and, to top it off, in terms of BTUs, I always undersold PG&E, Southern California Edison, and everybody else selling warmth "on the grid."

So all that couldn't help but swell my head some and, I don't mind admitting, I was always proud to be a woodcutter.

ACCIDENTALLY DRUNK

Properly speaking, I don't think you can get accidentally drunk. After all, it's not like those ice-cold, long-necked bottles of beer forced themselves down your gullet. Nor did those little jiggers of whiskey sneak up behind you. Still, were a person to set out to get accidentally drunk, he'd start by spending all morning long and half a hot summer afternoon felling oak trees, brushing them and bucking them into firewood sticks and rounds. Show up in the woods at dawn, crank up your chainsaw, and buck up three cord of firewood before the heat sets in. Then go down to the Boonville Lodge, relax, and sip a cold one to help you replenish your precious bodily liquids.

It's a Friday afternoon and the joint is packed with loud, out-of-order, keg-shaped lumberjacks. They are the hard-drinking kind that do all of their screwing in the woods and all of their logging in saloons. With a bunch like that, sooner or later, just for the hell of it, some yahoo is going to stand everybody a drink. Which will inevitably lead some other yahoo to match his magnanimity and, before you know it, there you are, accidentally drunk like everybody else.

That's what happened to the three of us woodcutters—my partners were an uncle and his nephew—that time we wound up getting stuck out there on the grade beside Duck Wallow. One minute we were up on the ridge atop the old Rickard Ranch, sitting down to lunch with our backs to the shady sides of tree trunks, and the next minute we were snockered in the Boonville Lodge. In those days the highways didn't belong to drunks like us until well past sundown, and by the time we realized the predicament we'd fallen into, the sun was still three hands above the horizon. Figuring we'd run out of money before the road back to Yorkville became safe for us, and thinking we weren't so drunk that one of us couldn't herd the others back home, we decided to leave while the getting was good.

Stepping outside the darkened Lodge and pausing to get our bearings, our eyes shriveled in the glare, the uncommon heat slapped us, the loud, crowded traffic assaulted our senses and, with seemingly the whole town teeming with people busy walking or driving this way or that, the three of us felt all out of sorts, downright baleful. But just when our situation started looking mighty bleak, up drove old Leon in his big, wide-open, top-down, two-toned 1957 Buick convertible. Leon was older and more responsible than the rest of us. Leon was also our neighbor and he could hold his liquor and so he could drive us home.

When Leon saw the three of us pilgrims standing there outside the Lodge grinning at him like he was some kind of fairy godmother, I could tell he was amused. After we'd run down for him the tale of how we'd gotten accidentally drunk, Leon nodded sympathetically and assured us that he'd be happy to deliver us safely home to our wives and babies—no problema. But at the same time, he hadn't driven up to the Lodge just to drive away and, if we didn't mind, he'd like to set a spell and sip a drink or two. Was that OK with us?

And of course we all thought it was A-OK with us. To prove it, we happily and thankfully followed Leon right back through the door of the saloon and stood him a drink at the bar.

Leon was a boomer out of Missoula, Montana. His father was a miner and his mother was a miner's wife. Like about every other penniless small-town boy with a hankering for the road, when Leon turned eighteen he joined the army. He spent a couple of years in Germany during the mid-fifties and, after seeing how much Bavaria felt and looked like home even though it was lousy with Bavarians, Leon was hooked on the road. Being part Indian, and thinking he might enjoy living in the big city, he became a steel walker. You know, the kind of guy who walks the naked girders of rising skyscrapers and bolts them together. Loving the money and the work but hating the city—like with most any other boomer, hearing Leon rhapsodize about his childhood home was enough to make you wonder why he'd ever left—he became like a hired gun. So long as a job was union, the project interesting, and the contract short-term, Leon would do about anything and go about anywhere. He'd operate equipment, excavate foundations, run cutting or welding torches, build pipeline or tear it up. He'd even break and tie rebar rods if he had to. So long as a job was in a place he'd never been, he'd take it if it was the best thing going. Like the cowboys used to say up in Montana, you'd always have a job so long as you were willing to work for nothing and you weren't particular about who you bunked with.

Not many folks in Mendocino knew anything about or appreciated desert, but Leon did. Once after I mentioned to him how I'd never much liked the Great Basin Desert, Leon asked me if I'd ever been up in the Ruby Mountains. When I admitted that I'd never even heard of them, Leon advised me that, if ever I was out Elko way, I should check out the Rubies because I just might be surprised. And the way he said it, he could have been talking about a plain-looking woman with a special kind of spark about her.

Years later, after Leon was dead, I made a special trip to the Ruby Mountains to see for myself what he'd been talking about. Laying my eyes for the first time on Ruby Dome was like seeing the Continental Divide in the northern Rockies. Up in Lamoille Canyon, what with its quaking aspen and avalanche chutes, towering sawtooth rims and hanging valleys, frozen waterfalls and beaver ponds, I realized how much the place must have reminded Leon of the Bitterroots back home.

From atop a rockpile on the spine of the range near Liberty Cap, with the desert spreading like a tablecloth at my feet and facing a thousand-mile-long wind, with just a bit of imagination I could see and appreciate what Leon had seen and appreciated all those years before. For a moment I could look through his eyes and see into his mind and finally know what he'd been talking about and why he'd spoken about it in that way.

"You just might be surprised," Leon had said with a playful gleam in his eye.

No shit.

After three or four hours of sitting in the Lodge, tossing back beers and sipping on whiskey, what with all of the yahoos and yahees, the jukebox twanging crying-cowboy music, the dice cups slamming the bar like wild turkeys shot out of the sky, the pool balls jumping, the elbow-to-elbow tottering noisiness, the dark and the smoke, Leon got to thinking that, after all the years and travels, all the jobs, women, and paychecks, he'd wound up right back in Missoula, Montana. Remembering his dad getting off a shift in the mine and hitting the corner watering hole, it was like Leon had never left home.

Sometimes you get drunk because you're young and irresponsible. Other times you get drunk because you're out to have some fun and lose your inhibitions. You might get drunk to be sociable, or because it feels like the right thing to do at the time. It might be to celebrate a holiday, or somebody's coming, or passing, or just to forget yourself, or to forget about whatever person, place, or thing that might be riling you, or troubling your mind.

But this night Leon got drunk to let out his mean streak. What good was an old boomer with a broken wing? Nowadays what good was a young boomer, for that matter? When all that counted was cheap, all you got was cheap. So why would a fellah hire a wily old pro like Leon when he could get a half-assed rummy kid at half price who'd get more than half, half-assed done? And finally, over and above everything else at the moment, standing way high like a granite cliff in Yosemite or a stand of virgin redwoods, stood the question uppermost in Leon's mind: What damned good were the three drunken puppies that had been thrust into his care?

Leon had figured that if he sat there long enough and got drunk enough, then we'd give up on him and he'd be rid of us and not have to take the trouble to deliver us back home. He wasn't in the taxi business. But as time and the drinks wore on and we all seemed perfectly happy to surround him and to chatter at him and to stay just as long as he pleased, more and more it pissed him off. If Leon had known he was actually going to get stuck into being our Designated Driver, he wouldn't have gotten so damned drunk.

I can't remember just what it was that got us out of there, though it was still before sundown when we all piled into Leon's Buick. We'd been drinking so long we felt nearly sober, or at least more sleepy than drunk. The uncle and the nephew sprawled out in the backseat and by the time we passed the gravel pit they were already blowing big Zs, their heads like loose coconuts, their mouths agape as if trying to catch flies on the wind.

I was sitting shotgun and helping Leon to navigate, and I could tell he was having trouble keeping his boat between the lines. Even though on the straightaways we must have been going something in excess of thirty miles per hour, it was like we were on a lake going crossways to the chop. Leon would shut one eye and drive that way for a spell, then he'd shut the other eye and try driving that way.

"How you feeling?" I'd asked him periodically, trying to keep him alert.

"You should try getting plastered in Montana and driving home on ice sometime," Leon sagely advised me.

Since I chose to ignore that comment, Leon said, "You know all those hundreds of frogs living in the pond below my place? These summer nights they'll all get to croaking so loud that I'll have to run naked out onto my deck and blast away at them with both barrels of my shotgun. And you know what? Every last one of them frogs shuts right up. Just like that, when that twelve-gauge barks, you won't hear another peep out of them."

After pausing to let that sink in, Leon continued, "Then from somewhere some frog will start feeling froggy again and he'll let out with a discreet little croak. And that's enough to get some other frogs to feeling froggy, and before you know it they're all back to happily croaking just like nothing happened. So all you've done is waste two shells of double-aught."

In my wicked way I knew Leon was trying to take my mind off his driving—already I'd told him to slow down twice—so his stratagem wasn't working. Long hours of hard drinking had reduced old Leon to quivering like Jell-O, and I could see it with my own eyes. Convinced that I could do a better job driving, I told him so.

"Ain't nobody driving my Buick," Leon let me know with an arched eyebrow.

Now, one of my faults as a person is thinking that just because something makes sense to me, it should make sense to somebody else. In other words, once I get ahold of a great notion, I have trouble letting loose of it. In the scheme of things my idea might amount to a guppy swimming in a goldfish jar, but still I might try to jump aboard it and ride it like a horse.

"I could get us home backward," I slurred haughtily.

"How's that?" Leon asked.

"I could slip this old Buick into reverse gear and drive us home backward and still do a better job driving than you're doing now." I started feeling queasy.

"While you're at it," Leon said, "you can come by my place next Sunday morning and polish my chrome."

"Come on, Leon. You know what I'm talking about."

"Don't you worry now."

"Come on, Leon. You know I—"

That's when Leon snapped. We'd made it past Fish Rock Road and we were climbing the grade there across from the massive moving mountain called Duck Wallow. Leon abruptly hit the narrow dirt turnout and brought us to a screeching halt. Next thing I knew, the Buick's black convertible roof was stretching over the tops of us like a bat's wing, and Leon was pushing buttons and sealing all the windows.

"I ain't going no farther," Leon announced, turning off his engine once we were battened down. "I'm too drunk to drive so I'm going to sit here and get me some sleep." Leon promptly set about doing just that.

The sudden silence and stillness awoke the uncle. He opened his eyes and cast them fuzzily about, ascertained that indeed we'd come to a solid and an unmistakable halt, then looked long and hard at the ugly, sliding face of Duck Wallow. His voice vague, he asked why we'd stopped in such a god-awful place. Next, as if suspecting that his nephew might help solve the riddle, he elbowed him in the ribs and took ahold of the bill of his baseball cap and shook it some to get him awake.

"Wake up, man. Look here. We're stuck at Duck Wallow."

Unlike Leon, who was single, shiftless, and lacking in schedule, we all had showers to take, suppers to eat, wives to make peace with, kids to civilize, animals to tend to, and beds to hit.

"What about us?" I protested. "We've gotta be to work in the morning."

And without even having the decency to open his eyes, Leon retorted that he didn't. Moreover, he asserted, if we were in such a damned hurry, then we could walk ourselves home and let him get some sleep.

By now my partners had regained their senses about as much as they were going to that night, and they added their voices to mine so that we had a veritable chorus of protests aimed at Leon. Between us we used about all the arguments we could think of to get him to see the light, and to do the right thing in the name of family, friends, and the American Way.

Realizing that in order to get us to shut up he was going to have to take drastic action, Leon took the keys out of his ignition, opened his door, stepped around the front of the car, and faced the steep gully the little no-name creek had carved beside that stretch of road. He stood there with his back to us and looked up into the canyon (the creek begins on a ridge up under Bloomfield's Roost), and then, as if he was throwing from deep center field to home plate, he flung his car keys into the gully.

For some reason Leon's action made us all feel obliged to go and see for ourselves what he'd done. So we clamored out of the Buick in a hurry and gathered at the edge of the gully and, after protesting most vigorously this latest revolting turn of events, we gazed forlornly into the void to see what we could see. There was plenty of land down there, all right, but we couldn't see any keys.

While we mentally adjusted to the fact that we'd now have to be walking home, Leon slipped back into his Buick, locked the doors, and promptly tried to get back to sleep.

This got us grumbling again—the very gall of the son of a bitch to lock us out—and I suppose we might have conspired to take some kind of violent action if we could have figured how it'd do us any good. Then it occurred to me that, because I'd watched Leon toss the keys and had marked their trajectory in my mind, I was probably seeing the spot where the keys had landed within, at most, a fifty-foot radius. So if the three of us managed to climb down the steep bank without tumbling into the creek, got down on our hands and knees and did a systematic box search, then within a few minutes, or an hour or two, we'd be bound to find the keys, almost guaranteed.

And maybe by then, with us rapping on his window and dangling our glittering discovery, Leon might have gotten enough of a nap to be refreshed, and maybe then he'd drive us home.

"I ain't getting bit in the nose by no damned rattler," the uncle remarked dryly.

"Plus all them foxtails down there," his nephew added helpfully. "I don't wanna be having to be walking home with a bunch of foxtails stuck in my socks."

And so the moment of reckoning finally arrived and we reckoned that, if we were going to get home at all that night, we'd best start walking.

After we'd walked about a mile and our mouths had become so parched that we'd stopped complaining, old Leon sped by us in his Buick. To show he was harboring no ill feelings, he waved to us and tooted his horn.

BLOOMFIELD'S ROOST

About twenty-five years ago an elderly gentleman told me a yarn his granddad had told him when he was a little boy. Since his granddad had been one of the original white settlers of Anderson Valley, I listened carefully. The storyteller had been named after a famous city in Arkansas, for a half century he'd been a successful sheepman, he'd spent his whole life living in the bottom of one wide mountain bowl, and there was no place you could see from his front porch where he hadn't set foot. He knew his locality and he knew the stories that came with it. And what was a locality beyond a collection of stories? Lose the local legends, lose the local folklore, and how do you not also lose your sense of place, of being and belonging?

As a boy the old gentleman had ridden his horse to school. He rode to the little whitewashed schoolhouse now rotting away on Stanley Johnson's ranch. Then when he got home from school there were always chores for him to do. The sheep and chickens, milk cow and steers needed feeding, and the hay crop, orchard, and garden all needed tending. There was firewood to be chopped, fences mended, stalls scrubbed down, dogs let out and cats brought in. A boy needed to help with the roundup and the doctoring, the shearing, tagging, and what all besides. Depending on the time of year, there might be pork, beef, and venison to cure, berries to gather, fish to catch and dry, apples, peaches, plums, and walnuts to harvest. Come spring more chores needed doing, and more chores needed doing before winter laid in or summer arrived.

That wasn't to say a boy was a slave or that ranching wasn't fun. According to his abilities, a boy was just expected to make hisself useful was all. Like with everything else in nature, a boy was expected to earn his keep. Yet if a boy had to study for a big test, or if there was a shindig in town, then so long as he tended to the animals as usual, a boy was free to put off the rest of his chores if he wanted to. He could even put off his chores a whole lot if that was in his character. If he wanted to be working Saturdays to get caught up, he was welcome.

So one day, when the old gentleman was about eight or ten years old, he was out working with his grandpa. They were up there by Teardrop Lake sorting through stacks of old redwood fence pickets, separating the salvageable from the too-far-gone, and he was none too happy about it, seeing how he always seemed to be missing out on the fun. His little boy mind being on anything under the sun except the task at hand, he got to staring at the face of the oddly shaped peak across the valley. Sharp and irregular and shaped like a crude pyramid, topped with a basalt crag like a black tooth and a solitary round oak tree, it was the sort of mountain that stood out from the others, a real eye-catcher.

Watching him gawking at the mountain instead of getting his work done, and knowing he was feeling sorry for himself, his grandpa took the opportunity to tell him about the young outlaw and highwayman by the name of Bloomfield for whom that particular mountain was named.

All full of piss and vinegar, wood-knot stubborn and as lazy as a potbellied otter, young Bloomfield had no use for the common ways of doing things. Figuring he'd live his own life according to his own rules and pay nobody else any bother, young Bloomfield took to robbing horsemen on the trail running between Cloverdale and Boonville. He'd let a fellah get up real close before he'd show himself with his leveled shotgun and his ivory-handled pistol gleaming in his belt. He'd take the fellah's money, his guns, and even his horse if he thought it was worth anything. Young Bloomfield also weren't above robbing a passing buggy or a stagecoach.

They say young Bloomfield robbed one stagecoach too many and that caused the local folks to get up a posse. Then again, along the way he'd made himself a good number of enemies and it could be that folks had finally gotten a bellyful of him and so decided to be done with him once and for all.

The posse spotted young Bloomfield on his horse ambling down along Beebe Creek and heading for the Ornbaum Opening. Seeing the posse in his way—there must have been five of them—young Bloomfield took off at a gallop up into the canyon of Rancheria Creek. He didn't know that another part of the posse was coming down that way, but he soon found out. With his escape blocked and the others hot on his trail, the boy had no choice but to abandon his horse and climb up the back side of that big steep mountain. While scrambling his way up there he'd occasionally turn to fire his Winchester to try to keep the posse off him, which he did fairly well since chasing a rifleman up a mountain was a mighty dangerous thing to do. No matter how many your numbers, no one wants to lead the way.

Young Bloomfield made it to the top of the mountain, all right. But it did him no good. An old boy with a rifle was hunkered down up there, hiding behind a rock. He fair enough got the drop on young Bloomfield and the boy dropped his guns, raised his hands to the sky, and that was the end of him. After the rest of the posse arrived at the spot, they promptly hung young Bloomfield from that round, solitary tree you see up there standing against the sky. They hung him from a limb and they left him for the buzzards.

When the little boy gazed up at his grandpa and scrutinized his face to see if that was the real, honest truth, his grandpa nodded in the affirmative and wiggled his fingers as if to say, "We'd best be getting back to work now."

"I AIN'T NO CATSKINNER"

Redwood logging was a seasonal sort of occupation, and that meant that when you signed on to a show it was understood that there'd be no days off except Sunday. Sunday was the one day you'd have to wash your clothes, replace, repair, or maintain your equipment, resupply your cupboards or ice chest, and generally relax if you got the chance. If you had a wife, then she'd take pity on you by waiting on you hand and foot and maybe even she'd get the town chores done herself so you didn't need to bother. If you had noisy, rambunctious kids, she'd go you one better by hauling the little rascals along with her, leaving you home alone to lie in your sitting chair, watch TV, and munch.

Because in the woods everything you did was something you could see, sink your teeth into, or stumble over, when Saturday quitting time rolled around you were always in the middle of something. If you were felling timber, you might have ended your day by leaving for the weekend's swirling winds an "outlaw" redwood tree (one impossible to properly fell) still standing only because of one skinny finger of holding wood plus the collection of wedges you'd pounded into its back-cut. And, sitting there at home on Sunday, you'd be wondering whether the outlaw would still be standing when you returned to the woods Monday morning.

If you were a loader man, then you'd be thinking ahead to Monday and how many trucks you had coming in and where you were going to find the logs to fill them. A catskinner might spend a part of

Sunday pondering the menu for his next week's feed bags. Come Friday, will it be a ham and cheese sandwich and Twinkies? Or will it be a can of Dinty Moore's beef stew and cupcakes? How about a meatball sandwich, wouldn't that be good? How about bringing along a big bag of *pee*-cans or a tin of Beanie Weenies?

A chokersetter will always be holding in the back of his mind his knowledge of the kinds of skids he'll be facing to start the week. Were they short skids? (A skid was the time it took the catskinner to deliver a "turn" of logs to the landing and return for the next one). Working short skids meant there'd be no kind of sit-down time for a chokersetter. There'd be none of that unless he had enough standing as an individual to be able to call a break on his own. Or, if the catskinner was kindly, then he'd see when his ground man was getting shaky and he himself would call a break. But even if you were a chokersetter in good standing working behind a kindly catskinner, if you rigged enough short skids back to back you were going to get tuckered out.

Yet, if the week ahead was packed with short skids, a chokersetter wanted to tackle the shortest of them straight out of the gate Monday morning. He'd want to have at them because Sunday had been his one day for rejuvenation. Since during the week you worked like a horse, on Sundays you ate like one to regain your strength. You ate like a horse and you licked your paws like a house cat.

So, if there was any fire in you, it'd come out Monday morning when your body was fresh. Monday, Tuesday, and Wednesday were your strong days and Thursday you started getting worn down. Friday you spent conserving energy to get through Saturday, and Saturday, even though you were getting paid time and a half (a logger's bulldog gravy), you only got done about two thirds of what you'd gotten done on Monday.

That's how it was with chokersetters, and every woods boss knew and accepted it. They accepted it by measuring your production by the week. So long as every week throughout the course of the season you got a good number of logs moved, the boss didn't much care how you did it.

Because redwoods grew in mountains, and since chokersetters worked from the top of the mountain down, the deeper the canyon, the longer the skids and the easier the job. A chokersetter's idea of hog heaven was a tall, hog-backed ridge corked with logs pointing at the trail and with the landings set way down yonder next to the creek. If you were a chokersetter and you were running a ridge top covered with pumpkins, then it might take the catskinner a half hour to make one round-trip. So you'd be able to scout your next lay of logs, sniff out the dangers, dig the holes under them, and still have plenty of time left over for sitting down.

Yet, for a chokersetter, there was no such thing as hog heaven. When the skids were that long you worked twelve chokers instead of six, one set to send down the mountain with the Cat and the other to set while it was gone.

No matter how you cut it, a chokersetter was the low man on the totem pole. You set choker on your way to becoming something else, be it a catskinner, timber faller, landing chaser, loader man, truck driver, donkey puncher, hook tender or—far more often than not—something other than a woodsman.

Still there were a few hardy souls who did make a career out of slinging steel. If they survived into middle age, they became legendary, even mythical creatures. ("In the deep dark woods are men who scramble up canyons like deer...") Famous for their great physical strength and agility, peasant pride, and simplicity, they were not the sort of fellahs you wanted to be messing with. Once in a saloon I saw one such legendary individual who weighed about one hundred and eighty pounds tongue-lash a giant, barrel-chested bear of a man who weighted at least two-sixty. Watching them go at it was like watching a sleek mountain lion spitting and clawing at a hungry grizzly with its hackles up. Except, in this case, the Griz had enough native sense to not want to tangle tooth to tooth and claw to claw. Even though the giant had hands big enough to fit around the top of the chokersetter's head, he used them to, by way of diffusing the situation, get out his wallet and stand the chokersetter a shot of whiskey and a bottle of beer.

Even though rip-roaring career chokersetters were a rarity in the woods, on every show the log riggers were divided into the greenhorns, the seasoned hands, and the genuine highballers, though all chokersetters highballed at least a part of the time. Because your degree of skill was measured by your production, on most shows there was an ongoing competition to see who could move the most logs. Or, if working conditions were particularly brutal, there'd be a competition to see who could last the whole season.

The only way to escape having to set choker was to either quit the woods or to master the moves and advance, and that meant stringing together some back-to-back seasons without getting hurt. For instance, before I moved on to chasing, timber felling, and hook tending, I slung steel for four full seasons plus parts of three others, and only once during that stretch did I get hurt. I was pulling bull-line down the face of a cliff and there was a little twelve-inch-thick, forty-foot-long log with its nose cantilevered atop a stump. I wasn't watching out and the cable just above the hook I was pulling on got strung underneath the log and caused it to roll off the stump. The log hit me on the top of my steel hardhat, dented it, knocked me all but out, and sent me tumbling twenty feet down the cliff. The log hit me so hard in the head that it put a temporary little tweak into my back that it took me ten years to get rid of. Though, even today, if I break out my old felling saw and cut enough firewood, I still feel the remains of it.

By the way, if you're wondering why the log didn't crush me after knocking me down the cliff, it was because, when it smacked me, it simultaneously got wedged into and held in place by the saddle made by a little six-inch-thick baby redwood tree growing out of the bottom lip of the stump. Maybe twenty feet tall and untouched by all of the commotion made by the clear-cutting timber faller, all morning long I'd been working around the sucker in order not to destroy it, my motive being to leave a tiny spot of standing beauty as a way of appeasing the woods gods. If you log enough seasons you are bound to get some pagan in you, and that was one instance when one of my superstitions seemed to pay off.

Anyway, as I mentioned in the beginning, during the logging season there were no days off except Sundays and some guys even worked them. The truck drivers typically worked five days a week and between sixteen and eighteen hours a day, but, while most of them had once been woodsmen, now they were a unique breed of critter: not quite loggers and their own brand of trucker. The catskinners and chokersetters usually worked six times ten, though most catskinners would take more hours if they could get them. The loader men worked between twelve and sixteen hours a day, except on Saturdays when, with no trucks coming in, along with their chasers they worked however many hours it took them to get the logs on the landings cleaned up, sorted, and ready for the push come Monday morning.

All of the above was "in the contract," and if you wanted to be a lumberjack then you worked those kinds of hours and you never took time off. The policy of no days off was about as inviolable as the Law of Gravity, and any logger who had trouble showing up for work in the morning had best be working for kin. In the woods, when it came to missing work, once was an accident, twice was a coincidence, and three times was an unacceptable pattern. The loggers on a show were the members of a team, and even single-jacking timber fallers—an ornery, loner bunch if ever there was one—were a part of it. The good timber fallers felled their trees so that the riggers had an easy time getting ahold of their logs, but even they would get run off if for whatever reason they failed to keep ahead of the riggers and so held up production. If necessary, a timber faller worked Saturdays, and even Sundays, if that's what it took to "get ahead."

The full-bore intensity combined with the nearly dark-to-dark workdays helped to make a logging operation into a "show." In the life of a lumberjack, it was show me the logs on the ground, show me the decks of logs on the landing, and show me the truckloads delivered to the mill. So long as you showed those three things, then there wasn't much to talk about and nobody was bossing anybody. The other reason why a logging operation was called a show was because it provided so much entertainment.

An uphill wind will help you to fell a downward-leaning tree up the hill, so even with the Law of Gravity there are exceptions. When it came to catskinners and chokersetters, there was the mythical Saturday you'd supposedly get off if on some sugar-candy Friday everybody, acting in malicious conspiracy in a sort of reverse strike, agreed to bust their ass all day long in order to "cork" the landings with so many logs that the loader man had no room to operate and the chaser no time to catch up. Supposedly, if we corked all of the landings simultaneously by quitting time on Friday afternoon, then the bullbuck would be forced to shut down the Cats on Saturday and give us the day off.

Over the years, I participated in a number of such conspiracies, but only once did we succeed in our coup. We got all of the landings hopelessly corked up, all right, but the old woods boss was so stubborn and ornery—it wasn't a stretch to say that some old-time loggers prided themselves on their great stores of stubbornness and orneriness—that, just to spite us, he made us come in on Saturday anyway. Not only that but he had the loader man and chaser stay Friday and work 'til dark to make room on the landings for more logs. And when, again out of spite, come Saturday morning we promptly re-corked the landings, the old coot had us go get more skids to cut loose and stockpile on the truck road. After, again out of spite, we instantly corked the truck road, instead of calling it quits, old coot sent us up the mountain to rig more skids to lay out on the mouths of our branch trails. Hopping mad now, in no time flat we corked all of the branch trails. Finally beat, the old coot allowed us to drag our raggedy, worn-out asses home what turned out to be a couple of hours early.

Except, looking ahead to Monday and also wishing to teach us a lesson, the old chattering badger had the loader man, chaser, one catskinner, and one chokersetter stay and work 'til dark and then come back out again and work all day Sunday in order to clean up the big mess we'd made. As the loader man and chaser spent the remains of the weekend uncorking the landings, the riggers uncorked the truck road and the branch trails as space became available.

In addition to the mythical kind of day off, there were two real kinds. Around here in those days, the logging season officially began on April 15 and ran until the rainy season laid in, which usually happened between mid-October and mid-November. During that stretch of time, other than Sundays, you got only two days off. One was Independence Day and the other was the opening day of buck-hunting season, which came on the second Saturday in August.

The bullbucks gave us the opening day of hunting season off because if they didn't nobody would show up to work anyway. If you were a bullbuck and you refused the day off, then on the eve of the opening day of buck-hunting season your whole crew would be calling you while you were home eating supper with your family. They'd call you claiming to be suffering from any number of unforeseen, but temporary, illnesses or infirmities. No kind of lie was beneath them.

Even if for some reason you wanted to work on opening day—say you wanted or needed the money or you didn't hunt—still you'd be unable to find somebody to work with you, and the bullbuck would be gone hunting anyway. And even if the boss didn't mind you working way out there all by yourself, still you wouldn't want to do it. With all of the yahoos scampering up and down the mountains with loaded rifles, itchy trigger fingers, and empty freezers (logging shows make excellent hunting grounds because of the forage and open terrain they provide), you just might get yourself mistaken for a buck deer and shot.

In addition to the two days off given in order to honor important holidays, there were also the days you got off because of who you were. Take Lester, my old catskinner. The season I worked behind him, when opening day of buck-hunting season rolled around, Lester got not a day but a whole week off. Lester got a whole week off to visit with his relatives, harvest blackberries, and hunt and fish to his heart's content.

And that's how I wound up working behind the show's star chokersetter, a gyppo boomer down from Oregon. On that show we had four Cat crews working, but one of them was owner operated and worked not by the hour but by "bushel rate," which meant they worked their own landings and got paid by the volume of marketable board feet that got loaded and shipped to the mill. Since the more logs they moved the more money they made, and because diesel, Cat parts, and rigging were expensive, no gyppo catskinner would ever tolerate working with anything short of a seasoned chokersetter with a powerful dose of ambition.

"Good and hungry" was the only sort of fellah who need apply.

Unfortunately for this chokersetter—I forget his name because we only worked together for one half of one skid—his partner and Lester were lifelong buddies and the two of them had gone off for the week gallivanting together, just as happy as clams but leaving the two of us to fend for ourselves.

"I ain't no catskinner," the fellah announced nervously as we shook hands.

"And I ain't no chokersetter," I lied, trying to make him feel better.

"You'd best keep a sharp eye on me," the fellah warned, seemingly speaking to himself as much as to me. "I told the boss I ain't no catskinner but he wasn't hearing me and so you'd better watch out because my hands and feet ain't trained to be operating no Cat controls and so you need to take care and take it to the bank and damn sure keep it there where you can get at it."

I wondered what he was so jumpy about. About thirty-five years old, sandy-haired, light-framed, muscle-bound, and fleet-footed, by reputation he was one of the very best log riggers you'd find anywhere, experienced in any kind of Pacific Coast timber growing out of any kind of ground. Also by reputation, he was said to be willing and able to kick up dust in a saloon with the best of them. Moreover, any kind of jumpy fellah was rare in the redwoods because, even if you were born jumpy or had gotten into the habit of acting jumpy, working twelve-hour days (as he was doing while gyppoing) meant you had no energy left over for it. Besides, over the previous months I'd gabbed with him some during lunchtime and he'd never let on that he was the nervous type. To the contrary, he seemed proud and cocky; cocky like you'd expect the senior man to be.

So when he reluctantly climbed up into the seat of Lester's idling Cat and waved me aboard, I hesitated, wondering whether I'd be better off walking up the mountain. Fear was contagious, and fear clouded your thinking. But I decided that there was no way the fellah could be that bad of a catskinner and I joined him up on the machine and sat down on the toolbox.

"Let her rip," I hollered recklessly.

Our first skid was atop the ridge where Lester and me had left off the previous day, and on our way up the trail I tried to put the fellah at ease by making small talk. Turned out he was from Arkansas by way of Fort Bragg and Roseburg, Oregon, though for the last decade or so he'd been mostly bouncing between the last two places, slinging steel behind Lester's old buddy and generally going wherever the timber and the money was best. He'd been married eighteen years, had three little rascals and a little plot of land up in the foothills above Roseburg; a plot of land and a handful of cattle.

Talking about himself and his land seemed to help set him at ease and, by the time we reached the ridge top, he seemed comfortable.

About the only time I rode the Cat was to get up the mountain, so when we arrived at the "flat" ground on the ridge top, I told the fellah to stop the machine so that I could climb off. It was a habit Lester had taught me right out the gate and one I followed my entire career. I had my water jug with me, wedged into the space between the toolbox and the seat, but I decided to leave it aboard the Cat.

Where we'd stopped was just shy of a narrow, treeless Y junction. The trail to the left continued slightly upward along the ridge top and the one forking to the right led gently down into a side canyon. Separating the two trails was a vertical cutbank that started off one inch tall but, as the trails parted company, quickly grew to a height of five feet. We'd stopped so the Cat's tracks were pointing directly at the point of the junction and, after I was safely out of the way, the fellah yanked on his Johnson Bar and the Cat lurched forward. He hadn't gone but a few feet when he spotted my water jug, picked it up with one hand, turned around to look at me over his shoulder, and shook it outside the cage, asking me with the gesture whether or not I wanted to take it with me. And while he was doing that and I was violently shaking my head "no," one of his tracks took the high road and the other track took the low road, and the bulldozer started tipping sideways with the growing height of the cutbank. By the time I realized what was happening and started frantically signaling him to stop, he'd felt the tilt himself and, letting out with a panicked shriek, he jerked his head forward, dropped my water jug like it was on fire and, instead of slapping his Johnson Bar, he lifted his blade.

As the uphill track rose and cracked daylight beneath it, the fellah decided to abandon ship. As the deck tilted so he couldn't stand on it, he stepped out onto the top corner of the uphill track. As the track kept rolling, he stepped onto the top of the blade's side arm and, as that gave way, he leaped for his life.

As the Cat tumbled sideways into the canyon, the fellah landed with one foot atop a stump hidden in the sluff just below the road. Even with the racket made by the tumbling Cat, I thought I heard his ankle pop. I certainly saw his ankle pop and his foot lay over limp. The sight made me shrivel like a raisin. I "cringed," I guess you could properly say.

I ran over to him as fast as I could and hit my knees on the road directly above him. He was crawling up the berm on his hands and knees, holding up high his flopped-over foot so that it wouldn't touch anything. I reached to give him a hand up.

"Go'n kill the damned Cat," he yelped angrily through clenched teeth, his voice breaking. "Go and kill that diesel engine before it burns up."

I rose up on my knees, looked at the Cat, and it was resting roughly upside down about fifty feet down the canyon. All that was holding it in place were two skinny standers, and both of them, having been partially uprooted by the impact of the machine, were leaning down the hill at about forty-five degrees, their trunks bent with gravity and their crowns limp and hanging. About the time I decided that the Cat could go on ahead and burn up if it wanted to—there was no way I was getting inside that thing—the engine mercifully died on its own and so preempted any argument.

I got back down and again reached my hand out to the fellah but, even though he didn't seem to be making much progress up the sliding face of the berm, again he waved me away. He waved me away, but this time very weakly.

"I'm awright," he tried to growl. "Get out my way."

And all I could do was stand up and step aside, for the first time noticing the head-to-toe outbreak of sweat coating me.

After the fellah had finally managed to get himself up onto the trail, he laboriously crawled to a spot of shade and, thinking better of trying to flip over to sit down, he just stayed there motionless on his hands and knees, his face ashen, his head hung low, his eyes shut, and his dangling foot held skyward like the flag on a flagpole.

I'd seen shock before in Vietnam, and I knew I had to get him down off the mountain. We were all by ourselves in a corner of the show, the active landing was far upstream, and by the time I could run for help and return with it, the fellah might be dead. But if I skidded him down the mountain, if I put my back into it and hurried as fast as I could, then I'd have him beside the truck road in no time flat. Once we'd reached the road, within a few minutes an incoming or outgoing truck would appear, and the trucks came with CB radios. The bullbuck's pickup truck had blankets and a huge medicine chest aboard, and once he'd gotten to us he'd know exactly what to do.

When in no uncertain terms I informed the fellah of my plan—I'd carry him to the top of the trunk trail and then, after carefully setting him down on his back with his head pointing down the hill, I'd grab ahold of his outstretched arms and skid him down the mountain like a log—he looked up at me like I was crazy. He then smiled wanly and puked, his flagpole swaying as he heaved.

"I warned you I ain't no catskinner," he gasped breathlessly, trying to sound brave. Sensing his own self slipping away, he looked up at me and nodded in defeat. Struggling over each word and pausing to rest between them, he managed to add: "Don't you go and drop me now because I think I've had about all of the falling down I can take for one day."

When I picked him up into my arms and started walking with him, it occurred to me that, with a foot dangling like his, he was no longer a chokersetter, either.

A CONVENTION OF CROWS

When I moved to Yorkville and folks warned me about the summer heat, I thought they had to be kidding. Mendocino County is the land of the redwood and the fog, the salmon and the fern. What did people living in Mendocino know about heat? If they wanted to experience real heat, I thought, they could go and spend a summer in the Mojave Desert. Go and spend some hot August nights out in Barstow or Blythe, Baker or Ludlow, then come and tell me about heat. It didn't matter that the heat down that way was a dry, desert heat, either, not when the thermometer topped one hundred and twenty-five degrees. Go wandering off in desert heat like that and, even if you're packing plenty of water, you won't get far before you're seeing spots and your tongue's hanging out. If you don't immediately turn back and nobody finds your blow-dried body, all that's going to be left of you will be shrunken like a shedded snake's skin.

I didn't expect heat like you'd find in Furnace Creek or Yuma when I moved out to the North Fork of Rancheria Creek. Taking note of the length and depth of the canyon the Rancheria had carved—its upper reaches are intermittent but prone to flashflood—I appreciated how it'd make for deep canyon quietude and so be a good place to camp myself and my wife and boys. But I hadn't considered how, when summer came, the canyon would become an oven and us roasted chickens. Once while we were living out there the thermometer broke over one hundred degrees for ten or twelve days running. Though any one day never registered over one hundred and sixteen degrees, it wasn't a desert heat but a steam bath heat. Get out to working in heat like that, stretch your collar, take a peek inside of the front of your T-shirt, and you're liable to see a little rainstorm going on inside there. Look closely and you might see some fleas kayaking. While out in the Mojave the dry heat instantly stole the sweat off your back, out along the North Fork the heat was so wet that you swam in it, lugged it around like baggage. Once you started seeing spots out in that country, they'd have water spots on them.

When it got god-awful hot like that out along the North Fork it meant that the superheated air rising over Nevada's Great Basin had broken over the rim of the Sierra and had pushed westward, chasing the Sacramento Valley air over Yorkville and Yorkville's air out to sea. An invader wind, it was, and it breathed fire. The foliage on the trees hung low and the creeks seemed to quiet as if hiding out until it passed. The animals, from the small fry to the wild pigs, mountain lions and bears, found shade and stayed put, awaiting the sundown and the shift in the wind.

That was another difference between the Mojave and the North Fork. During a heat wave in the desert, at sunrise the temperature might already be one hundred degrees. But in Anderson Valley, even way out along the North Fork, the hottest day couldn't keep the cool ocean air from sneaking back in overnight. As night fell, the Great Basin wind died, and the hot air rose, it sucked in fingers of ocean air that followed the canyons like uphill-running creeks. The wet ocean air blew out of the river mouth's stands of redwoods and over the town of Navarro. It filled the wide flatlands of Anderson Valley proper before, beyond Boonville, it pushed onward over the valley's south wall and, rejoining the fat finger of ocean air pushing inland inside of the Rancheria Creek Canyon, it kept advancing upstream until topping out at the divide at the Oaks Cafe in Yorkville. Once the cool currents reached those coming up Dry Creek and those coming over the mountain from the Russian River Valley, they blended into each other and stilled over the mountains. So even out there along the North Fork at sunrise during the hottest day, we'd still see fog lying in a pool in the bottom of the canyon. What would be a one-hundred-and-ten-degree day started off at about sixty-five degrees.

So when the crows showed up over the valley one blazing hot

August afternoon, it seemed like a sorry bit of timing on their part. Why begin a migration in the middle of a heat wave? The crows were flying in a long, strung-out line, and I could tell they were laboring because only occasionally did one of them squawk, and then only with one or two low, guttural, straining "caws." Even with the dry tailwind, their wings were flapping vigorously as if they were having trouble keeping aloft in the thick air, or as if the slow ones were being forced to keep up with the fast ones instead of the other way around.

Since the crows were flying across the canyon and not down it, and because they seemed to be aiming directly for Bloomfield's Roost, I figured they were out to rejoin the Rancheria there in the wide valley where it meets the Beebe. Following the canyon down from there, the crows would break over the south wall of Anderson Valley and, continuing downstream, soon be relaxing in the cool Pacific breeze.

The next afternoon another string of crows flew over the canyon, and the next day after that. For days the crows kept coming and always they made their appearance in the afternoon, always they flew fast and quiet, and they always aimed for Bloomfield's Roost.

So one day I asked my boss about it. He'd been born and raised out there along the North Fork and he knew all about such manner of things. The crows were no doubt from parts east, he informed me, and they were coming from all over that way and that's why there were so damned many of them. The crows always came in August, too, the rancher let me know, though some years they'd come and others they wouldn't for reasons nobody knew. But maybe once a decade the crows would gather to have themselves a huge hoedown. They'd arrive from all parts and perch up there on the ridge above Elk. There might be hundreds of them crows, even thousands of them. And they'd perch way up high in the redwood trees where they could overlook the ocean. They'd make one huge commotion, too, a racket so loud and nerve-racking that they'd disturb the sailors standing on the decks of the passing ships at sea. And you talk about making a mess of things. Those crows covered the dirt under their trees with so many droppings that mushrooms grew up that were the size of bongo drums.

When I asked the rancher why he thought the crows gathered like that, he looked at me like I was missing the obvious.

"They're shooting the shit," he declared.

Something about his answer tickled my funny bone and I started laughing at him. No boss likes getting laughed at for whatever reason—part of being a boss is thinking you ain't funny—and I could tell I was hurting his feelings. But I couldn't help it, his explanation just seemed totally absurd to me. Finally I affectionately tapped him on his shoulder and managed to ask just what he thought the crows might be shooting the shit about.

The rancher shrugged his shoulders, shook his head, and remarked that, since he didn't speak crow, he couldn't tell. Though he strongly suspected that, sooner or later, the crow's conversation would turn to the subject of a farmer's corn.

THE COWBOY AND THE TRAPPER

Old enough to be my grandpa, Ole Claude was one of those rarest of breeds: a cowboy with ambition and an education. Ole Claude also had a serious sense of humor and he loved telling riddles. Like, he'd ask, it's Friday night, the saloon has shut down, and three cowboys are making their way back home to the ranch. They are sitting three across in the cab of a pickup truck that's rolling dust down a long dirt road. Now, which one of them fellahs is the real cowboy?

And after you'd scratched your head and gazed at him in slack-jawed befuddlement, he'd answer that it's obviously the fellah riding in the middle. That one ain't gotta drive the pickup truck and he ain't gotta get out to open the gate.

Claude having himself a college education meant he knew there was more to life than just cows, horses, and dogs. There were sheep, for example. Contrary to what folks thought, Claude didn't mind explaining, sheep weren't all that much stupider than cattle. Like with any other sort of social critters, the degree of an individual sheep's intelligence relied upon the size of the herd he was running with. The larger the herd, the rule was, the stupider the individual critter.

For instance, Claude would point out, if you get up one horse and one dog and you take after one wooly maverick buck that has gotten himself used to running free in these hills, you'd best be ready to expend some effort. For if the buck's half wily you can count on him heading for ground too steep for a horse and too brushy for a dog.

"You take after a lone old wooly up here in these hills," Ole Claude would volunteer, "you'd best remember to pack a lunch."

Whereas if it was one hundred head of sheep you were after, why, sometimes just the sight of your ambling horse was enough to get the whole bunch of them all turned and heading the right way.

I suppose if I'd've asked Ole Claude if the same rule applied to us humans, we being social critters and all, he'd have frowned as if he'd never thought of it that way. He might pretend to ponder the question long and hard before answering in a gentlemanly tone something like, come to think of it, he reckoned he'd have to allow how that just could be some kind of possibility if you looked at it in the right way. Then he'd grin at you with a crooked little glint in his eye.

I used to love listening to Ole Claude telling stories. During the 1970s and early '80s up in Yorkville, just after quitting time most days, Ole Claude would shuffle into the Oaks Cafe. Back then Yorkville was still mostly working ranches, and when the day was done lots of us ranchers and hired hands, both newcomers like myself and old-timers like Claude, would polish our elbows on the bar. Some, like Marvin, would keep his black Stetson cocked low over his eyes and silently nurse cups of coffee. Others would sip beers and still others, mostly us young bucks, would knock them back.

When Claude was in his seventies, he'd sit in the Oaks Cafe long enough to sip on a beer or two. But after he turned eighty and his body started quitting on him and his shaking hands told him the end was coming near, he'd just sit and sip a cup of coffee or a bottle of what he called "sody pop."

During the 1920s and '30s Claude did some rodeoing. He was too tall to make much of a bronc buster or bull rider, but those long, skinny arms of his did help make him into a fair-to-middlin' roper. I remember once Claude told me about how, unlike in the Hollywood movies where all of the cowboys were Anglo-Americans, in real life, blacks, Mexicans, and Indians did a lot of the heave-ho both out on the spreads and on the rodeo circuit.

Like all professional sports in those days, rodeo was racially segregated. If a fellow's complexion looked to be passably white, they'd let him compete. But if he looked to be something less than that, they'd turn him away. Rodeo was a white man's sport and the others were allowed along to muck the stalls and to tend to the livestock, to do the setup and the takedown, perform as clowns, wranglers, animal doctors, blacksmiths, and the like. But none of them were allowed to compete in the arena for those big pots of prize money.

So naturally, things being that way, lots of real good cowboys were kept out of competition. Claude remembered this one black fellah who was probably the best damned bronc buster there ever was. He was a liddle-biddy squirt who was so skinny that he needed to hang his socks over the rims of his pointy-toed, tooled, high-topped cowboy boots. But boy he could sure ride horses. The black dude developed a clown act where he'd come out the chute aboard a bucking bronco sitting it backward. No lie and that's God's honest truth. Seeing him coming out the chute riding backward was the damnest sight, and once word got around that the rodeo had itself a black dude fool crazy enough to ride a bronc like that, why, the stands filled with gawkers and rubberneckers, and pretty quick this fellah's getting rich off his appearance fees.

And if that weren't sweet enough, Ole Claude was glad to tell, to put icing on the cake the black fellah used most of his fee money to make side bets saying that he'd come out the gate and stay aboard his bronc for the full eight seconds just like a frontwise-riding cowboy. And since most of the professional cowboys thought the whole idea was asinine and somehow not right, or proper, or even conceivable unless you'd just clunked your head on a rock, the black fellah had no trouble finding cowboys willing to match his money. And because most always the fellah made the horn and the cowboys were forced to pay up, for a while there the black dude was the best-paid damned cowboy on the whole damned rodeo circuit.

So, talking about Claude, one time a bunch of us were sitting in the Oaks and this brand-new young-buck government trapper walked through the door. A pack of coyotes was slaughtering sheep up on Sanel Mountain, and the trapper had been brought in to fix the problem. He sat down next to Claude and they got to talking, and it came out that the trapper had just come from trapping out in northern Nevada. Claude knew a fair bit about that country himself, him having once worked out along the Humboldt River downstream from that glittering diamond of a desert oasis with the sweetly sonorous name: Winnemucca. And hearing them carrying on about the Basin and Range country made Ole Stanley, who'd spent most his life out in Surprise Valley there east of the Wagner Mountains, start telling his own Great Basin stories, and soon, listening to the three of them talking made you feel the open-range wind and smell the sage.

You want to graze a cow out by Empire? Well, you just set her aside two hundred acres and you cut her loose.

I remember Ole Claude mentioning to the trapper how, what with people being so scarce in those parts, the *ki*-oats were easy pickings. Give them a full moon and, just like a bunch of drunken cowboys on payday, they'll be out there in the wide open howling like there was no tomorrow. Or set yourself out there in the scrublands in the middle of a black night, switch on your rig's headlights, and the *ki*-oats will gather around you just wondering what in tarnation you're up to and how that might be of some benefit to them. Or go out there all alone, make yourself a little campfire under the rimrock, start cooking yourself some hot dogs, and soon the *ki*-oats will be sitting in the shadows just beyond your flickering firelight. They'll be out there licking their chops at the prospect of wolfing down your leave-behinds. And if you were to ask them nice enough, why, they'd come in out of the shadows and join you next to the fire and shoot the shit with you and, if you didn't watch out, they'd drink up all of your coffee.

Now Yorkville's *ki*-oats, Claude assured the trapper, they were of a whole different sort of background and personality. For one hundred and some odd years folks in Anderson Valley had been trying to kill off the *ki*-oats any which way they could think of, plus some other ways based just on hunches. As a result Yorkville's *ki*-oats, Claude authoritatively declared to the new trapper with just a wee bit of pride showing through, had all got themselves college educations. A college-educated Yorkville *ki*-oat, Claude swore, would as soon walk into a trapper's trap as show mercy to a three-legged lamb, or overlook a wild turkey with his head stuck in a chicken wire fence.

Well, the young trapper took a slight bit of umbrage, if umbrage it was, and I suppose I couldn't blame him none. Him being a young government trapper meant his whole professional life folks had been offering him little tips on how to go about his business and how he could better earn his money. So I could excuse the trapper if in this case he missed the fact that the old fart talking knew a little bit more about Yorkville's *ki*-oats than he did.

Ole Claude, who most always wore a "too old to care" sort of expression, still didn't mind jumping on a joke when he saw one. Sensing the trapper's wounded pride, Ole Claude saw the chance to have some fun with it.

"You don't go off in the brush with your truck keys in your pocket, do you?" he asked the trapper

"No," the trapper answered hesitantly, sensing a trap.

"And you leave your wallet in your glove compartment so you don't lose it while you're out there rooting around in the hills, am I right?"

Against his will, the trapper nodded.

"Well I'll tell you right now you can't be doing that around here and, if I was you, I wouldn't even try."

"Why's that?"

"Because if you do then while you're up on Sanel Mountain setting your traps them *ki*-oats are gonna be down in Cloverdale joyriding in your pickup truck and thumbing through your credit cards."

WHACKING WEEDS

I think it was Lily Tomlin who first said it was a good thing us baby boomers never got our childhood wishes. Because if we had, we'd all be cowboys, firemen, and ballerinas.

Since I was born in 1949, I know what Ms. Tomlin was talking about. In the neighborhood I grew up in, we little boys played "cowboys and Indians" about any chance we got. Like most everybody else my age of the male persuasion, I had me a cowboy hat and a leather vest, spurs and holsters, a Winchester '73 rifle and pair of pearl-handled Fanner Fifty six-guns. My heroes were Wyatt Earp, Bat Masterson, Wild Bill Hickock, the wagon master, the shifty-eyed bounty hunter with the funny-looking scatter gun, and—my favorite—Paladin, the San Francisco perfumed dandy who, with a change of costume and scenery, became a black-clad hired gun with a heart of gold.

Always happy to celebrate our pioneer heritage, us little boys in the neighborhood regularly got together and staged bloodbaths. I was one of the best "die-ers" on our block. Put me to running across somebody's front lawn, shoot me with a cap gun, and I'd tumble down dead and lie there with my eyes shut.

Depending upon our numbers and mood, we'd hold up imaginary stagecoaches, shoot snipers out of trees, pull off jailbreaks, and rob banks and trains. If there were only two of us, we'd set up a showdown on main street at high noon.

None of which, as you might have noticed, had anything to do with cowboying. In fact "cowboys and Indians" was a euphemism for war games, and what we really wanted to be when we grew up was gunfighters and soldiers. For what future was there in being some high-plains-drifting, dust-eating, flea-scratching, bean-spooning, horse-smelling cowboy? I mean, what fun was there in babysitting some fat, clumsy, bow-legged, moon-faced, snot-nosed, shitty-assed cows when you could be in town raping and pillaging?

Only once in my life did I ever really want to be a cowboy, and even then the feeling—so warm, wholesome, and sweet—lasted only a moment.

It was a hot spring afternoon and I was whacking weeds out along the Elk Horn Road on the back end of the Diamond Dee Ranch. Weed whackers had just hit the consumer market, and the rancher I was working for was so impressed by them that he'd bought a half dozen. Dotting his very large spread were all kinds of buildings and outbuildings, yards and boneyards, Christmas tree fields, pastures, fence lines, roads, avenues and such. So every spring, once the grasses had headed out, thrown their seed, and were turning brown, a bunch of us would be out running weed whackers, working full time for maybe two weeks straight before getting it all done.

Now, if first thing in the morning you pick up a weed whacker and you work it all day long, and if you string together a few days like that, then pretty quick you get real good with a weed whacker. And the better you get, the easier it becomes, the quicker it goes, the more fun it is, and the more proud you feel. It gets so you think you can strike a match with a weed whacker.

We Americans are nothing if not industrious, and a weed whacker is the quintessential American tool. In a weed whacker we see the ancient scythe modernized and motorized, miniaturized and somehow popularized. In this totem of our techno-culture we have industrial science applied to prove once again the age-old equation that weight plus speed equals force. For while the machine's plastic whips are virtually insubstantial when compared to the weight of a traditional steel scythe, because of their nearly supersonic velocity they obliterate all of the grass they touch.

After working a weed whacker for eight hours you'd be able to look back and see exactly what you'd accomplished. You'd left your mark on the land, by golly, and there was no mistaking it.

Everywhere you'd stepped foot you'd left behind naked, crew-cut, scrubbed, scoured, and domesticated earth.

While the process of whacking weeds can be broken down into various physical operations that are elementary in their mechanical simplicity, that doesn't mean the task can't be a cause of wonderment. For instance, if you examine your spinning disk from above, it looks to be spinning clockwise, whereas if you look at it from the grass's point of view, it looks to be spinning counterclockwise. But here's the real kicker: no matter which side you look at it from—east, west, north, or south—the disk always appears to be spinning the same way.

When the morning was young and the air chilly, my body rested and my mind fresh, whacking weeds made me feel like a big-screen Dominato Americano, Conqueror of Nature, Scourge of the Spring Grass, Lord of the Magic Ring. If you were tiny and you had roots in the ground, my disk zoomed in on you like a lethal flying saucer out of the movie *War of the Worlds*. I didn't just chop the grass—with my whips I terrorized it. Piloting my flying saucer, I vaporized a path through the stalks, toppling them over wholesale and laying them out flat like logs. Neither mere weed, nor leathery stand of English Harding grass, nor even the mightiest clump of Norwegian thistle stood a chance with me striking from overhead, my weapon swooping down on them, my whips slashing and my titanic shadow looming.

"Zoom-zoom, you helpless little suckers," I'd growl scornfully, drunk with power.

Of course whacking weeds wasn't all an uninterrupted march toward inevitable victory. Bad things could and did happen. Once, I hit the dirt with my whips and they shot a pebble into my wanger and—"yippie-yi-yo-ki-yay!"—that put me to rooster-walking. Then a friend of mine, who worked with goggles instead of a face mask, once kicked up a rock that smacked him square in his two front teeth. From then on, whenever he smiled, it looked like some hippies had come and pitched a black teepee in his mouth.

Sometimes, in order to properly operate a weed whacker, a person needed to be what's called in the profession "counterintuitive." For example, the old-timers, when they ran their phone lines between their shanties, liked using copper wire, which conducted well, was cheap, bent easily, and so quickly wrapped around things. Once while whacking weeds I ran into a long length of old copper telephone wire that was hiding in the grass like a snake. When my whips came over the wire's crumpled head, it jumped up out of the grass, struck at them, wrapped around my disk, and about yanked me out of my boots. And while I was airborne my instinct was to tighten up and brace myself. Which meant, by the time it occurred to me to let go of my throttle, I'd already belly-flopped some twenty feet down the road.

I looked up through the settling dust to see what had happened, and around my invincible disk I saw a bound-up wad of pioneer "telly-phone wire" about the size of a bowling ball.

Another thing that was embarrassing was when your whips got to galloping along two-by-four-inch horse wire. There'd you'd be, edging the fence, making it look all nice and tidy and antiseptic like a Kentucky stud farm, your disk slowly and carefully grooming back and forth, back and forth, when suddenly, with all of your might and without you even knowing it, you're swinging a golf club. Your whips have somehow ricocheted off the wire and now your flying saucer is arcing way up over your head. A friend of mine claimed he'd once knocked a bird out of the sky that way. It was one of those crazy wild doves that liked to hide out in the grass until the very last instant before blasting off in an explosion of feathers and scaring the snot out of you, if that's any consolation.

Still, when things were going well with the weed whacker, things were going easy with me. Like with swinging a scythe, there's a natural rhythm to whacking weeds. There's a cutting stroke and a clearing stroke, a forward and back, a fore and aft. Almost on its own, your disk adjusts to the terrain, banks with the slopes, swings into the gullies, and sinks low between rocks. Your two-stroke powerhouse whines between its combusting peaks and valleys, its tenor voice lilting, its whips singing, grass flying, and toxic fumes rising to high heaven. Running weed whacker is like making industrial music, artificial surf or tornado jazz. Like the micro-buzz of an electric toothbrush, or the blast of a blow-dryer, or the grating whir of a leaf blower, your engine's two-stroke whine is a part of America's tribal song—a bit of the racket we make to keep ourselves company.

On this particular afternoon out on the Diamond Dee, I was feeling at one with my machine. My weed whacker was an organic extension of my hands and fingers and its gas-fueled essence was coursing through my worker's soul. Back and forth, effortlessly and seamlessly swinging my conductor's wand, my strokes mirror images, my cosmic pendulum ticking and tocking in perfect balance, its tone and rhythm exquisitely true and in tune and—boy, I was feeling like a genuine native son just then, a good old-fashioned go-getter or go-withouter. And because I happened to be a rooting, tooting go-getter—look at all of the grass I'd killed and it wasn't even lunchtime yet—I was feeling like I was a part of a grand enterprise, like all alone in that canyon I was a living slice of the good life in the home of the industrious.

I was feeling my wild country oats, I was, until out of the corner of my eye I caught sight of a ragged herd of animals moseying my way. Their appearance was so unexpected that I absentmindedly shut down my engine as I stood and watched. My machine's choked-off silence allowed a sudden splash of canyon silence to wash over me and fill my ringing ears. And the overall depth and breadth of the silence was enough to make me immediately appreciate just how strangely quiet this weary, worn-out procession was.

They were the dozen of maverick cows that had escaped the Cooley Ranch a couple of months before. Now and again I or somebody else living out that way would momentarily glimpse the mavericks at some long distance, either topping a grassy ridge on the skyline or clamoring up a brush-choked draw. Still, for two months the cows had been living as free as the deer and the rabbits.

But now the cows were heading up the Elk Horn Road with their heads swinging low, their ears lying flat, and their hoofs dragging. Trailing them were two painted, panting, wiry, short-haired dogs that, with their heads and tails held low, loped in time with the cows. Bringing up the rear were two back-leaning cowboys aboard lathered, low-slung horses that slowly clip-clopped in time with the dogs and the cows. And watching them amble by showed me what real harmony and real natural rhythm was. The lyrical serenity of the scene was so inviting that I couldn't help but want to be a cowboy, to experience for myself what it was like to be a part of the living landscape.

After that, I never could look at my weed whacker the same.

TO FELL A CORNCOB

Once, a bunch of us loggers sat down to lunch next to the creek out there along the South Branch of the North Fork of the Navarro "River" (folks Out West like to lie about things like amounts of water, with puddles commonly christened "lakes" and creeks titled "rivers"). Out there where we were, the canyonsides were smooth and steep, and across the way the boss's son was in the process of felling a big old redwood tree. A small giant, the redwood must have been six foot thick on the butt and something like two hundred and fifty foot tall. It being a "seeder tree" left standing by the loggers who'd come clear-cutting through the canyon during the 1950s, it was used to having its own spot of sunshine and plenty of room to stretch its limbs. Its columnar trunk had very little taper, was ruler straight, nearly perfectly plumb, and its first limbs were hanging a good sixty foot above the ground. Yet, again because it had its own spot of sunshine, once the limbs got started, they grew to about a foot in diameter on the butt, forty foot long, and thick together like the kernels stuck in an ear of corn. A tree with a thick canopy like that was called a "corncob," though what it really looked like was a sculpted Christmas tree. But once the tree was felled and de-limbed, the logs bucked out of its crown looked just like corncobs, and that's how they got their name. All and all this particular corncob was a beautiful stander, especially considering how high up the mountain it was growing since most giants grow along the creek bottoms.

A big redwood like the one the boss's son was "chopping" needed to be felled up the hill in order to "save it out"—to keep it from shattering upon impact. Even though, because of the downward-sliding ground, nearly all canyonside redwoods leaned at least a bit down the hill, if you felled them that way you'd break them to pieces. By "gunning" (aiming) the tree up the hill, you halved the distance of its fall and so more than doubled your chance of saving it out. Yet, even felled more or less straight up the hill, a big redwood pumpkin was awfully fragile. If the "lay" was on flat ground, or on a gentle slope, then you'd have a Cat tractor come in to make you a "bed" to lay the tree down on. Beds were big mounds of fresh, loose dirt pushed together one behind the other so that when the tree landed on them they acted as shock absorbers. But up on a steep canyonside like the one the boss's son was working, even if you could get a Cat up there pushing dirt, whatever mounds it built would slide down the mountain.

Working without a bed, just felling the pumpkin up the hill didn't guarantee you'd save it out. If the tree landed on a stump or a rock outcrop, its trunk would break. If where the tree landed there was a bend in the middle that made the butt-half impact the forest floor before the top-half, the tree would break. And a giant redwood wouldn't break like a giant fir or pine tree, either. Drop a big pine or fir on a stump and its trunk will snap like a carrot. But do the same thing with a redwood and it'll shatter vertically along the grain and leave you with hundreds of long shards called "toothpicks." Though useless for lumber, the piles of toothpicks could be bucked to length and hand-split into fence rails, fence posts, grape stakes, pickets, shake shingles, and palens (3/8th inch thick, by 4 inch wide pickets). Yet, because the piles of toothpicks were rarely handy to a road or even to a serviceable foot trail, most of the time they were left in the woods to rot.

If a timber faller wanted to shatter a giant redwood from top to bottom—and get run off the show to boot—then he'd fell a pumpkin across a canyon or a swale. Make it so the top and the bottom land simultaneously with nothing to support the middle of the trunk and you're going to reduce virtually the entire redwood to rubble.

Because the corncob tree was almost perfectly plumb, to get it to fell up the hill the boss's son was using his ax to pound a set of six foot-long plastic wedges (faller's axes have a blade for chopping wood and a flat head for driving wedges). Using six wedges to spread the load and alternately tapping them like piano keys—the wedges set near the middle of the tree for power and those at the rear for lift—the poor fellah'd been swinging his ax for quite some while and still the tree was standing.

I suppose I should explain just how it was a little six-foot-tall, two-hundred-pound man swinging a six-pound ax-head into six pounds worth of plastic wedges could lift and eventually topple a giant, waterlogged redwood tree weighing maybe eighty tons. To begin with, you needed to make a face-cut that sawed away more than 50 percent of the trunk. By way of illustration, fill a glass full of water and slide it so that it overhangs the edge of a table. The percentage of the glass over the edge represents the depth of your face-cut. Extend 45 percent of the glass over the edge and it stands there. But extend it 50 percent plus a fraction and it tips right over.

To account for this pumpkin's slightly downhill lean, substitute the glass with a full coffee mug with a heavy handle and let the handle represent the lean. No matter where you position the handle, whether it's overhanging the edge, opposite the edge, or anywhere in between, if you overhang the cup more than 50 percent, it will topple.

After you'd cut out your face-cut's "pie" (the wedge of wood you removed from the trunk to make a void for the tree to fall into), you'd begin your back-cut, its leading edge advancing into the center of the tree parallel with the straight edge made by the inside of your face-cut. As you cut deeper into the back of the tree you'd start setting your wedges, tapping them deeper as you neared the end of your cut. When you were finished with your chainsaw, all that would be keeping the tree upright would be your wedges and the narrow strip of uncut "holding wood" that you'd left between your face- and back-cuts. The narrower the strip of holding wood, the easier it was to pound your wedges but the less control you had over your tree. Leave too little holding wood and your tree might snap off the trunk sideways in a gust of wind. Or it might go over backward, "eating" your wedges on its way to the creek. Or—this was about the worst thing that could happen to you—your tree could "barberchair."

With a thunderous explosion of fracturing wood, the trunk of your tree would split up the middle, the separation opening in your face and instantaneously racing up the center of the tree like a crack in ice, the rear half of the butt rising skyward with the falling top, and the front half still standing and acting like a towering pivot for a teeter-totter until, when the top impacts the ground, both sides crash to earth, dropping out of the sky like boulders.

When a redwood barberchaired on you, usually the front part of the back half of the trunk remained standing. Sometimes the remnant was just a few yards tall, and other times it was fifty yards tall. The sight of the straight, split-out center of the tree facing the level floor of your old back-cut (now the back of your stump) once reminded some fellah of a high-backed barber's chair, and so that's why it was called that when you accidentally split a standing redwood tree up the middle. A process named for a thing, in other words. Go off hiking through the redwoods and you're bound to see some barber chairs still standing, each a monument to some poor boy's folly.

Or worse. When you were sawing in your back-cut and your tree barberchaired, all you could do was run for your life. In fact, about anytime you felled a tree in the redwoods, you always had stored in the back of your mind at least one place, and sometimes four places, where you could escape to and find secure cover. Before you began felling a particular tree, you'd scout the ground all around it searching for hazards. Once you'd decided how you were going to gun your tree, you'd hike up to the top of its lay to see whether or not you'd chosen the right spot. Also, you'd want to take at least one careful look at the entire tree (you never saw the tops of the trees as you were felling them). How healthy was the treetop? Were there dead limbs hanging loose up there that might break free when you started pounding your wedges and sending shudders up through the foliage in the crown? Or, because a one-inch-thick wedge sunk to its head into the back of your back-cut will "swing" the spiked top of such a tree a few feet, sometimes just tipping the tree was enough to make loose limbs fall to earth. Needless to say, falling limbs were fairly common, and it didn't take much of one falling from much of a height to drill you. Hence their name: "widowmakers."

Standing near the top of your lay and taking into account your whole tree, you'd try to imagine how much commotion it was going to cause when it hit the forest floor. Would it break loose some rocks, logs, or baby trees that might tumble, roll, or slide down on you? Or what if you missed your lay by some degrees to one way or the other—what would happen then? Nearly always when you felled a tree it would "wash" other trees on its way down, their limbs tangling, snapping off, and floating, tumbling, and spinning to earth. Where would they likely land? Also you'd search for dead, rotten treetops crowning the little ones that might get washed. One of the most spectacular—and deadly and terrorizing—things that could happen to you was to have some of your tree's limbs wash a skinny, rubbery stander with a dead-top in it so that, after getting bent backward like a limbo dancer, it sprung back upright and spat its severed dead-top at you, it flying like the broken, wingless hull of an airplane.

Sometimes among the big trees on steep ground you'd use your chainsaw to cut yourself an escape trail through the brush and debris good enough to allow you to sprint away from your stump running full speed. Just about always, before your tree hit the ground, you wanted to be far away from your stump and already bunkered.

At the beginning I mentioned that the fellah working this particular corncob tree was the boss's son, and so I needed to explain a bit about the tree felling craft so you wouldn't take my meaning the wrong way. Out in the big-tree redwoods, the boss's sons were usually among the best all-around lumberjacks on the crew, and this fellah was no exception. Born to the woods, on his twelfth birthday he'd gotten as a present a little McCulloch chainsaw so in his spare time he could go out in the woods and cut the family some firewood. Since when he was growing up his dad was a timber faller, by the time he was sixteen years old he'd already been out bucking logs behind his dad—bucking logs and learning how to fell trees. While growing up he'd also slung steel, skinned cat, and chased on landings before taking up timber felling full time. And that had been some while ago since the boss's son was already getting past what you'd call being a spring chicken.

Not that any of that seasoning did him any good during what happened instantly after his corncob hit the ground straight up the hill exactly where he wanted. To the contrary, all of his previous experience had set a trap for him by making him lazy and a gambler. What happened was that he'd gotten to the point in his career where most everything about the woods seemed predictable to him. So long as he kept a close eye out, he'd convinced himself, nothing could get him. Where a greenhorn saw only chaos, he saw logic and order, gravity and inertia, weights and measures, cause, effect, and margins of safety. He knew when he could stand and gawk and he knew when to hightail it out of there. And, because logging was so brutally physical, a good part of mastering the craft amounted to knowing when you could save moves and stay put.

His decision to stay put under the stump as his pumpkin was falling straight above him wasn't the smartest thing he'd ever done. He'd left a tall stump with a wide mouth and, out of the end of the bottom lip of it, he'd cut a parallel "snipe" (notch) to help hold the bottom edge of the severed butt in place against the stump. Also, because he wanted to gently ease the pumpkin down into its lay, he'd left a thick strip of holding wood so that, as the tree began its slow-motion descent, the holding wood bent, moaned, stretched, growled, crackled, squealed, and whined in its fight to hold up the tree against gravity. Now acting as a hinge, his holding wood didn't let go until the last instant, and that too should have helped to keep the butt locked to the stump.

I still don't think the boss's son had intentionally planned on taking cover below the stump. One thing wrong with leaving lots of holding wood was that pounding wedges gets to be a whole lot more difficult, and he'd been swinging his ax most of the time we'd been sitting down to lunch, listening to his whacks, munching our food and feeling sorry for him. It had been brute strength and stone hillbilly stubbornness that had gotten his wedges sunk and his tree successfully tipped—instantly after your tree tips you want to whack wedges for all you're worth to make sure it doesn't change its mind—and by the time his tree started its fall he was just plain too tuckered out to try making a run for it. He was so winded that all he could do was kneel down below the stump to catch his breath.

When the crown of the corncob tree hit the canyonside way up the hill, its limbs were so stout and thick that, as they shattered, they kept the butt of the tree from fully hitting the ground and locking into the snipe. The trunk bounced, rolled sideways on the limbs and, having cleared its stump, started sliding butt first down the hill, gaining speed with its descent. Within a blink of the eye, the tree was racing and its bottom limb smacked the snipe on the stump and snapped off, and immediately it was like a string of firecrackers going off as more and more limbs snapped and got piled above the stump while the poor fellah was holding his head and cowering below.

From where we were sitting it looked like his only chance of surviving was to run away before the space above the stump filled and limbs started slapping over the downhill side of the stump and pounding him into hamburger. But just when I covered my eyes with my hand, the butt slammed into the creek bottom and the tree froze like an arrow stuck in a bale of straw.

Even after the swinging standers, falling limbs, tumbling rocks, small boulders, chunks of wood, and all of the rest of the commotion had settled down, the boss's son was still frozen beneath the stump. And seeing him unhurt and yet still petrified, absolutely and genuinely scared stiff, made us all roll in the dirt and laugh our asses off.

"You can come down now," an old catskinner finally called up to him, his voice disguised to sound like a mother's.

Finally the boss's son climbed down to us on wobbly legs. After something like that happened to you it was customary to call it a day, and he was feeling mighty customary. He sat down in a loose heap on the ground among us and, even though some of the guys kept making fun of him, you wouldn't have known it by watching his face. Judging by the moon-eyed expression on his face, you'd have thought he'd just seen the Virgin Mary.

THE TURKEY AND THE RAVEN

The other day I watched as a tom turkey took after an old skinny raven. Ravens have a reputation for raiding the nests of other birds, but I doubt if this tom turkey had much in the way of paternal instincts, or cared much about the raven's reputation. It seemed to me the tom turkey just plain didn't like the looks of the old raven and that was enough for him to not want him to be hanging around.

In order to drive the old raven away, the tom turkey puffed up his chest, noisily beat his wings, stretched out his goofy neck, and then shot straight up into the air like a bottle rocket. Next, his wings clumsily flapping, his talons out, he tried to land on the old raven with both feet.

And each time the tom turkey dropped out of the sky, the old raven waited until the very last instant before he, with a single flash of wings, hopped out of the way.

Missing his target would get the tom turkey so mad that he'd chase after the old raven, even though he stood no chance of catching him. And when the tom turkey stopped chasing, the old raven stopped running. Standing just out of reach with his head cocked sideways, he'd stiffen his back and plant his feet. Regarding the tom turkey with one sharp eye, the old raven seemed to dare him to take another lunge.

It occurred to me that what was riling the tom turkey wasn't so much the old raven's raggedy looks but his haughty attitude.

Like every time the tom turkey shouted "Goodbye!" the old raven whispered "Hello."

Whatever it was that was really going on inside of their heads, clearly they were enjoying themselves. Tom turkeys are lazy critters, so any time you see one of them jumping up and down you know he's got to be having fun. As for the old raven, he'd lived a long time, passed through a lot of places, and he liked keeping his cool. He'd move along soon enough, no sweat. But only after the flustered tom turkey was all tuckered out and he himself was feeling good and ready.

TENDING HOOK

I remember the first time I laid eyes on a yarder. I was felling timber up along the headwaters of the Albion River. The canyon I was working in was steep and narrow like a wedge of sunlight driven into the mountains. The cutbank above the haul-road below my strip was tall enough to hide the logging trucks barreling in and out, though the rising rooster tails of dust told me which way they were heading.

I was beyond cutting my teeth as a timber faller and I was having the time of my young life. Though I'd been at it for some months stretching over two seasons, still about every tree I felled was teaching me something, especially those that landed exactly where I'd gunned them. How'd I do that and why couldn't I do it every time? I was working the tall, skinny residual redwoods that the old-timers, in polite company, called "dog's hair," and they'd warned me that while I was "clipping the dog's hair" there'd be less money, more work, and more danger.

Facts I already knew. Using a jack, wedges, or both, a redwood that is three foot thick or more on the butt can almost always be put down with precision atop any point on the compass. But while working a strip of dog's hair, trees that big were few and far between. Most trees were too skinny to fit a wedge and a chainsaw into their back-cuts at the same time, baby redwoods being mostly bark and sapwood with not much heartwood. So about all you could do to pull them away from their lean was to cut extra-deep face-cuts and hope they didn't sit down on your bar, or a gust of wind didn't fill their canopies and cause them to barberchair.

On the bright side, while clipping dog's hair, you didn't have to worry about breaking any logs. How do you break a paper straw? You could put a baby redwood over sideways, backward, or dump it straight down the hill dead center atop a stump, and still you'd have to get mighty unlucky to break it, much less shatter it into toothpicks. Again on the bright side, because the trees were so young and insubstantial, few of them had powerful downhill leans. Unless a tree was a limb-locked part of a "sucker clump" (the root shoots growing in a ring around the massive weathered stumps left to us by the pioneers), virtually all of them could be felled almost perfectly side-hill, which eliminated most all of the up-and-down climbing, limbing, and log bucking that the old-timers had taken for granted.

As an added bonus, working dog's hair meant you could sometimes "shotgun" your trees. Because in the mountains the prevailing wind blows either up or down the canyons and never crossways, stands of trees leaned slightly with the prevailing wind. The way the forest leaned with the prevailing wind was called its "lead" (as in "leader"). Since you could usually count on the prevailing wind to come up off the ocean early every afternoon, you could use the wind plus the lead to simultaneously knock down a whole bunch of redwoods and, no matter what their individual leans, send them all crashing the same way.

To shotgun trees first you'd find a biggish tree that you could put side-hill with the wind. Next you'd calculate how many standers your tree would wash on its way down and, if those trees fell, how many more trees they would wash on their own ways down. If your shotgun tree is one hundred and fifty feet tall, and if there are plenty of smaller trees in its lay, then, using it as a domino, you can slice a crease into the canopy that is one hundred yards long.

After determining the exact number of trees you can knock over, beginning with the farthest of them and working your way toward your shotgun tree, you'd put an extra-wide and -deep face-cut and a liddle-biddy back-cut into each of them, leaving just enough holding wood to keep them upright in a gust of contrary wind. Finally you'd work up your shotgun, tap a couple of wedges into it as insurance and, leaving your saw in the back-cut, shut it down and take a breather. You'd sit and listen to the wind and watch it bending the treetops. If the afternoon wind was coming up strong and steady, you'd see its gusts rippling the forest as they advanced up the canyon in waves. If that was the case, then after you'd caught your breath and a gust was just about on you, you'd crank up your saw, hot-rod through the rest of your back-cut, and let her rip.

You talk about raising a commotion.

So there I was up on the canyonside taking a break while waiting for the right push of wind to come and help me knock down one tree and a half dozen pecker poles. The instant I'd cut off my chainsaw I heard a humongous racket coming up the haul-road. It was a noise so big and loud and unpleasant that it distracted me and I decided to stay put so I could see just what kind of gigantic machine could be putting out so much god-awful, steel-track-screeching sound.

Above the cutbank appeared a bright yellow armored steel box that I'd have mistaken for the pilothouse of a tugboat if it hadn't've been preceded by a forty-foot-tall steel-girder tower that advanced though the forest like the neck and head of a Trojan Horse. I'd heard the rumor of such a mechanical monstrosity coming out to help us move logs, but I hadn't given it much thought, and I was surprised by how quickly it had arrived.

"Yarder logging changes everything," the old hands all swore, remembering their yarder days in the lumber camps up north. At the time I had no idea what they were talking about.

• • •

The next day, the bullbuck hiked up into my strip. His name was Mike, I'd been working for him for three years, and we were on friendly terms. At first I thought he'd come to inspect my work, or just to gab, or maybe to tell me about my next strip of timber since I was about finished with this one. But, after catching his breath, Mike told me he wanted me to do him a favor. He sat down in a spot of shade and gestured for me to join him.

Now, I'm as suspicious of doing a favor as the next guy, but in the woods everybody does favors, and that's about the only way anything ever gets done. If you're getting set to dump a tree on the landing and a fellah drives up and parks his truck in your lay, then once he's outside with his feet on the ground you'll gently holler down to him, "Say, can you do me a favor? Could you please move your truck out of my way so I can fell my tree?"

Likewise, a seasoned chokersetter will stick with a particular catskinner mostly because he likes him and wants to do him a favor. Or, if a timber faller takes a show and winds up making less money than he's used to, then he'll tell you it's because he's doing his brother-in-law, an old buddy, or somebody else a favor. And gyppo catskinners, they being of a breed famous for its pickiness when it comes to signing on to any particular show for any length of time, are always doing somebody a favor just by showing up for work.

So when Mike asked me to do him a favor I knew he was issuing me an order and, my heart sinking, I strongly suspected it had something to do with that giant clattering contraption I'd watched move in the day before. When I sat down beside him, I did my best not to show my disappointment.

Firstly, Mike wanted me to know, he considered me to be an outstanding chokersetter, an excellent landing chaser, and a fair, if novice, timber faller. Those qualities made me a good all-around woodsman and so I was just the sort of fellah he needed to break in and honcho that newfangled machine. He knew I was enjoying myself felling timber and he assured me that, as a "hook tender," I'd continue doing some felling and bucking, at least enough to keep me from getting rusty.

Yet, no matter my desires, the plain fact was that Mike had timber fallers a lot better than me sitting at home and licking their paws and waiting for a job opening. And it wasn't right for me to be filling their boots, at least not while I could be helping him out in a bigger way. Mike would like to do one of them old coots a favor plus me one besides by giving me the honor and the pleasure of getting my teeth cut by a master hook tender that Mike was importing down from Washington state.

Given the rudimentary state of my single-jacking skills, Mike assured me, I'd be making more money working under the yarder. I wouldn't have any more equipment expenses and, since I could rejoin the crew riding to work in the crummy, I'd have no more travel expenses. I'd have no more break-down or "plumb stuck" time, and I'd be back to working sixty-hour weeks, which included the customary twenty hours per week of overtime pay.

Throw it all together and, Mike promised me, I'd be making at least 30 percent more money per week tending hook than I was clipping dog's hair.

Finally, Mike added with a challenging gleam in his eye, tending hook was fun.

"So what you say?" Mike asked me.

What could I say?

• • •

The particular kind of yarder I went to work under is called a "heel boom." The "boom" is the tower and the "heel" describes the boom's ability, during skidding operations, to swing about one hundred and twenty degrees either left or right. To get an idea, imagine you are still-fishing from the steep shore of a mountain lake with a plastic float on your line. The angle of your fishing pole is about the angle of the boom. Now drain the water out of the lake so that what you have left is a V-shaped canyon. In this case your fishing line is a one-thousand-foot-long, one-and-one-eighth-inch-thick steel cable called a "skyline." You run out your skyline to the bottom of the canyon and up the opposite face far enough so that, once you've hitched the end of it to a stump and once the yarder, by engaging its winch, reels in the slack and pulls the line tight, you've got "lift." Depending upon the shape of the canyon, your skyline might hang between ten and seventy feet up in the air, though fifty foot high is ideal.

The logs covering the canyonside below the skyline are your fish. Since when you hook logs they are going to exert pressure on the skyline, and because the boom will not bend like a fishing pole, to keep the machine from toppling over into the canyon its ass end is filled with tons of steel counterweights. Plus, and this is crucially important, the yarder is anchored in place by two massive steel cables called "guylines" that, spreading from the "guy tower" backward at forty-five degrees from the boom and anchored to "immovable" stumps on the hillside just above, act like a deep-sea fisherman's harness does when it keeps him from getting yanked overboard by a big fish.

Riding inside a carriage and below the skyline was a second, one-inch-thick steel cable called the "haul-back." The carriage was a heavy-duty steel collection of rollers and brakes that skated up and down the skyline like a trolley. From its mouth dangled the haul-back's big steel hook, and from the hook dangled a collection of chokers. By stopping the carriage at a particular spot along the skyline and releasing the brake holding the haul-back with its hook and chokers, you could have your rigging air-dropped to you anywhere under the cable.

Since the yarder operator in the pilothouse could rarely see his chokersetters (yarders employ two of them) "down in the hole," they communicated with each other using a code transmitted with electronic whistles. Usually worn around the waist like gun belts, the whistles emitted electronic beeps that had been scientifically designed to grab and hold the operator's attention. For if a catskinner was like a trained elephant with his own mind and temperament, a "donkey puncher" was a trained elephant that was totally blind and, judging by the volume of the beeps firing out of the loudspeaker on his tower, about stone deaf.

Actually, that's unfair. The donkey puncher has the noise of his giant diesel engine to contend with, plus the buzz of his chaser's chainsaw and the whine of his log loader. And that's not to mention the mind-numbing boredom that comes while putting your hands and feet through the same routines over and over during the course of a ten-hour day. So it takes a little persuasion to keep a donkey puncher alert and on task. One reason why yarders are called "donkeys" is because sometimes you have to whack a donkey on the head with a two-by-four to get its attention. Another reason is that, in the early days, yarders were so weak you couldn't really say they had "horsepower." "Donkey power" was more like it.

Another reason the beeps were so loud was because they enabled everybody working down in the hole to know when logs were flying.

For safety reasons, everybody in the hole was equipped with a whistle and everybody knew the code. But, barring emergency or special circumstance, only the senior chokersetter was authorized to send signals. Called a "whistle pump," or sometimes a "whistle punk," the senior chokersetter ran the show when it came to moving logs. He not only controlled the actions of the yarder, he also decided what logs went when and how many at a time.

Because, at least back then, no greenhorns were allowed to work under yarders, and given the propensities of seasoned "Cat-side" log riggers, usually the whistle pump and his helper shared responsibilities and worked equally hard, the first taking the lead but the second free to occasionally have things his own way. Still, if the whistle pump got too bossy or lazy, or if the helper got too lazy or bossy, then, well, it isn't a stretch to say that simmering feuds between chokersetters working under yarders were about as common as pulled muscles and barked shins.

"Yarding" logs is a lot simpler than skidding them behind Cats. With the skyline tight, using gravity, the carriage delivering the haul-back line and rigging is skated down into the hole. When it has reached the point where the whistle pump wants it, he lets off with one beep, which is the signal for the operator to apply the brakes and stop the carriage. Next, after another single beep, the operator slackens the skyline, which lowers the carriage so that the chokersetters can get a hold of the rigging. After setting chokers on however many logs the machine can handle (you want to run a yarder at about 90 percent of capacity), the riggers move away, find cover and, once he has double-checked everything, the whistle pump blows two beeps, which is the signal for the operator to tighten the skyline. As the operator revs his engine and engages his spool, the skyline tightens and the logs lift into the air. Once the dangling logs have stopped swinging back and forth under the carriage, the whistle pump gives his final signal, three beeps, which tells the operator to reel them on up to the landing.

Naturally the job was a whole lot more complicated than that. For instance, if the load was uncommonly light, or if the puncher got too heavy-footed on his accelerator, then when he tightened the skyline the logs exploded out of the woods and leapt into the air. Once, when we were first learning what the yarder could and couldn't do, we blew a "tight line" and five skinny forty-foot-logs jumped up into the sky and, their noses dangling from their leaches and their butts circling, they promptly wrapped themselves around the trunk of a stander. Once they came to a stop, like tetherballs they instantly started unwinding, their speed and arc growing while we ran for our lives.

Chokers bite into the bark of redwoods and, especially during the spring and early summer months when the trees are full of rainwater, sometimes the bark breaks free and logs slip the lasso. What happened was sort of like if you pulled on the choke chain of a big dog and his head fell off. Get a forty-footer swinging or circling in the sky and it breaks bark, then there's no telling what's going to happen. Once I watched a skinny twenty-footer sail by me like it had been shot out of some kind of catapult.

One of the strangest things I ever saw happen under a yarder was a solo fat forty-footer weighing about four tons go absolutely still under the slowly eased-up and tightened skyline and, before I could whistle the operator to reel it in, break its bark. The log dropped the few feet to the ground and just stood there erect, perfectly still and perfectly plumb. Just when I started wondering what I was supposed to do now, the log finally toppled over.

Another time I watched as a log getting reeled in broke bark, landed straight up and down the hill on its belly and, using the canyon's side-hill-laying logs as rollers, skate eight hundred feet down to the creek, most of the way gone out of sight. Another time the same thing happened to a tall, skinny redwood tree that was in my way and I dumped straight down the hill. Watching its newly polished butt receding into the void, it was like watching a man in a rowboat who has just hooked himself a three-thousand-pound Marlin. I cocked my ear and—*bam*—I heard my tree splash in the creek.

Even more curious than watching flying logs was watching people tumbling down the hands-and-feet-climbing steep canyonsides. Watching a lumberjack bouncing down the mountain like a half-full keg of beer could be more fun than throwing rocks.

Easily the best time I ever had watching somebody take a tumble happened while I was setting choker under the yarder. My partner was walking down a ten-foot-thick buckskin log pointing straight up and down the hill when the spikes on one of his boots picked up a piece of dead bark that acted like a banana peel. My partner landed hard on his back, bounced into a ball, and instantly started rolling straight down the top of the buckskin as if it was a bowling lane. The ground was cliff steep, and as he gained speed I was sure he'd get killed even before he hit the creek. But, maybe five stories down, he bounced and disappeared behind the wall made by the buckskin. Even over surrounding industrial hubbub, I heard his body crashing into the brush.

I was standing roughly side-hill when my partner started his tumble; I was way up the hill when he finished it. Afraid of what I might see, but knowing he might need my help, I ran down the hill, leaped atop the buckskin, and in a flash I was looking down at him. And what I saw I'll never forget. My partner had landed head first in a mat of huckleberry bushes covered with a bed of crisscrossed broken redwood limbs, and all I could see jutting above the thicket was the bottoms of his spiked boots, one of them with the banana peel still firmly stuck in place. And—what a great sign!—the boots were wiggling. In fact, his boots were thrashing so fast it looked like he was running upside down. I leaned over and stretched my neck and I saw his face all scrunched up down there and—it was a miracle!—his eyes were open and he was looking plaintively up at me. Red-faced and blinking rapidly, he was looking at me like he was aware of the fine mess he'd gotten himself into and sorry for the trouble he was causing me.

I tried to ask him if he was OK, but I didn't see any blood, except the blood rushing to his face, and with his legs wiggling like they were—like his body knew it had to do something—I nearly fell off the log laughing. Ashamed of myself, I was hysterical nevertheless.

"Help me," he managed to call. "Help get me up out of here."

Which only made me give up all pretense of having a just and noble character, slide like a snake off the buckskin, loll in the dirt like a pig, and laugh my ass off like I'd just won the lottery.

"I'm gonna kill you," my partner yelled in a weak, strangled voice, his flying spit slapping his forehead. "You'd best hurry." Then, after heaving a huge, heartrending sigh, my partner went silent and his legs stopped thrashing the brush.

After regaining my composure, I climbed back atop the buckskin and took another peek at his face. Now beet purple because of all of the blood leaking in from his twisted neck, I figured all of the fight had gone out of him and so it was safe for me to climb down there and help him untangle himself.

After I got my partner back on his feet, he ignored me while he weakly staggered up to a little flat spot above a stander and collapsed in a heaving heap, his hands shaking and lower lip quivering. I tried to tell him how sorry I was for laughing at him, but seeing him sprawled there got me to laughing some more and, not wanting to further provoke him or disgrace myself, I walked away to give him some privacy while I worked the giggles out of me.

When after a couple of minutes I turned back around to see how he was doing and how pissed off he was, he'd come back alive. He was sitting up, his eyes were twinkling, and he was methodically working his neck, hands, legs, and the rest of his body parts to see if any of them were broken, or if any particular part of him hurt more than any place else, him having bumps, bruises, and contusions covering his whole body save his feet. He glanced up at me, slowly shook his head, and chuckled as if he was beginning to understand just what sort of critter I was.

Next, having more important things to think about than me, he twisted around and gazed up to the spot on the buckskin where he'd lost his footing. He allowed his eyes to follow the course down the log he'd taken, and he wound up staring for a long time at the thicket he'd landed in. He turned back up the hill, ran his eyes along the course again, and I could tell he was calculating just how far in feet he'd fallen. He stared at the thicket again and his mouth stretched into a big, self-knowing, self-satisfied grin. He glanced past me like I was a tree and, raising his chin to the sky, he let out with a loud, joyful "HEE—HAAWWW!"

• • •

About all we know about picking up and transporting heavy objects we learned from sailors. Thousands of years ago, how did sailors hoist thick, heavy, waterlogged hemp ropes up and over the tops of fifty-foot-tall masts? They did it by tying one end of a little rope to the end of the big rope and the other end of the little rope to a man and sending him climbing up the mast with it. At the top he'd run his rope through a pulley and ride it back down to the deck. With the help of his mates, he'd use the little rope to pull the end of the big rope up and through the pulley and back down into his hands.

Using the same idea (rope A pulls rope B pulls rope C), American engineers during the 1930s stretched the massive, mile-and-a-half-long steel support cables up and over the towers of San Francisco's Golden Gate Bridge.

The idea has so many everyday applications that the lead rope is universally known as a "pilot line." Except, that is, when used to run out the spooled-up skylines of yarders, in which case it's called a "straw line." But if you have the ends of two straw lines shouldered and you are monster-stepping them down into the bottom of the canyon, then what you are doing is called "running hay wire."

Three-eighths of an inch thick and two hundred foot long, on each end of the spaghetti-like cables are loop, twist, and hook mechanisms known as "Hindus." Made of the doubled-up cable bent back on itself and a tiny hook, a Hindu is designed to be flexible enough to get wound up and buried in spools while being strong enough to keep hold while pulling tons of weight. Why the connectors were called Hindus is anybody's guess. Once, an old hand explained to me how, lying loose in the dirt, two Hindus hooked together looked like the profile of Ali Baba and his forty thieves, what with their baggy pants, baggy shirts, and belts cinched down the middle. When I informed him that Ali Baba was a Muslim and not a Hindu, the old hand regarded me like he was wondering what that had to do with anything. Whether Muslim, Hindu, Chinese, or Greek, who cared? We were talking about the origins of the lingo.

Two hay wires pulled out and connected through a pulley on your tail hitch acted like a clothesline strung between two tenement buildings. Pull one side of the loop toward you and the other side moves away. So, after you'd muscled your two straw lines down to the creek, you dropped the end of one straw line and pulled more length out of the other, carefully coiling the slack at your feet. Once you calculated you had enough slack coiled to get you up the opposite canyonside to where you needed to go, you'd blow a stop to the operator and he'd apply the brakes to the spool and take himself a break. Meanwhile the landing chaser, who'd been helping to keep the lines coming smooth out of the spools, disconnected the appropriate Hindu and hitched it through the eye of the skyline and, his work done, he also took a break.

Back down in the hole, depending upon the steepness of the canyon's opposite face, you'd shoulder the end of your hay wire or, using the Hindu, cinch it crossways to your body like a bandolier. Taking the most direct path offering the least resistance, you'd bull the cable up the mountain to your preset pulley. You'd run the end through the pulley and ride it back down to the creek. Once you connected the two Hindus your clothesline was complete and, using the diesel power of the yarder to re-spool the straw lines, you'd simultaneously run out the skyline.

But they didn't call it running hay wire for nothing. Given the limits of a human's physical strength and endurance, the complications could seem endless, one hang-up following another. As with the other aspects of tending hook, whether finding the right "tail hitch" for the skyline (a tail hitch is a massive stump that, using your chainsaw and ax, you notched to seat the looped and shackled cable), or finding and working up the stumps used to anchor your guylines, or actually running out the guylines, or felling trees out of your way, or bucking the tree lengths left for you by lazy or superstitious timber fallers, or scouting ahead through lays of logs for your next "setups," or pinpointing the precise location for the machine, or helping the riggers, fixing or replacing broken rigging or equipment or, sometimes, just finding a safe place to sit down and eat lunch, running hay wire was a lot easier said than done.

What was unique about tending hook was the amount of time you spent hiking up and down canyonsides covered with loose logs. Timber fallers worked their strips from the bottom up to avoid having to work under logs, and rigging crews worked from the top down for the same reason. But as a hook tender you came after the timber fallers and before the riggers and you used logs as pathways to get you where you wanted to go. Nearly always you were below logs, and sometimes you dropped into the hole, or climbed back up out of it, without once touching the dirt. And that aspect of the job alone made it exciting. If the amount of excitement is determined by the degree of danger, then tending hook is one of the most exciting jobs on earth.

I'll mention one example because, framed within the rest of my experiences, not just as a hook tender but as a woodsman, the incident helped convince me to quit logging and go back to something safe and sane like ranching. I was running hay wire and, because I was nearing the creek, I was monster-stepping with my back into it, and my body was perpendicular to the slope. I stepped down onto the nose of a log that gave way under my feet. Instantly I dropped my hay wires and found myself surfing, holding my balance while getting carried down the canyonside. Before I could gather my wits, the log stopped moving, I stepped sideways onto solid ground and, free of my weight, the log swung back up to where it'd started.

Thrilled and amazed, I gazed up at the log I'd ridden and saw what had happened. A skinny sixty-footer, the log was held on the slope by a single stump located at its exact center of gravity that had acted like a fulcrum. What had felt like an elevator ride had been a ride on a teeter-totter. Struck by the elegant simplicity of the physics, while climbing back up the hill to fetch my straw lines I was sorely tempted to ride the log again, to see if I could get it to act the exact same way. The temptation was intoxicating until I remembered my wife and my two little boys back home. And thinking about them made me realize just how addicted to danger I'd become, and just how selfishly and irresponsibly I'd grown used to living my life.

Back up the hill with my straw lines and looking down on the nose of the wonder log, I saw where my spikes had left their patterns of holes in its bark, and I tried to get my body to leap back aboard. And while trying to decide what to do it felt like I was trying to decide whether or not to stay in the woods. Which would it be?

Though it took me another couple of logging seasons to finally make up my mind, I picked up my Hindus, shouldered my hay wires and, moving a bit side-hill to stay out from under that particular log, I pulled them the rest of the way down to the creek.

THE ANGLE OF REPOSE

Geologists have a concept called the Angle of Repose. What it means is the maximum degree of steepness a particular type of earth can achieve. Clay can stand steeper than sand, and rock can stand steeper than clay. In the redwoods, aside from the occasional rock outcrop, the steepest parts of the steepest canyons are called landslides. Landslides stand at the exact Angle of Repose.

• • •

Back when I was setting choker behind a Cat, I got to know a pair of elderly timber fallers who were of Swedish descent. Brothers in their late fifties or early sixties, tall, round-faced and round-shouldered, their blond hair tinged with silver and their blue eyes wide and lively, as young men they'd come to America, like thousands of their countrymen before them, to make some easy money logging the redwoods. Based in the town of Willow Creek up in Humboldt County, the brothers lived next door to each other, raised their families together and, them being what used to be called "eager beavers," they hit the road when they had to and returned home only after a job was done.

Known as "The Swedes," by reputation the brothers were two of the most accomplished timber fallers left in what remained of the big trees. And that said something special about them because, unlike most aces, they didn't single-jack adjoining strips but worked together in the same strip. Back then, because of the size of the timber, "partnering" wasn't too uncommon among timber fallers. The usual arrangement was that one fellah did the felling and got ahead a tree length while his partner followed along doing the limbing, bucking, and scaling.

But the Swedes worked the same tree at the same time. If the tree was big enough, they'd even cut their face- and back-cuts together, one brother working his side of the tree and the other his own. After the tree was felled, one brother would go ahead and knock off the limbs while the other followed along up the trunk, stretching out his tape, bucking and scaling.

What was even more peculiar about the Swedes was they talked all the time. If you think that Swedes, what with them being used to long, frozen winters, arctic nights and all, are the silent and stolid types, you never met these two. To make money they needed to keep their chainsaws constantly singing, and sing they did. But at the same time, having found a way to throw their voices over the racket, all day long they yakked at each other like magpies. While sawing logs they discussed their wives and kids, nieces and nephews, in-laws, friends, and neighbors. They chatted about hunting and fishing, the prospect of an early winter, the price of chisel-bit chain, and anything else that popped into their minds. One of them might be bucking a log, his sawdust sailing, and giving the other a progress report: "Sound wood here I've got me, by Jimmy. Not too soppy wet, eh? She's ah cutting like ah buttah now, she is. Buttah in de sun, yo-see."

Another interesting thing about the Swedes was how they mangled the lingo. While the redwoods drew adventurers from all over the European world, the flavor of the lingo was provided mostly by the Sons of Arkansas and those from the adjoining territories. For instance, instead of saying "yes" or "no," a logger typically said "yip" or "nah." Except the Swedes, who, when you said something they agreed with, or at least understood, nodded in unison and thoughtfully uttered, "Yaaap, daat's tooo." Or, if the contrary answer was appropriate, they'd shake their heads and say, "Naaap."

Now, the ground we were working was the sort of steep that brought out the best in a mountain goat. The ground was so steep that, if you took a gander down into the bottom of the hole, your tin hat would topple off your head. Your hat would ping and pang down the mountain and you'd have to climb down after it. Once you'd climbed back up to where you started, if you happened to take a gander up the hill searching for the skyline, then off you'd go again chasing after your hat.

Which raises the question: Why didn't tin hats come equipped with chinstraps? Whether you were running to get out from under a falling tree, or just looking up the trunk of a tree, or running to get out from under a rolling log, or just stumbled, the first thing that happened was your hardhat fell off. It's curious that when OSHA outlawed tin hats in the woods and forced us to all wear plastic hardhats painted in the loud, Day-Glo colors that they insisted would make us more visible and so a whole lot safer, the new hats didn't come with chinstraps either. Even OSHA wasn't that smart. Or, for that matter, that stupid.

Just for laughs, I wish they would have tried to force us to wear chinstraps. Boy, I can hear the howling now.

"How's a fellah to look up his own tree without strangling hisself?"

"How's a man to look over his shoulder without snagging his chinstrap on his suspenders?"

"What if a Jill-poke gets wedged in all down under there?"

"If they're so damned smart out there in Washington, D.C., why don't they force rodeo cowboys to wear football helmets?"

"They may as well wrap us all up in life preservers."

"Yeah, them big puffy kinds of life preservers so when we get to tumbling ass-over-teakettle we can be bouncing down the mountain like beach balls."

According to a rumor I heard recently, as of April 15, 2010 (you've got to allow folks time to adapt to things), everybody working in the woods will be required to come equipped with a new, scientifically designed kind of hardhat. Called the Woody Woodpecker Model '08, it will be painted with Proceed with Extreme Caution Government Orange—the kind of orange that makes your eyes shrivel and your skin crawl. It'll also come with a wraparound black mesh mask to protect your face and eyes from flying sawdust and wood chips. The Model '08 will also come equipped with a pair of ostrich egg–sized earmuffs, half an egg for each side of your head. Still—wouldn't you know it?—the new Woody Woodpecker will not come equipped with a chinstrap.

Instead, the Model '08 will come with a patented haul-back feature. It will operate like a Slinky with one end attached to the webbing inside of your hardhat and the other end attached to the sweatband cinched around your head. To get the sweatband adjusted right, you'll turn a clamp with an Allen wrench. With your sweatband properly cinched and adjusted, whenever you lose your hat you won't have to chase after it because it'll automatically spring right back to you. In fact, whenever you feel a tug on your sweatband, you'll immediately drop whatever you're doing so you can have your hands ready to catch your hat. After a bit of practice—the instruction booklet will advise you to practice this maneuver at home, after work and on your own time—you'll cock your head and your hat will land right back atop it, all screwed down and pointing the right away.

In addition to the steepness of this particular canyon, its mouth opened into a wide swath of the Pacific Ocean. "Russian Gulch," the place was called. It was the Russian Gulch that's just north of the Russian River in Sonoma County, and not the Russian Gulch up in Mendocino. Anyway, every afternoon off the ocean the wind came up at one o'clock sharp. In Russian Gulch the afternoon wind was cold, wet, and steady, and every morning at starting time the canyon was wet with dew, snot slippery, and hidden in a blanket of fog. When the areas inland were sweltering in the summer heat, overnight the rising air sucked into the canyon fog so dense you could kick it up with your feet. You could kick up the fog with your feet even as the mist falling from the canopy was so thick that, if you peeked at the sun rising over the rim of the canyon, it was ringed with a rainbow.

As timber fallers go, the Swedes were exceptionally organized, disciplined, and methodical. Fog or no fog, wind or no wind, they were the first ones in their strip in the morning and among the last to go home in the afternoon. So one exceptionally foggy early dawn the Swedes parked their pickup on the shoulder of the truck road above their strip and, after upending the dregs left in their coffee cups, proceeded to get to work. After filling a canvas satchel with every spare wedge they had, they dove off into the canyon below their truck.

That morning the fog was so thick that the Swedes hadn't gone a log-length before they disappeared from sight. Yet, their voices receding, you could still hear them yakking back and forth as they worked their way down the mountain. The deeper they got, the thicker the fog became, a fact that made little or no impression on them since they were used to being unable to see the tops of the trees.

By the time the Swedes reached the bottom and their cached gear, they were already discussing the tree they'd be starting their day with. A giant pumpkin about twelve foot thick on the butt and three hundred foot tall, it was a bonanza tree; the sort of redwood that, even back then, made not just your day but also your week and month.

The jackpot tree was growing exactly where the toe of the mountain disappeared into the floodplain edging the creek. The previous day the Swedes had gunned the pumpkin straight up the hill, and when they were finished with their face-cut its lower lip met ground level. But, because the ground was so steep, to saw in their back-cut first they had to notch in springboards to stand on. They'd notched in two sets of six springboards that reached an elevation of twelve feet above the ground and ascended the tree like a pair of spiral staircases that met in the middle.

To get the sort of reputation the Swedes enjoyed you had to be making lots of money compared to the other fallers. As for the hungry young bucks just coming up, if any of them could put down the amount of timber the Swedes did, day after day and week after week, then they knew they had themselves a boy who just might have a bright golden future ahead of him, by golly. That is, if the boy survives long enough to gain enough practical sense to stop chopping timber for ten hours a day instead of just six or seven. Still, having once been cocksure young bucks themselves, the Swedes knew if the boy held up working those kind of hours then the other fellahs on the show would, by virtue of just being associated with him, swell with pride and start spinning the boy's legend. If the boy really was all that lickety-split, they'd be bragging about him in saloons as if he was their own son. "Ain't no steep ground stopping that old boy," one might say, raising his drink in toast.

The Swedes were nothing if not lickety-split. In no time at all they had their back-cut into the pumpkin, their saws were stashed, and they were back up on their springboards pounding wedges, their swinging axes swirling the fog, the sharp *cracks* swallowed by it. The fog was so thick they couldn't see upward much past their own eyebrows. But that didn't bother them none because, with each brother working six wedges into his side of the back-cut and the two of them working apace and sharing the load, felling the tree should have been a cinch.

Except it wasn't a cinch. Their wedges sank into the back-cut easy enough and the tree lifted and tipped but, even after they had all of their wedges buried up to their heads, the tree was still standing.

Deciding what they needed was to activate Plan B, one brother stood and waited while the other fetched and returned up the springboards with their satchel full of extra wedges. By "sandwiching" their new wedges one atop the other and pounding them, they got enough lift to free their original set of wedges and, by sandwiching them and driving them home, they'd get twice the lift and that, by Jimmy, would be enough to get the tree to fall.

Except, once they were done and all of their sandwiched wedges were buried, still the tree stood there. Dejectedly admitting defeat and retreating down off their springboards, the brothers started complaining to each other and, pretty quick, castigating each other. Like, why hadn't they hauled down their hydraulic tree jacks now sitting useless way up yonder in the bed of their pickup truck? Because the rule was never to hump around blue-steel-heavy tree jacks when you could swing axes, drive wedges, and get the same result—that's why. It was a rule they always followed and both of them had agreed that, since the jackpot tree was alone and way down at the bottom of the canyon, it would have been silly for them to hump their jacks.

But now, forced to activate Plan C and go and fetch their jacks, it turned out they really hadn't agreed after all. One brother asserted that he knew right off that they should have brought their jacks, which made the other brother demand to know why, if that was so, hadn't he piped up? And the other retorted that, even though he had doubted the wedges would fell the tree, the other seemed so certain of it that he went along because he hadn't wanted to hurt his feelings.

And away they went, climbing up the canyon all lickety-split, angry, frustrated, humiliated, and arguing back and forth. They got so much into arguing—they both were unused to outsmarting themselves—that when they suddenly reached their pickup truck they had to bend over on the truck road, prop their hands on their knees, and wheeze.

After they caught their breath, they were still too spent to immediately return to the hole lugging their jacks. Agreeing that, given the special circumstances, it wouldn't hurt them to tack a bit of recuperation time onto the length of their workday, they dropped their tailgate, poured themselves cups of coffee, and sat there silently sipping on them. One cup of coffee led to another and, by and by, they forgave each other and started yakking again just like nothing had happened.

When they finally returned to the butt of their jackpot tree the fog had lifted and, dropping their jacks and staring upward in awe with their mouths agape, they saw what the problem was. They'd had so much trouble felling the tree because they'd already felled it. The ground was so steep that the tree was already resting on the ground.

• • •

Because in the 1970s most of the remaining big trees grew on the steepest ground, I spent a good part of my hook tending career working near, at, or a couple of times, beyond the Angle of Repose. Without the logs covering the ground like a jumble of fiddle sticks, there was no way, at least without using a rope and grapple, that I'd have been able to climb up some places, much less get down them. I had to use logs as walkways to get about anywhere.

Even the skinniest log has a top to it, and once you've learned how to stay plumb and to keep one foot directly in front of the other, traversing logs is as easy as gliding down a sidewalk. Because your spiked boots, if set properly, made you surefooted, after you've taught your body how to lope while keeping your movements fluid and easygoing on your joints, you could cover a forty-footer in ten or eleven steps. Moving straight side-hill, leaping from log to log, you could run if you wanted to.

My favorite part of tending hook was scouting ahead along the bottom of the canyons, especially when I could round a bend and put some mountain between myself and the yarder's racket. Sitting next to a cascade in the creek with my back resting against a tree, I might spend a half hour getting away from it all. Sometimes, if things were going smooth and I was enough ahead of schedule, I'd go off exploring. Usually the canyonside opposite the one we were logging was still green with standing trees and, if I came upon a side canyon leading that way, I'd hike up into it just to see what I could see. If there was water up in there, I'd get down on my hands and knees, put my lips to it, and drink. Once in a side canyon I found a pioneer's rusted rigging chain with hand-forged rings and hooks (it's now in my rock garden). Another time I came upon a redwood burl, a slab of which now sits as my coffee table in my living room.

Occasionally, instead of scouting ahead, I'd return to the areas we were finished with. Standing next to the creek and gazing up at the damage we'd done to the canyonside, I'd feel ashamed. I never did like clear-cuts because, like all but the most gullible of the "company men," I knew clear-cuts amounted to liquidation sales and lost jobs. Then the idea of clear-cutting the remains of previous clear-cuts, mowing down baby redwoods to make pulp as if they were limby little Georgia plantation pines struck me as plain stupid—the kind of stupid born of greed. Also there was no getting around the ugliness we left behind, the eyesores we'd made.

When I first started in the woods I pretty much ignored the environmental issues. In Vietnam I'd seen rich, cultivated mountain valleys deserted and pockmarked with bomb craters and ruined empty villages. I'd seen jungles not just blown to bits but burnt to a crisp. So skid trails, stumps, wounded trees, and slash piles seemed small-time to me.

But it was one thing to knock down a forest to provide folks with the lumber to build beautiful outdoor decks to picnic on or to use as the ridge beams of churches. It was another thing to have your redwood trees be ground into oatmeal, pumped full of glues and chemicals, and rolled out as painted particleboard. That was a waste.

Because I wasn't afraid of bears or mountain lions (the ground was too steep for a rattlesnake's liking), and since I was used to listening for snaps, crackles, and pops, just naturally I moved quietly. And when I was off alone scouting, I made it a point to move as silently as I could. Logging shows were magnets for deer and, one day if I was lucky, I wanted to get close enough to touch one. I'd seen big bucks balancing their racks of horns and traipsing down logs like they were wearing spiked boots. I'd seen deer perched atop a tree stump with their necks stretched and their ears perked as if they were fixing to board a bus that had just pulled up to the curb. I've stirred deer out of thickets and, mistaking me for a hunter, I've heard them crashing through the underbrush to get away from me. Once, I was sitting down resting and an unsuspecting doe appeared down the hill from me. I playfully threw a rotten stick at her and—bull's-eye—it broke over her rump. After skipping a frame and reappearing a log-length away, the doe turned and glared at me with a scowl that put me to shame.

The first time I thought I saw into the soul of deer was during my second season setting choker. By then having my woods legs set firmly beneath me, it had been months since I'd fallen down, and I was to the point were, if ever I did fall down, I just hoped nobody was looking. We were working the swell-butted residual redwoods and skinny grow-backs left from a 1950s clear-cut, and the ground was choked with brush. Between the standers the huckleberry bushes grew so thick that, unless you dropped a tree across them, or you hacked your way through them, you were forced to go around them. Blocking the sunnier, rockier spots (we were working inland near the eastern limit of the redwoods) were stands of ceanothus, or California wild lilac, as it is known in nurseries. Out in the woods the tree-bush is called blue blossom or tick bush yet, growing so thick and impenetrable, it always reminded me of bamboo even though by outward appearance the two species were not alike.

While everything under the sun, both living and unliving, earns its keep—tick bushes hold and fertilize poor soils and (if the legend is true) provide valuable habitat for ticks—still I never liked them. Unless you used your chainsaw, there was no way to get a tick bush to lay down flat. Even wielding a chainsaw and having murderous intent, because the bushes were twenty foot tall, skinny, multi-trunked, and tangled, you still never had an easy go of it. Touch the bar of your chainsaw to a trunk of tick bush anywhere much above the butt and, instead of cutting it, you'll get it to violently bouncing like you'd lit it up with a bolt of electricity. And you'd have to back off to stop your saw and your arms from violently bouncing right along with it. Or, if you managed to stick the nose of your bar down into the heart of the shrub to fell its trunks like trees, they were so interwoven that, even if a particular stick was leaning away from you, if you didn't watch out its severed butt might spring back and bop you on the nose.

That's why—ticks or no ticks—the same timber faller who takes pleasure in smashing mats of huckleberry and who could care less about how many invading, trespassing little tanoaks or pepperwoods he knocks down or smashes to pieces—that very same timber faller will pound wedges before he'll drop a tree into a thicket of tick bushes.

So there I was "mopping up" this extremely degraded canyon. The Cat was on its way to the landing and I was scouting ahead for my next skid. I was walking side-hill on a log and, unnoticed by me, I came upon a doe. Standing just above me and fronting a knocked-down tanoak with brown, withered leaves, she was well camouflaged and I suppose that's why she froze and held her ground as I approached. I was looking down at the logs arrayed on the canyon below me and, when I accidentally got too close to her, she exploded into motion and flew past me, scaring the shit out of me. She flung herself headlong into the canyon, bounded over logs and stumps and dodged standers, never missing a step or hesitating in a flash of indecision. She reached the canyon bottom, leaped the creek and, without breaking stride, she climbed the opposite wall. When she reached the same elevation as where she started and where I was standing—and she kept on going—it had taken her ten seconds flat.

Watching that doe convinced me on the spot and without a doubt that you could take all of humanity's best scientific minds, fund them with the wealth of nations, and give them a century to do it in, and still they couldn't design a machine that could match that. Never in a million years could they come up with a machine or a human strain that could mimic such awesome strength, confidence, balance, and grace. As I was learning, animals, plants, and even patches of terrain have their own personalities, their own kinds of awareness and magical abilities. In the case of deer, they seemed a kindred spirit to me, even more so than badgers, mountain goats, *ki*-oats, and mules. The deer seemed to be my wise and gentle teachers of the inner ways of the woods, the gatekeepers of the secrets of the forest. And that's why I wanted to touch a wild mountain deer. I thought it'd bring me balance, surefootedness, and luck.

Once while scouting ahead of the yarder I actually did get a chance to touch a deer. I was sitting on a log lying side-hill with my feet dangling into empty space. Below me, ending at the creek, was a sheer, one-hundred-foot-tall landslide and, piled at the bottom of it, a jackpot of logs. The landslide was blocking the path I needed to use to run out the skyline, and I was wondering what I could do about it.

Hanging above me and providing shade was the canopy of a knocked-over pepperwood tree. The "knock-down" was also hiding me from view and, with the pepper-like fumes rising from its smashed, dehydrating leaves, it was also disguising my scent. I heard a slight noise to my left and, standing on the log just above me, I saw the head of a buck deer with a big rack of horns. We both froze and I pretended I hadn't seen him, since if he'd have wanted to he could have butted me and knocked me over the cliff.

Without moving a muscle, I tried to relax and communicate to the buck my imperturbability, how comfortable and at ease I was with our chance meeting. After a few seconds the buck stretched out his neck, put his nose to my ear, and sniffed. Then he raised his head back up, daintily stepped off the log to the uphill side of me, ducked under some limbs, and resumed his journey just as if I'd been nothing more than a bump on a log.

Now, if you think experiences like that were making me a little bit crazy, you wouldn't be far from wrong. Sometimes I'd watch a raven glide through the redwood canopy above the creek like a blind bat flying with precision through a maze of piano wires. Never touching a limb, or a needle, or doing more than bending a wingtip, the raven might soar at twenty-five miles per hour. And I'd wonder how the raven did that, and I'd want to be able to do it myself, not as him but as a kindred spirit soaring in my imagination. How far could I fly without touching a twig? How would the forest look from a raven's eyes?

My encounter with the buck I took as a "touch" and I convinced myself that some of his grace had rubbed off on me. He had become my spiritual ally, I thought, and he would help keep me safe.

And so, a few days later when I came upon another, not-so-tall landslide and saw a deer trail traversing it that led to where I wanted to go, I didn't hesitate to follow it. As always when I was scouting ahead, I'd cached my gear, including my whistle belt and hardhat, so I could travel light.

I got about halfway across the landslide when the trail, which at that point was about three inches wide, gave out. Recently a little landslide had broken off the face of the big one and that had erased about six foot of trail. Not only that but the slope had gotten so steep that, to stay plumb, my shoulder was brushing the wall. Finally I took the opportunity to take the measure of the ground below me and, seeing a sixty-foot straight-shot drop to the sharp rocks and boulders lining the creek, my heart sank as I realized that I'd gotten myself into a good bit of trouble. No way could I leap the breach and—this is what scared me—it seemed I couldn't turn around.

I'd've hollered for help if I thought it'd do me any good. But the yarder was behind a bend in the mountain and the fallers were long gone. So all I could do was stand there with my knees knocking, trying to get my suddenly shaking boots to grow roots. Below me was a certain, gruesome death, ahead was the void, and to stay put was impossible. I needed to get down off of there and the only way to do that was to turn around and to face the way I'd come. And so, afraid to lift a foot and steadying myself with my fingertips touching the wall above me, I slowly pivoted around. Just like the army had taught me, I executed an about-face. Then the trail ahead looked like a freeway and, careful not to hurry, I followed it back to solid ground and, once I was back in forest duff, I picked up a handful, kissed it, and flung it in the wind.

My God, how could I have been so stupid?

Remembering how a few days before the buck had sniffed my ear, I realized that whatever luck he'd bestowed upon me I'd just used up.

BADLANDS

The landslide coming down off the Johnson Ranch was so massive and powerful that, after rolling over Rancheria Creek, it kept on going up a side canyon for another quarter of a mile. When the cloud of dust settled, over two acres of Mitchell-X land was buried beneath about six foot of Johnson Ranch dirt.

After standing up on a bluff and surveying the extent of his good fortune, old man Johnson promptly set about fencing off his new acquisition.

Some version of the above story is often told in law school in order to illustrate the absurdities underlying our notions of private property. A mountain might live for thousands of millennia, and a landslide may take millennia to wash away. And here's a man or a woman who might be lucky enough to live through eighty earth revolutions around the sun.

Who owns what?

Observing that no one lives long enough to own a mountain is like telling a newcomer to Anderson Valley about the badlands out past Yorkville. The concept just doesn't compute and, after staring at you slack-jawed, they'll get suspicious of your motives. What are you, some kind of communist?

Yet you can't blame them much because, being from the city and all, they wouldn't know about such things because they simply don't care about such things. Out of sight is out of mind, and off the highway is off the map. "The Badlands"—what's that, a new restaurant?

It was a whole different story if you'd ever lost a knot of cattle up in those tangled, chaotic scrublands. Go and lose your hunting dogs in that gnarly stuff and then you'll know what the badlands are. In the old days if you were coming up the trail from Cloverdale and your horse went lame, if it was summer you'd wish you'd brought along more water. If it was winter, you'd wish you'd brought along more clothes. Even today if you venture out there and your four-wheeler breaks down, or gets stuck, then to reach an outpost of civilization you're going to have to hike for some miles. And were you fool enough to leave the road and attempt a shortcut cross-country through the scrub, you'd be reduced to advancing on your hands and knees, your progress marked like the tracks of a mole burrowing under a crew-cut lawn. Head off under that stuff and nobody is ever going to find your body. They won't even find your buttons or belt buckle.

"Rabbit Country," the old-timers called it. That was on account of all the rabbits that darted out in front of you anytime you were traveling a ranch road out there. But actually the animal ecosystem rests on the backs of the furry little small fry called rodents. Being on the bottom of the food chain, the mice, ground squirrels, and the like are not particularly adventurous creatures, and never will one dart out in front of you and try to pace you up the road like a rabbit. If ever you do see small fry on the road (they usually only come out at night), they'll be crossing in a beeline with their afterburners blazing and their little paws kicking up tall rooster tails of dust.

Other critters common to the badlands are quail. In fact, when the old-timers said "Rabbit Country," they could just as well have said, "Quail Country." Go out into the badlands in the springtime and, just like a crazy jackrabbit, a mama quail and her herd of egg-shaped hatchlings will all jump out in front of you and start running away from you in panic. They'll be looking back over their shoulders and taking evasive actions, juking left, juking right, but refusing to get out of your way.

Were I to have a quail made available to answer me why they did that, I'd also want to know why, once they decided to escape your tires, they all tried to dive through the same hole in the brush? Not only that but just how they did it so lightning quick and without banging into each other?

The main reason why the badlands grow only scrub is, I suppose, because of volcanism. From up high around those parts you can see Mount St. Helena, Cobb Mountain, and Konocti, ancient volcanoes all, so who is to say that Yorkville's Big Foot Mountain is not also an old volcano? Looking up at Big Foot Mountain from the depths of the badlands, it sure looks like one. I've heard of stranger things. Once, a few years ago, way down at the Deep End on the ridge overlooking the North Fork of the Navarro, I found a piece of volcanic rock called pumice. Sitting by itself on a spot of bare dirt under some blue blossom, milk chocolate brown and pitted like a crumpet, it was about the size and shape of a large grinding pestle except it had a big bend in it. When I picked it up to give it a closer examination, it was so full of air it weighed nearly nothing.

Even if Big Foot Mountain isn't an old volcano, it's still tall enough to catch and wring out the rain clouds blowing in off the ocean, and that makes the leeside of the mountain dry, and that dryness adds to the poorness of the soils. That plus the all-around steepness of everything and the generally no-telling-which-way-running creeks and creeklets gouging the land like knives. Canyonsides too steep to hold grass ain't going to grow much more than brush, and erosion being a constant means the zigzag ridges and sub-ridges are sliding downward into the arroyos. The occasional trees that have taken root out there nearly all have huge bends in their trunks. That's because while they've been growing skyward the dirt beneath them has been sliding into the creek. The old-timers called them "pistol butts" because of the shape they take. On the steepest and quickest-moving slopes, a tree's trunk might grow so bent that it comes out of the ground nearly horizontal and you can stand up on top of it.

You combine poor, steep dirt with dryness, exposure to the wind and sun, and periodic wildfires and what you get is like a chunk of Great Basin chaparral butted up against the redwoods and the fir, tanoak, and madrone. One side of the ridge is in Mendocino County and the other side may as well be in Nevada.

So one time I was maintaining ditches along the fire road on the western edge of the badlands when, way down below like a crooked finger pointing into a deep, barren defile, I saw a razor-backed ridge with two parallel-running dirt roads topping it. The ridge marked the boundary between two very large ranches, and along the very top of it ran a cattle fence, three foot of sheep wire topped with two strands of double-nasty barbed wire. Because to build a fence you needed to import your materials to your line, and because once you'd built a fence you had to maintain it, one of the ranchers had punched in a road flanking the fence. Then, as if in some perverse way to go his neighbor one better, the second rancher had punched in his own road on *his* side of the fence.

Now the funniest part was, soaking in the ugliness and taking into account the lay of the land, it was obvious that without the roads there was no way some chubby cows were ever going to be able to reach the top of that ridge anyway. Not that they'd ever want to. So there had been no need to build the fence in the first place. Yet, there it was, a sharp, rusting steel line squeezed in between two gouged-out yellow dirt roads leading to nowhere.

I wondered how much time and money the ranchers had sunk into their enterprise and what they'd ever gotten for it. Whatever little bit of graze they'd opened up to fatten their cows was more than offset by the amount of weight they'd lose while getting herded all the way back to the main ranch and to the trucks that'd take them to market. Opening up the badlands to the cattle also meant that, come roundup, some boneheads were bound to be hiding out in the farthest, thickest reaches of them. Therefore, in addition, you had to factor in your own travel expenses, be they aboard a horse or inside a pickup truck.

So just what could the old coots have been thinking? Were they afraid of squatters usurping their rights to that scraggly-assed, razor-backed ridge stuck out in the middle of nowhere? With all of the land they owned, why would they give a rat's ass about that crooked little brushy finger? Or was it just each other they'd been thinking of? Each knowing the other weren't above selling a lame horse or a watered steer, what was to keep one of them from grabbing up a piece of loose land if the other fellah wasn't watching out for it? So maybe the roads were mirrors facing each other and the fence line the fold in a sheet of paper.

Then again, just possibly the old coot's folly could be laid at the feet of Western Pioneer Tradition. Out West you fenced your land and you did it because a man did what a man had to do. So maybe the source of the ugliness was as simple as that. Make yourself gullible enough and you can even see how their line works were not a waste of time and energy, materials, environmental vandalism, or anything else beyond a necessary capital improvement. Whether the result of suspicion, self-defense, greed, vanity, or spite, not by a long stretch could you call their excavations a mistake since nothing a man *has* to do in this world can ever be called a mistake.

Looked at that way, the fence and the roads are sure signs of Progress, a necessary and noble attempt to tame the badlands. They were just one more way the old coots had left their marks on this world.

WATERBIRDS

Two summers ago waterbirds invaded this place. Beside the house we're renting sits an old agricultural pond, and the owners of the ranch wished to drain it in order to remove a few decades' worth of accumulated sediments. Small yet deep, spring fed and situated at the shady mouth of a steep, creek-running, redwood-forested canyon, the pond attracts all kinds of birds. The local birds return to the pond at the same time most days, while the migratory birds show up at the same time every year.

But, once the owners started draining the pond, it became a veritable waterbird magnate. Ospreys, herons and egrets all made appearances. And because our porch overlooks their flyway, we had front-row seats.

The first newcomer I noticed leaving the pond was a giant gray pelican. When it sailed past our porch, it was only about twenty feet off the ground. It wasn't long before I realized that all of the waterbirds leaving the pond and passing by our porch were sailing at that same height at that point. Also, they all elevated at the same rate and followed the same path, though it wasn't a road in the sky but a series of imaginary hoops for them to sail through.

Once I'd taken into account the shape of the land and the weather, it made sense that the waterbirds, them being economical creatures, would stick to their flyway. The mouth of the canyon sits on a rim overlooking the valley's flatlands. In the grasslands below the pond and the dam the watercourse slopes downward and is hidden beneath a sixty-foot-high wind wall of oak trees. Above the pond the canyon drains a fair amount of forestlands, so near dusk the canyon's mouth gives off a "mountain wind." The canyon mouth, in other words, exhales. At dusk during even the stillest, hottest summer day, a cool wind ripples the surface of the pond and rustles the limbs in the overhanging trees. Stand on the dam at sundown, face up the canyon, and you'll feel the river of cool air washing over you.

Dusk is also when waterbirds start thinking about returning to their roosts for the night. So when the birds lifted off from the pond, the canyon wind caught them and blew them over the dam. Suddenly airborne, their wings still and outstretched, they rode the river of air until it emptied into the valley's thermos and they were soaring one hundred feet above the flats.

As anybody who has ever flown in an airplane over Anderson Valley knows, the land has so many little manmade ponds it looks like a kid with freckles who's been left out in the sun too long. So how did all of these waterbirds find this particular little pond? How come, as the summer went on and the water lowered, more and more of them came? Why did two egrets become four egrets, then eight? And why would the egrets leave nose to tail making a line as precise as if they were riding a toboggan?

Summer shrank into autumn, the winter rains arrived, the birds disappeared, and the feeder creeks came alive. The pond was full by Christmas, and the next spring, after the storms were over, the grass had thrown its seed, and water had become scarce, the waterbirds didn't return to the pond. Since that summer when the pond was drained, I haven't seen another pelican and only rarely have I seen an osprey. Herons and egrets are not uncommon, though nearly always they are silent and solitary. Never again have I seen any type of waterbird in a flock.

So why is that? Why don't the waterbirds return? More properly, why did they gather in the first place? For the food, surely, but how did they find out about it?

It occurred to me that maybe two herons had been sitting on that big, mostly submerged log at the mouth of the Navarro River. The day was sunny, the wind down, and they were just lazing. One heron turned to the other and asked, "Have you tasted those fast-food frogs they've got up there by Boonville?"

THE BLUE REDWOODS

Ask a person how many different kinds of redwoods grow in the world and, if he or she was educated in California, they'll probably answer "two." There's what's called the Sequoias growing up in the Southern Sierra, and the Redwoods that grow along California's North Coast. A smart aleck might add that, actually, there's a third kind that grows in China known as the Dawn Redwood. Though closely related to the others, the Dawn Redwood is a relative dwarf and it is deciduous.

But mention the Blue Redwoods and chances are that all you'll get will be blank stares. Or, with a sniff, you'll be informed that, scientifically speaking, there is no such thing. And that'd be right when it comes to species but dead wrong when it comes to "strains" or "subspecies." Fact is the Aptos Blue Redwoods are a scientifically identified strain and they have been for some while. The strain is named after the city of Aptos that's perched on Monterey Bay. Squeezed between the Pacific Ocean and the sharp toes of the Santa Cruz Mountains, Aptos is located at the southern end of the Redwood Belt, a slender finger of ocean-hugging primordial forest stretching five hundred miles long and sometimes only five miles wide. Because the Coast Redwoods are the earth's most voracious fog eaters, the trees don't grow at elevations higher than 3,300 feet above sea level.

Because the Santa Cruz Mountains are so close to San Francisco and to the last stop on the Transcontinental Railroad, the redwoods in the mountains above Aptos were among the first to get chopped down. So it was that up there the Blue Redwoods were first discovered, recorded, and studied. Hence the name Aptos Blue.

One interesting thing about the Blues is that, while they are common in the Santa Cruz Mountains and are sprinkled throughout the Redwood Belt all the way up to the fingernail reaching across the Oregon border, the farther north you go the less you see of them. Why that is, nobody knows.

Now if you were to ask an old-timey North Coast hillbilly—a fourth generation woodsman born with one leg shorter than the other to help him get along on side hills—what a botanist was, or where the city of Aptos was, chances are all you'd get would be a blank stare. Mention to him an arborist and he'll likely think you're talking about some kind of city-slicked tree-hugger sitting off in some ivory tower somewhere.

But ask him about the Blue Redwoods and his eyes will light up and he'll tell you all about them—they're the damnest, most beautiful things! If you show enough enthusiasm for the subject, he's taken a shine to you, and he's got the time for it, he'll offer to take you out into the woods so you can lay your own eyes on some Blues. Around here he might take you up into Dago Gulch, or over to the shady side of Lone Tree Ridge.

But that doesn't mean the Blue Redwoods ain't rare or their existence mostly secret. Along with the regular kind of redwoods, over 95 percent of the "ancient" Blues got chopped down, and baby Blues ain't near so distinctive. Considering that, above the creek bottoms coursing like veins, the redwoods grow on some of the steepest and slipperiest mountains on earth and that, with the passing of the lumberjacks, huge swaths of forestlands have returned to "untracked wilderness," it's not a stretch to say that most folks living on the North Coast nowadays have never even heard of the Blues much less noticed any.

Woodsmen see the redwoods better than other people do. To an outsider the redwoods seem tall, round, fat, and pretty. They are scenery only. Parkland trails through remnant groves of giant redwoods are fine, and even the least of them can make all but the most citified folks feel like they're passing through God's own wondrous creation. And that's good, very good. But the real forest is off the trail and up on the steep ground where a person feels fortunate to find an animal track to set his or her feet on. Unless a person is taking a living from such unforgiving ground, there ain't much reason to go up there.

But once you've worked in the redwoods long enough, every tree takes its turn in your eye and every forest sound tells you something. Whether you're out to fell the giants or their small-fry stump shoot offspring, every tree has its own way about it, its own personality and possibilities. Some trees are fat pumpkins waiting to get plucked—seemingly thankful to get plucked (you're only giving them haircuts). Others are "outlaws" that will fight you every step of the way if you're fool enough to tangle with them. And always in the woods there's the possibility that you'll encounter that one tree, that singular tree that's different from all of the others in the forest. You just might meet the tree that has your name on it.

The Blue Redwoods stick out because they are darker than the ordinary kind of redwoods. Their bark is thicker and more deeply furrowed and shadowy. Their foliage is also a deeper, darker green, the individual needles plump almost like the needles of cedars or junipers. The old-timers say what makes for a grove of Blues is the bountiful groundwater they are tapped into, an underground reservoir of upwelling, nutrient-filled liquid, and their needles feel heavy with it. Pick off a sprig of needles and hold their undersides up against a cloudless sky and they will show blue.

Stand back at a distance and a grove of Blues appears saturated, sodden, and overripe. Not only is the foliage fatter and darker but there is more of it, so much more that the trunks of the trees are hidden behind heavy hanging curtains of it. Tall, erect, sturdy, and yet shaggy, from afar a grove of Blues on the skyline can look like a grazing wooly mammoth.

But it is how they appear out of the dawn that gives the Blues their name. When the first light of day reaches them and the fog is lifting, when the hanging foliage seems to be steaming and wisps of ground fog are swirling upward like campfire smoke, when the frost on the meadow grass shines white and the shadows are shrinking, that's when the trees radiate blue—pure watery blue.

THE WILDMAN OF PARDALOE PEAK

I'd just about given up hope when finally I spotted him through a window in the redwood forest. Perched near the top of a sheer shale cliff, he was barefoot and naked except for a faded, tattered loincloth. Leaning over a tiny, pale green wild succulent plant growing out of a crack in the rock, he was carefully pollinating it with the whittled tip of a wooden chopstick. So intent was he on his work that he hadn't noticed my deliberately noisy approach (mountain lions and hungry bears prowl around out there on the shady side of Pardaloe Peak). Not wanting to startle him, I held back.

The man who I will call Billy Bones is famous for having spent a year wandering around with a begging bowl through the Punjab region of India, and I guessed that's where he'd picked up his loincloth. It looked like a fuzzy version of a clown's balloon, you know, the long, skinny hot dog–shaped balloons they'd twist and bend and wrestle into the forms of animals like poodles or flamingos. Except the balloon Billy Bones was wearing must have been fifty foot long. As near as I could tell, to dress up in a loincloth you'd start by sticking the middle of the thing between your legs, then you'd wrap one tail around one leg, then the other tail around your other leg, then both around your waist a couple of times, then back between your legs and so on until when you were done and you stood erect you looked like you were wearing a giant, puffy diaper.

Now I was used to folks wearing strange getups. Over the years I'd seen burnished belt buckles the size of Frisbees, pointy shoes, high heels, size A haircuts riding atop size Triple-D heads, hats worn sideways or backward, starched collars, pierced noses, the nooses some men cinched around their own necks every morning—to cite a few examples—and so I was accustomed to folks' seemingly infinite tolerance for physical discomfort and stone impracticality. Still, try as I might, I couldn't conjure even one logical reason why a person would want to wrap himself up in a loincloth. With the possible exception being, I suppose, if ever some person was scrambling down a scree slope, lost his footing, and landed on his ass, maybe being able to bounce back up to his feet.

The onetime dean of UC Berkeley's School of Paleo-Psychology, winner of the Altmond Award for his pioneering research into Mesoamerican mysticism, and an internationally recognized authority on the culturally transmorphic qualities of electronically broadcasted ritual and taboo, I took to calling him Billy Bones because his personal hygiene was preindustrial, his hair was long and matted, his beard scraggly, and his near naked body a collection of reddish bumps and knobs.

Living without electricity or refrigeration in a redwood stump house four miles by a winding and nearly imperceptible trail through deep canyons and impenetrable thickets, and past pounding waterfalls, Billy Bones also had a powerful appreciation for cheese. White cheese, yellow cheese, orange—bring Billy Bones a chunk of cheese and he'd literally jump for joy.

"Is that Limburger?" he'd exclaim, excitedly rubbing his hands together and hopping in anticipation. "You've brought me Limburger? Oh, dear! Oh, dear!"

When Billy finished pollinating his succulent, he holstered his chopstick, stood up, and stretched his back. Standing perfectly plumb and holding on to the cliff with his toenails, he sniffed the air, looked around, and finally noticed me down below him sitting in a beam of sunshine. Folded into the half lotus position with the thumbs and forefingers of my hands making perfect circles, my other fingers outstretched and my palms facing skyward, I looked like I was giving the double A-OK secret hand sign to the angels floating above me.

Billy Bones had been expecting me because I'd gotten him a message. Maybe once a month Billy would hike out to Fish Rock Road to meet an anonymous friend who brought him supplies, and near the end of his trail stood a giant, goosed-out redwood stump. Inside the cavernous goose pen was a badger den, and next to that was a big rock, and under that rock you could leave written notes for Billy Bones.

Once Billy's eyes adjusted to the exquisite brightness encircling me, he gave me a hearty wave, grinned widely, and called down, "Did-you-bring-cheese?"

When I nodded in the affirmative and tellingly patted the bulge in my shirt pocket, Billy seemed so overcome with delight it looked like he might swoon.

I'd hiked all that way in to see and report upon his creek works and, while we sat and jawed some and he was sampling my cheese (Gouda), Billy agreed, after he'd snacked to his heart's content, to give me the full fifty-cent walking tour.

"There's a hint of bacon," Billy dreamily announced, munching my cheese like he was sampling caviar. "Beyond the bracing aroma of a Highland Scottish glen, I do believe I detect an oh-so-slight hint of bacon."

With Billy Bones leading the way, his leather-hard bare feet gripping the steep trace like tiger's paws, and with me huffing and puffing to keep up behind him, we arrived at his camp.

Now you'd think a hermit like Billy Bones would get at least a little bit lazy, he having only himself to care for or even consider. Erase vanity as a motive and all of humanity's works wouldn't amount to much, civilization meaning only that status-seeking has replaced the ritualized hunt for big game. Left by yourself and living only for yourself, just what would you need, anyway?

But Billy Bones was a scientist systematically studying many things simultaneously, including what it meant to be a hermit, and everything he did was for a reason. Not only that but everything he did was duly recorded in his widely read (if annotated and abridged) journals. No hermit had ever worked as hard or had experimented with so many new ways of doing things than Billy Bones, and his reputation for innovation was international.

Take, for example, the newfangled kind of chicken coop Billy had invented since my last visit. Firstly, I must admit that I've always considered chickens to be the price paid for eggs, buffalo wings, and chicken tenders. Fowl-smelling, fowl-tempered, prideful little bipeds, you can also eat them whole once they'd outlived their usefulness. Even the old ones taste tolerably decent boiled down in soup. In addition, to be charitable, I have to admit that chickens do eat grasshoppers and other sorts of greedy bugs, and that has to be worth something.

Still, who'd have ever thought to corral chickens using rabbit wire? You know the type of wire I'm talking about, the finely meshed, stiff, heavy, galvanized stuff you used to cage cute little furry bunny rabbits to prevent them from hungrily chomping off the tips of the poking fingers of heedless little kids.

While I'd been gone, on his back and over hill and dale, Billy Bones had not only hauled in what must have been at least two dozen rolls of rabbit wire, he'd also encircled his flock of chickens with it and had used it to run a ceiling over the tops of them, effectively sealing them off from the rest of the world. When I asked Billy why in tarnation he'd go to all that trouble just to enclose some skinny, sun-starved chickens (he'd already built them a safe and secure henhouse), he answered that he wished to produce vegetarian eggs.

"Eggs without Bloodshed," he called them.

Though it occurred to me to further inquire why either a chicken or an egg would wish to become a vegetarian, out of courtesy I withheld any more of my probing questions.

Nearby Billy had hung an old redwood wine barrel atop two stout limbs about sixty feet up the trunk of an old redwood tree, and taking a shower under the nozzle of the garden hose leading down from it Billy got so much water pressure that he had to brace himself against the blast to keep from getting washed off his feet. So I commented admiringly upon that.

By and by I followed Billy down his switchbacking track to the rushing creek in the bottom of the lightning-bolt canyon. Billy's main project was to document what one able-bodied person with one shovel, one pick, and one long, straight, and stout fir limb could accomplish toward the restoration of a silted-up and sterile creek. Working most every day for at least four hours over a period of less than ten years, by his own calculation Billy had removed from the creek 7,170 cubic yards of accumulated sediments. Not only that but on his back he had hauled the stuff up out of the canyon and had made a mountain of it on the ridge top. Face to face with his manmade mountain atop a mountaintop, any objective outside observer could take his own scientific measurement of the amount of material Billy had imported and piled.

But the true indicator of Billy's success was seen in the pristine condition of the creek. Using the power of the currents during high water plus his stout fir pry bar, Billy had rolled one-ton boulders and set them where he wanted them. In one place he'd made a semicircle of a half dozen boulders, and in the glory hole beneath them were suspended a school of fat steelhead lazing in water so cool, deep, clean, and crystal clear that it looked like they were smiling and wagging their tails like puppy dogs. So healthy, rested, and contented were the fish that it was like they were affluent retirees in a resort community in Arizona, or rich tourists in Vegas or Orlando. So bucolic was the scene that if you saw a fat steelhead fish happily fluttering by on silver wings, it wouldn't have struck you dead with surprise.

As my eyes filled with tears of admiration, and as I promised Billy on my word of honor that, once I arrived back in civilization, I would spare no opportunity to sing his praises, and to publicize his noble enterprise, I noticed that Billy Bones was getting more and more uncomfortable, and more and more downcast. I sensed that he knew that I was missing something and, not wanting to keep the real truth from me much longer, he had a confession to make. Finally I stopped rhapsodizing about all of the great things I was going to do long enough to ask him if something was wrong.

"Yes," he admitted, relieved to be able to spill the beans. "Recently Big Foot has been assisting me. Yes, you've heard me right, old Sasquatch himself has been lending me a hand, though his friends call him Squash. He's why I've gotten so much done recently." Billy paused and I could tell he was envying the physical strength of his new helper.

"You talk about being able to swing a pick and shovel," Billy remarked admiringly, almost dreamily, gazing at me with his mouth bending into a faint smile. "You talk about being able to haul dirt or to manhandle boulders."

(Originally published in the Anderson Valley Advertiser *on April 1, 2005.)*

MILD HORSES

When the old-timers warming their favorite seats in the Boonville Lodge learned I was going to work on a horse ranch, they were all full of warnings. And when they found out that the horses on the ranch I'd hired on to weren't cutting horses, or even trail horses, but Thoroughbred racehorses like they've got running around down there in the big city, the old-timers took time from their drinks, turned from the bar, and looked me up and down as if they'd decided I must be feeling mighty sure of myself.

Thoroughbred horses, they all warned, recounting their various tales to each other while kindly allowing me to overhear, were bigger, stronger, and faster than the regular kind of horse. Thoroughbred horses were also more skittish, unpredictable, witless, and prone to panic. Why, sometimes just the sight of their own shadow was enough to make a Thoroughbred bolt. Like collies or greyhounds, Thoroughbreds were so inbred that whatever native sense they'd once had was long gone out of them. Why, if a Thoroughbred stallion caught a scent and took a notion, he'd gallop full bore headfirst into the side of a barn. And, the old-timers all wisely agreed, knowing the blockhead would do that meant he wouldn't think twice, or even one half of one time, before running me over if I didn't get out of his wild-assed way.

Just like most mules and some people, the old-timers swore, Thoroughbreds turned nasty when they got old. As if I was the one who'd done it, an old retired racetrack gelding might pin back his ears, bare his teeth, chomp down, and take a bite out of me. Then, him being a strict vegetarian holding to high standards, he'd spit it out and glare at me like the taste of me was my fault, too. They talk about these modern-day pit bull yard dogs having themselves some powerful jaws. *Shee-it*, the bite of a pit bull dog was like a newborn baby gumming his mommy's nipple next to the bite of a horse.

If all that weren't bad enough, or at least enough to give me legitimate pause, while I was gently adjusting that old gelding's leather halter, or combing the hay out of his forelock, he might shift his left front foot forward, plant it atop mine, shift his weight onto it, perk up his ears, and gaze intently at something way off beyond the farthest reach of the farthest pasture. And while I was frantically flailing at him, beating him with fists about his head, neck, and shoulder trying to get him to raise his foot off mine, he'd pretend that whatever it was he was looking at he just couldn't take his eyes off.

Or, while I was feeding that old gelding coot carrots and trying to be friendly, or at least let him know that, like it or not, we were on the same team, he might up and for no reason throw his head into mine, light me up from head to toe and send me flying.

And while I was trying to figure out how to use my hands and feet to pick myself back up out of the dirt and the settling dust, that old gelding would be eyeballing me wondering why I was being so stingy with the carrots.

If I knew what was good for me, the old-timers in the saloon all agreed, I'd never turn my back on a Thoroughbred. A stupid and vicious horse good for nothing but canned dog food would be kept alive and in top physical condition if he was a Thoroughbred and he was making money at the track. A mean, stir-crazy, tree-stump-stubborn, no-brain horse an ordinary rancher would shoot in the head and be done with before breakfast will get a likeness of himself done up in bronze and planted atop some granite pedestal back in the Bluegrass Country if that no-good nasty beast was a Thoroughbred and he'd won the Kentucky Derby.

Finally, it went without saying, never under any circumstances was I to allow myself to get kicked by a Thoroughbred horse or even by the ordinary, worthy kind of horse. Because whoever it was who first said that a horse "kicks like a mule" knew what he was talking about, and there weren't no two doubts in anybody's mind about that. Allow myself to get double-barreled in the head, chest, or between my shoulder blades—the very thought put the old-timers to mournfully shaking their heads and reaching for their drinks—and I may as well forget about supper, breakfast, lunch, and everything else for that matter.

Listening to those old coots razzing me made me feel mighty fortunate that I hadn't hired on to babysit the "stable" of horses. (We averaged thirty head). I was thirty-six years old at the time, well-seasoned, responsible, and mostly law-abiding, and my wild and wooly ways were years behind me most days anyway. I was a settled settler in Anderson Valley, in mostly good standing, a father and husband, and I couldn't afford to be laid up in traction in some hospital bed at one thousand dollars per night just because some spoiled bit of livestock decided to take his life out on me.

Moreover, if ever I was going to pay one thousand dollars for one night's bunk and one day's worth of grub and entertainment, then it'd damn sure never be to camp myself in some hospital bed where my hosts charged me an hour of my hard-earned wage just for a tiny saucer of split pea soup delivered bedside with no salt, no pepper, just two salt-free saltines and no bacon. Even in Reno, young again, single-jacking, and feeling a whole belly full of oats, to spend one thousand dollars in one day I'd have to leave my family home, get laid by a beautiful stranger woman with a nice smile and a business attitude, and then go and eat like a pig in the best carpet joint in town before getting myself mightily drunk in all kinds of places and, just before daybreak cracking somewhere over in Utah, get mighty snakebit at the crap table and afterward overgenerous with my sunrise sunny-side-up-eggs-toting waitress.

So I wasn't about to go and get my fingers chomped off, or my backbone broke, my head split open, or even my foot flattened and splayed by or for some high-bred, broom-tailed horse (if you don't comb out and barber a Thoroughbred's tail then, pretty quick, it gets to looking like a Nevada Mustang's).

For what good was a ranch hand without fingers? What good was a gimp if what you needed to keep was somebody used to hard physical labor and using his common sense? I wasn't about to have my working, breadwinning days ended by some neurotic horse—that much I knew without saying.

• • •

If anybody should have been scared of horses, it was me. The very first time I got behind a horse it kicked me square in the nose. I was vacationing with my family in Baja and I was eight years old. My dad was a wholesale salesman whose territory extended southward to the Mexican border below San Diego and then eastward to Yuma City, the Desert Mecca of Arizona, and then northward along the Colorado River from there. So, unless it was dead winter and the weather was inhospitable, if my dad had business down in San Diego and school was out, he'd bring us along on his business trip: my mom, my big sister, me, and sometimes his mother. He'd park us just south of Tijuana at Rosarito Beach and, come morning, my dad would recross the border to run through his list of appointments. He'd return to Rosarito in time for an early supper and then we'd play on the beach during the evenings. Us kids would build sand castles or wade in the shore breaks while my dad surf fished.

In 1958 Rosarito was a tiny pueblo built around El Hotel Rosarito, a mob-owned resort built in the Spanish Mission style. The El Rosarito offered "luxury accommodations" and, at the bottom of a staircase descending the bluff, a wide-open, sandy, warm-water beach. The hotel had its own private landing strip for shuffling in and out celebrities, VIPs, politicians, narcotics, and laundered money. For favored customers the hotel had a very private casino and, lining its opulent bar after sundown, some of the finest young prostitutes in all of Baja.

Southward and across the creek from El Rosarito was Rene's Motel. Owned and operated by Rene and his kin, his place was more reasonably priced, family friendly, and that's where we usually stayed. Rene's had a restaurant that served excellent fresh seafood and a cantina with a parquet dance floor fronting a low stage that, after sundown every night, held a mariachi band soulfully singing and playing ballads of love and loss within empty, windblown desert landscapes.

The hills above the beach were cattle lands, and farther south from Rene's was an old-style cantina that sold bottles of liquor to go. Built of worn-out wood planks teetering above a foundation of rocks and cracked concrete, atop a short, bowed staircase hung a covered porch with batten chairs. Sitting in the chairs were a half dozen dusty vaqueros sipping warm beers and passing the time in the shade. Out front were two hitching posts and tied to them were a half dozen saddled, tired horses.

When my dad parked our car beside the horses, he turned around and told my big sister and me sitting in the backseat to stay put while he went inside to make his purchase. We nodded and he disappeared up the stairs and through the swinging front doors of the cantina.

Once my dad was out of sight, I asked my mom if I could go and pet the horses. She and my dad had just been arguing, she was preoccupied with her own thoughts, and she waved her hand dismissively as if she didn't care one way or the other.

So I opened my car door, stepped outside, slammed my door, and—*bam*—a horse raised one hind leg, kicked me in the nose, and sent me sprawling. More shocked and humiliated than hurt, nevertheless, feeling warm blood pouring from my nose and seeing it splattering the front of my brand-new Mexican cowboy shirt, I let out with a loud, bloodcurdling, eight-year-old scream that put my dad to running. He flew out the swinging doors, leaped the stairs, and in an instant he had me on my feet. And while my dad was inspecting my face and knocking the dust off me, the vaqueros on the porch all burst into spontaneous and uproarious laughter. They pointed at me, slapped each other, dropped their beers, and three of them had to struggle up out of their chairs to keep from suffocating. You'd have thought that seeing a little kid getting kicked in the nose by a horse was the funniest thing any of them had seen in many a long moon.

Holding back his temper, my dad returned me to the backseat of the car, got behind the steering wheel, rooster-tailed dust speeding out of there, and immediately lit into my mother for ignoring his instructions. I was used to hearing them battle and so I glued my eyes to the passing shrubs and cactus.

What's funny is, today, I can't remember what the horse looked like other than to say that it wasn't painted with stripes like a Tijuana

Zebra. But I do vividly remember some detail about each and every one of those laughing vaqueros: a jiggling beer belly, a toppled beer bottle, a loud shirt, a sculpted handlebar mustache, bowed legs, a tipped-back sombrero shaking, another sombrero slapping a thigh, a giant tooled-silver belt buckle heaving in and out, gold-crowned teeth gaping, whiskers, a knife scar, a vest studded with glass prisms and turquoise, a pair of brand-new, dusty cowboy boots.

I'd left the cantina thinking that—my parents were convinced of it—I'd have been killed if I'd been standing just a few inches closer behind that horse when it kicked me (actually, just out to teach me some manners, the horse pulled its punch). And, of course, it took me years to realize that the vaqueros were laughing at me not because I'd gotten hurt but because I hadn't; that had I been sitting on that porch sipping beers with those guys, I'd have been laughing right along with them because good luck is always something to laugh over (unless it's your kid who got the bloody nose).

Not wanting his son to grow up scared of horses, the next day my dad got me up in the saddle. Beside the cantina was a horse rental business, which was a single-rail bowed-willow-log corral pinning maybe a dozen saddled and tied horses. I can't remember how exactly I felt about my first horse ride because, once we'd returned from the cantina to our room at Rene's, I'd again been sternly reminded to always do as my dad said without question and no matter what.

Because Rosarito Beach was so close to Los Angeles, and because my parents were a part of a clan of people that had left the old neighborhood in Chicago and had moved to the West Coast, at least once per summer all of the adults and their kids gathered at El Hotel Rosarito for a vacation. The adults would pass the time drinking liquor and playing poker in their suite and, since poker was the sort of game that required a bit of peace and quiet, us kids would spend our days riding horses. Back then one horse cost one dollar American per hour, but if you rented a half dozen horses for the whole day you could get the price down to eighty cents, or even less if business was slow. As an added benefit, when you put a half dozen tinhorn kids aboard a half dozen rental horses, it was the horses and not the kids who called the shots and you could trust them to keep the kids safe.

Like when it came to determining the speed of travel. Kids never wanted to walk and rental horses never wanted to run, and so we walked. We walked unless we turned the horses around back toward the corral and gave them a little kick. If we did that, then even if we were getting bounced so much we wanted to walk, we ran. I remember once, thinking we'd trick the horses, we turned them for home, got them to running, and thought we could turn them back once they were tired and had gotten up a lather. No way. We'd rented the horses for the whole day but in a cloud of dust we were all back where we'd started from an hour before. The poor wrangler had to jump aboard his own horse to lead our reluctant mounts back into the hills.

Which reminds me of a story an old horse logger told me about the personality of the broom-tails they teamed with up in Idaho. If you were on the landing and it took you and your horse a half hour to make a skid and the clock said it was fifteen minutes before lunchtime, then your horse would refuse to return up the mountain. Just like everybody else on the logging crew, your horse would want his nose in his feed bag and his feed bag empty before he was going anywhere.

Over the coming years, both in Baja and elsewhere, I'd ride horses a fair amount, though not long enough to ever get thrown from one. Rental horses are as tame as they come and all of them will show more patience with an obnoxious little kid than they will with an obnoxious adult. And, once I learned to team with my horse and pay some attention to its feelings and its way of seeing things, I never gave a horse a reason to throw me. Though, due to inexperience, I did occasionally lose my stirrups and ride dangling from the side of my saddle. And, I must admit, one time I rode a galloping horse a fair ways with my arms and legs wrapped around its neck and holding on for dear life. But that was just once and the old mare didn't run so far that I lost my grip.

Even before I hired on to the Thoroughbred ranch I'd spent most of my adult life sharing land with horses and other types of livestock, and I considered myself an experienced animal person. I'd even spent a short period of time working with Belgian draft horses (you talk about getting your foot squished) and a virgin Arabian stallion (you talk about getting nipped and kicked). But none of that made me a real horse person. I'd known some rodeo cowboys and a couple of Nevada buckaroos and they'd forgotten more about horses than I ever learned.

But even they were not real horse people. Ask a rodeo cowboy to name all of the bones, muscles, and tendons in a horse's anatomy and, if he's in a good mood, he'll turn his back on you. Ask an open-range cowboy to massage his poor nag's tired and aching muscles and he'll stare at you like you was some kind of weirdo. And ask either one to explain to you something of horse psychology and, after shrugging his shoulders in baleful acknowledgment of a lifetime spent full of vexation, he'll likely tell you that, while he couldn't be sure about any such things, his own particular horse did seem to have some kind of inborn knack for counting cards.

It wasn't until I went to work on the Thoroughbred brood ranch that I found out what a real horse person was. Real horse people are kinder, gentler, more sensitive, intuitive, and caring than ordinary dudes. They are more in tune with nature and its rhythms, a horse's thoughts and feelings. Real horse people, it turns out, are women.

HORSE WOMEN

The minute the new ranch manager showed up in her big new Ford-tuff diesel one-ton pickup truck pulling a rusty, windowless, two-horse trailer stuffed to the gills with her furniture, linens, kitchenware, tack, and a whole bunch of assorted cardboard boxes piled on top, I got a bad feeling about her. Instead of pausing to say "howdy-do" to me (I was standing beside the hay barn to greet her), she whipped her rig around so that she could back her trailer up to the open breezeway of the stable. I'd cleaned the corner stall she'd be storing her stuff in and, knowing she was coming all the way down from southwestern Oregon just a spit above the California border, I figured she'd ignored me because she was in a hurry to get her stuff off-loaded so she could relax. She wanted to "officially arrive," in other words, and I could sympathize with that.

I myself had put in over one hundred and fifty thousand miles hauling precious hoofed cargo all over the southern two-thirds of California in a four-horse, fifth-wheel trailer, and never during my travels had I stopped for anything other than fuel or fast food to go, or gone for long with my trailer empty. I'd drop off a mare here, travel two hundred miles, drop off a mare and foal there and, on the way back home, pick up a mare and foal here, cross the mountains, and fetch another mare and foal there. And all the time I'd be sharing the interstates and backroads with drivers who wouldn't know a fifty-thousand-dollar filly from a baby strapped in a car seat, and who nearly always were either in a big old hurry or no kind of hurry at all. My long hauls lasted between ten and eighteen hours round-trip and once I even wheeled it for twenty-five hours straight. Since I was working by the hour, that was the most money I ever made in one day.

So I knew about road weariness, and getting the cold shoulder from the new ranch manager didn't bother me much. I figured she was just putting first things first as I did when I returned from a long haul. After my horses were safely bedded down in their stalls and happily munching on their horse candy and I was back behind the wheel of my own rig, I'd make a beeline for the Boonville Lodge. I'd be out to get the road out of me—the crazy focused intensity and the built-up body tension. I was accustomed to using my jump muscles, and driving truck I had to use my anti-jump muscles.

Dropping down the steep dirt road connecting the ridge-top ranch to Highway 128, without a trailer behind me, I'd drive extra slow, reacquainting myself with my rig's fingertip steering and smooth ride. When I reached two-lane blacktop, even though it was still fifteen miles to the Lodge, I'd drive extra slow and careful. I'd take it easy because I knew my concentration was shot and my mind was wandering. Imagining the humiliation of coming off a thousand-mile run just to smack into a redwood tree standing a few miles from home, I'd keep both my hands on my steering wheel and force my eyes to keep between the lines. Only once do I remember rushing, and that was because I'd arrived so late at night with the horses that I was afraid the Lodge would close without me.

Inside the saloon, standing belly up to the bar, I'd sip between two and three shots of Tullamore Dew and chase them down with two or three bottles of beer. Only after my backbone had unscrewed and the tip of my nose got numb would I consider myself to be mentally fit enough to get myself the few remaining miles home and snuggled under the covers with my wife (without the booze, I'd be lying there wide awake, my eyes like headlights).

So the new ranch manager's lack of dirt-road etiquette didn't bother me much, and I was still ready to graciously welcome her to her new home. She'd been hired sight unseen because of her long list of impressive references, and even though when I was a little boy my dad had taught me that having a long list of references meant you couldn't keep a job, I certainly wasn't holding that against her.

But, as I watched her try to back up her little two-horse trailer square to the breezeway, I got the first indication that something was seriously wrong. I'll grant that backing up a trailer is tricky, but still, after a bit of practice, it's not an impossible task. Yet here was the new ranch manager jackknifing her trailer left, pulling ahead and jackknifing it right, and pulling ahead and then jackknifing it I-couldn't-predict-which-way next.

Because of the Law of Averages I figured she'd get it right sooner or later and, sure enough, after maybe eight tries, she got her trailer positioned just right. When she dismounted her rig I could see she was frazzled and possessed with worries, for her knees were knocking and her body was trembling like she was a shaky two-month-old foal just off-loaded out of a trailer after having endured a ten-hour ride.

"She must have had quite some trip," I thought to myself.

Though I was standing a respectable distance away, still the new ranch manager looked right past me. She opened her passenger side door and out jumped a giant Irish wolfhound. But once the giant dog hit the dirt he just stood there as if the ground was covered with eggs and he was afraid of breaking them. He was also shivering and, even though through my teeth I blew him a tiny whistle of wind to try to tweak his interest, he too refused to look at me.

The new ranch manager promptly produced a ridiculously long and gaudy Hollywood cowboy bandana and wrapped it around the poor dog's neck while he held perfectly still for her, his neck stretched out and his head held at attention. After tying the bandana with three half-hitches, she slid her palm under it and, as if it was a chest strap and the dog was a rodeo bronc, she led him to the nearest empty stall to lock him up for safekeeping.

"Ain't you going to help me?" she asked me, after sliding the stall door shut on her blinking dog. My helper had already dropped her tailgate and he was beginning to off-load her stuff, but still I could read the insult and the hurt in her voice.

"Yabetcha," I lied cheerfully. "But right now I'm in the middle of something. I'll be back in a minute."

After pivoting and quickly disappearing behind the barn, I lit up a cigarette. I hated smoking and I'd been warned not to smoke around the new ranch manager or to do anything else that might make her unhappy, but I had no intention of off-loading her stuff, and instinctively I knew my fifteen years in the trot-trot business were drawing to a close. A person that won't allow a dog to be a dog won't allow a horse to be a horse, and if you put such a person in charge of a large herd of hot-blooded horses, the results ain't going to be pretty. Even a scrawny-shrimp six-month-old filly is still a lot bigger, faster, and stronger than a man or a woman, and even a shrimp is not the type of critter you want getting pissed off at you.

Moreover, I'd always carried a warm soft spot in my heart for Ireland's wildgeese, boys like me who for centuries had fought wars in all corners of the Diaspora. Oftentimes when the wild geese returned home—*if* they returned home—they fought the bloody English and I liked that, too. So seeing that gangly Irish wolfhound acting like a scared showdog puppy I took as a personal insult. Moreover, after I'd turned my back on her and before I disappeared, I heard her start in on my helper, a "no English"–speaking Mestizo who knew what he was doing.

"Be careful with that," she ordered. "Easy now, put that over here, not there," and that really got my blood boiling. There's the corporate world and there's the hill world, and she'd come into my hills uninvited. Uninvited by me, anyway.

But the plain fact was that I was too old and I had too many years on the job to have any stomach left for breaking in a new ranch manager. I'd already gone through a handful but this was the first one I knew was, straight out the gate, downright delusional and nasty to boot. Saddled with her I'd feel like a short-timer platoon sergeant in Vietnam stuck with a cherry lieutenant platoon leader fresh out of college and filled with book learning and ambition. Except, with this here cherry, during her first firefight, instead of keeping her head down and her mouth shut, she'd be up and leading the charge.

And, sure enough, within a few days the new ranch manager got kicked by a docile old sweetheart mare that was extremely heavy and overdue with foal and so was in no mood to be messed with. The mare's kick was a one-legged, gentle kind of kick like she'd use to shoo a horsefly buzzing her tail. But the woman got two cracked ribs, she couldn't work anymore, and so she, her dog, and her stuff were down the road again.

• • •

I don't know what it is about women and horses. I've heard various dudes advance various theories about the reason for the connection, but I've never listened much to dudes when it comes to women. Still, if I were to venture a guess, I'd say the connection is cultural. Teenage boys get into cars or jump aboard motorcycles, and teenage girls take to horses. I know that when my little teenage stepsister got her own horse and my house was suddenly filled with little teenyboppers chirping like songbirds, that's when I quit riding.

There's the short answer, anyway.

Because the absentee owner of the ranch was convinced that only a woman could be given responsibility for the herd of horses, and because the herd became a "stable" during the long, rainy winter months—horses were kept indoors during the worst of the weather and therefore needed plenty of food deliveries, fresh water, and cleaning up after (horses are, after all, mobile organic grass processing units)—and not to mention that because each horse needed attention, strokes, exercise, grooming, and doctoring, to run the stable we needed a crew. And since women were the horse experts and not many men worked well under women, especially if they became nags (as in an old mare that's become more trouble than she's worth), over the years nearly all of the stable hands were horse women.

Because the pay was low, the labor strenuous and dangerous, and the working conditions what you'd expect while being outside under a giant, blowing North Pacific downpour, the turnover rate was such that over the years I worked with or around maybe twenty horse women. Some of them stayed a while, others a half-while, and some stayed for years. So I feel qualified to say that what ties all horse women together is their powerful appreciation—love—of horses and, logically, animals generally. And that love of animals puts them on common ground with ranchers and farmers everywhere. The horse women knew that their charges were more than just commodities to be bought and sold, tools to be used, or objects to be exploited. And it was that precise attitude that the owner, himself a blue ribbon–winning horse trader, always counted on.

Beyond their powerful appreciation for animals—horses, dogs, cats, bummer fawns, bummer lambs, baby coons, injured birds—there wasn't really all that much to tie them together, especially considering that the stable drew women from as far north as Dakota, as far east as Indiana, as far west as Hawaii, and as far south as Michoacan. When it came to the Theory of Horses, most disagreed on some things and some disagreed on most things. Given their varied backgrounds and diverse schools of thought, simple stuff like just naming the color of a particular horse could be cause for controversy.

For example, my own idea of a beautiful horse is a sorrel with a blond mane and tail, a good-looking, narrow white blaze, and four tall white socks. If I was to buy a horse for its looks, that's the kind I'd want.

But tell that to a horse woman and she'll likely correct you by saying that there's no such thing as a sorrel-colored Thoroughbred. The horse I was admiring was properly called a chestnut or, maybe, upon closer inspection, a chestnut-roan. And if I protested that Out West (scrap the tops off a couple of ridges and we'd be looking down on the Pacific Ocean) a horse of that color is called a sorrel, she'd take that as a point out of order.

So—because I liked being rambunctious and, I suppose, obnoxious—I'd ask her to put herself in that poor filly's hoofs. There you were, your coat glowing golden in the morning rays of sunlight. What would you rather be called? Something sweet like "sorrel" or something sharp and edgy and slightly insulting like "chestnut?" But then, to be fair, the horse certainly was "chesty," and "nuts" if that meant acting at times in unpredictable and illogical ways. So I could live with "chestnut" if she could live with "sorrel." (Eventually I started calling them chestnuts like I was supposed to.)

Every kind of people develops their own lingo, and Thoroughbred horse women were no different. A chestnut was not a chestnut-roan, and that wasn't a strawberry-roan, or a blue-roan, or just a plain roan either, though it took a practiced eye to see the differences. Like with corrals. Over my working career I built all kinds of corrals for various types of livestock (including, once, a holding corral for buffalo), but never once did I ever build a corral for a Thoroughbred. If I built a state-of-the-art and perfectly safe enclosure and I kept an Appaloosa in it, then it was called a corral. But take out the Appaloosa and put in a Thoroughbred and it's no longer a corral but a "paddock." Appaloosas get corralled, you see, and Thoroughbreds get paddocked.

Now, there's a small minority of horse women—every craft has its lunatic fringe—who so love horses that they hold a much lower opinion of people, especially the two-legged male kind of people like me: crude, macho, burly, dirty, smelly, callused, scarred, bulldog strong, and white-trash sassy.

Once, while leaning on a pasture fence and watching a two-year-old filly stretching her muscles by running laps and using redwood trees as barrels to pivot around, one such woman, charmed by the sight of the filly, came and stood side by side with me. Feeling rambunctious and wanting to get her goat, with awe in my voice I purred admiringly, "Now that there surely is one fine piece of livestock."

Well, the horse woman recoiled from me in shock and, judging by the way she was eyeballing me, she was wondering how she was going to be able to pick me up and throw me off the mountain.

After that never again did I get up the courage to utter the word "livestock" in front of any kind of horse woman. Some things, I learned, weren't to be joked about.

If I was to divide horse women into two groups, there'd be the Western Saddles versus the English Saddles. The Western Saddles were mostly homegrown hillbilly girls. They knew horses the way they knew the hills; they were possessed with "horse sense" plus common sense, and they saw no reason to make things any more complicated than they already were. Some could talk the bark off a tree, and others hardly said a word. But all of them kept their focus, didn't complain much, and felt completely comfortable around horses. Even though all horse people carry somewhere deep down a fear of horses, they never let the horses know it.

My favorite ranch manager was a homegrown hillbilly who, like me, enjoyed keeping things simple and harmonious. She liked working alone, in other words, and she never hired somebody to do something she could do for herself. During the dry months, when most of the horses were pastured, she often worked alone, making the rounds through the pastures, delivering feed and checking in on everybody.

Once, just after she'd taken over the herd, I came up out of the woods at quitting time. I was reforesting the steeper slopes and when I emerged up out of the hole I saw her truck parked in its usual spot but she was nowhere to be seen. After searching the stable, the barn, and nearby corrals and still not finding her, I figured she was out in one of the pastures and I started searching those. On that ranch we had eight pastures and, after searching the most likely of them and still not finding her, my wicked imagination took a hold of me and a worm of panic started wiggling in my belly. What if she'd gotten kicked and had bled to death?

About that time I spotted her emerging out of the redwood tree line beyond the back fence of the ranch. Out that way were hundreds of square miles of wildlands, and she'd disappeared somewhere along the edge of those. In one hand she was carrying a Winchester rifle, she was being escorted by her Jack Russell nose dog, and she had a big grin on her face. She'd nearly gotten off a great shot on a beautiful buck deer, she happily announced. It was a beautiful buck with a huge rack of horns. But it wasn't a sure, dead head-shot so she never squeezed her trigger. Though, she smiled wistfully at the memory, she'd been sorely tempted.

The homegrown women were nearly always gentle with the horses and they hated whips and twitches the way I hated No Trespassing signs and barbed wire. But that doesn't mean one of them couldn't occasionally get cross with an unruly horse. Once I saw a gelding kick at a woman's head and (thank God) deliberately miss her while still sending a gust of wind past her ear. Well, that woman instantly dropped her feed bucket, turned on the gelding, and smacked him on the nose with her fist so hard that his knees buckled, his ears dropped, and for a second I thought he was going to keel over sideways, his ass end having already been knocked out.

Another homegrown woman, a young mother as gentle as a dawn breeze, once explained to me what to do when a horse set its foot down on mine and refused to get off it. I was to bite the horse as hard as I could on the lip, she sagely advised me. I was to draw some blood and see how fast that horse raises its foot off mine. For emphasis, she opened her mouth wide, bared her teeth, and slammed them shut so hard that the "click" startled the horse she was working on.

Occasionally I'd be walking down a breezeway in the stable and from around the corner I'd hear frantic hoofbeats. Knowing by the sound that we had a roped horse running backward, I'd stop shy of the corner, yielding to the horse the right-of-way. And so it would come, its tail dragging, its ass low-down, and its nose straight up in the air. Next came a ten-foot length of woven cotton lead rope, steel-cable taut, and hanging on for dear life to the end of it would be some skittering little sprig of a woman, her legs furiously running backward even as she was getting dragged forward.

Once the coast was clear—I figured if the woman had wanted my help she'd have asked for it on her way by—I'd carry on with my business.

One time I watched as a backward-running horse pulled a woman clean out of the stable, down the road, around a corner, and down an aisle between two pastures, around another bend, and then down a long, straight backstretch. The sight was so peculiar that I ran along at a distance so I could watch to see what happened. Half of me was betting the horse would suddenly stop running and the woman would smack into its chest, ricochet, land on her ass, but still tenaciously keep ahold of the rope. As a variation on that betting proposition, she'd land on her ass but, tweeting and circling birds flying around her head, she'd let go of the rope. The last possibility was that the woman, finally realizing that the horse was ten times as big, twenty times as strong, and just as stubborn, would give up the ghost, let go of the rope, and let the beast go free.

If she did that, or if the horse broke free, then I'd decide whether or not I'd volunteer to help recapture the runaway, basing my decision more on the temperament of the woman than on the temperament of the horse.

But in this case the horse didn't stop back-thrusting and the woman didn't stop back-thrusting or let go of the rope. They both just sort of disappeared into the sunset. And watching them go—

all out of breath, I couldn't keep up with them any longer—I had the strangest vision. Somehow it seemed the woman was facing the wrong way. If only she'd turned around, it seemed, they both would be on the same cosmic wavelength.

Anyway, unlike the Western Saddles, the English Saddles came off the show horse circuit or the racetracks. They were suburban, they had more money and education, more rules and regulations and, certainly, more opinions about everything. The Western Saddles and the English Saddles usually got along kind of OK but, given my ex-GI prejudices, I was partial to the first group and somewhat ill-disposed toward the second. I knew that horses were dangerous and so establishing various Standard Operating Procedures was necessary in order to help ensure public safety. But I didn't need anybody to tell me how to lead a horse, or how to talk to one or how to correctly put a big smooch on his cheek. While the Western Saddles knew all about ranching, the English Saddles knew all about Organization. Get enough of them working in the same stable and pretty quick you've got a manager, an assistant manager, a shift manager, and a substitute manager. And me, because I was in charge of everything but the horses and I had my own (male) crew, schedule, and responsibilities, I was a loose cannon.

Respecting neither experience, age, or seniority, and power hungry in the way of a meticulous housewife who wants everything in its place and a place for everything, with the worst of the English Saddles I felt like I was a stranger intruding into their kitchen just as they were putting the final touches on a masterpiece feast.

To give just one example of the types of stylistic conflicts that occasionally arose: We had two ranches (we called them the "top ranch" and the "bottom ranch"), which between them held sixteen double-fenced horse-wire pastures. The smallest pasture was an acre in size and the largest was twelve acres. As was traditional with American ranchers—our forefathers and foremothers had learned it from the natives—the names we gave the various pastures were descriptive. We might name a pasture for its size and location: the "front four" or the "bottom eight." Or we might name a pasture after some feature: the "foothill pasture" because it was in the foothills or the "orchard pasture" because of the scattering of pioneer apple trees still growing within it. Or we might name a pasture because of what was beside it, like the "bullpen pasture" ("bullpen" was slang for the round corral we used for "breaking" colts and fillies) or the "pond pasture" because, located above the irrigation pond, over the years half of its churned-up and muddied-up topsoil had washed down into the pond. Or we might name a pasture for its function, like with the grassy little pasture next to the top stable that we kept rested during the winter so that, come time, the newborn foals would have a safe place to learn how to run while their mothers, their bellies suddenly feeling empty, got to munch on lush spring grass to help them produce milk. That pasture we called "the nursery."

So along comes a new English Saddle ranch manager and she doesn't like the sloppiness in our system. She tells me she wants to number all of the pastures, one set of numbers for the top ranch and another set of numbers for the bottom ranch. We'll begin our catalogs with the westernmost pastures on each ranch and work clockwise from there: one, two, three, and so on. That way, she assured me, everybody would be on the same page. I was to manufacture nice-looking, painted, numbered signs—would beveled plywood look good? Whatever sort of nice-looking sign I could think of I was to hang beside every one of the fifty pasture gates. I was to hang the signs on the latch sides of the gates and not the hinge sides because they'd be easier to read that way and that would make everything uniform.

Since I didn't like being told what to do, and since neither paint, plywood, nor my time came cheap, and because I enjoyed creating beauty rather than ugliness and preferred chaos to regimentation, not to mention the fact that I thought the whole idea—even if a fancy stack of fifty readymade numbered signs magically appeared in my hands—was plumb loco, I had no intention of doing as I was told. I mean, while we were at it, why not spray paint numbers on the sides of the horses? We could spray the same numbers on both sides of every horse so never again would there be any confusion about who was who.

I don't mean to make too much of such stylistic conflicts because it takes two to kick up dust, and whatever troubles I had over the years I had my own hand in creating for the reasons I've explained. I worked with some catskinners who were no fun to be around, and so it was only natural that, given my peculiar ways and my long years in the horse biz, I'd also run into some horse women who made me feel the same way.

CONVERSATIONS WITH HORSES

There's a breed of pony-player who goes around bragging about all of the money he makes betting on the horse races at the track. Some of them claim to have some magical mathematical formula that allows them to beat the laws of probability. They claim to have the power not only to beat the laws of probability but also to beat the house percentage (the cut the track takes in exchange for providing the amenities and the action).

Other pony-players claim to have developed through long experience a winning way with their hunches, meaning an ability to know in a great flash of insight which horse in a race is the ringer and then having the guts to go and bet the farm on it. But even the "winningest" of them have trouble putting their thumb on just what it is that makes them winners. Although that hasn't prevented a whole slew of these guys from marketing books offering to share with you their divine gift. It boils down to having an eye for horse flesh, they'll tell you. That and the ability to see into a horse's mind.

Sometimes called "paddock flies," before each race these guys gather around the rail of the giant paddock where the horses and their jockeys are paraded for their benefit. After having checked off, underlined, blotted out, and otherwise tattooed the pages of their Daily Racing Forms, and after having studied the shifts in the odds being displayed on the tote board—my horse opened at three-to-five and now it's down to two-to-one!—they commune with the horses circling in the paddock. They have conversations with the horses, exchanging bits of information while leaving the surrounding crowd of tourists none the wiser.

"How you doing, Eddie?" the man will ask. "Are you ready to take a little spin? I made a bundle betting on you last month and I'm thinking about going strong with you in this race. So how you feeling, old pal?"

And the horse, using his body language as the window into his soul, replies, "I'm feeling my molasses, boss. I'm feeling my molasses, alfalfa, and my oats to boot, if you really want to know and you can keep a secret. Running with these bums, I'm already back in my stall getting massaged and slurping champagne, if you know what I mean." Then the horse winks and the man bets his money accordingly.

Or maybe the paddock fly is out to see a particular horse that he's won and lost with in the past but hasn't seen race in a while. In which case the man will say, "Hey, Marty, remember me? How you doing, man? Long time no see."

Recognizing the man, the horse smiles and replies, "Not too well right now, boss. They promised me retirement to stud in green pastures but here I am running with these youngsters chomping at their bits. I'll tell you something else if you want to know a secret: If I wasn't looking forward to retirement, I'd charge the rail, stop on a dime, and throw this skinny-assed, whip-flashing, smart-talking, heavy-sitting jockey off my back and up and over my ears. If I was any younger, I'll tell you, I'd head-butt him on his way over me to put some arc in his flight."

And the horse, returning to reality, groans and the man bets his money accordingly.

As for what I think about those sorts of conversations with horses, I don't know because I live in the sticks and I seldom get to the races. The few times I've watched Thoroughbreds on parade, about all I could tell about them was that they all appeared physically sound, muscular and beautiful—horses sleeked down to look like greyhounds. Some horses in the paddock seemed nervous, others were feisty, and still others acted like they were glad to be out of their stalls and outside in the fresh air. As to what any of that said about their willingness to run—to run for the pure primal joy of it—how would I know?

But I do remember my dad, a serious card player and gambler (my dad divided his gambling activities into business and pleasure), making sure that I understood that if anybody—long term—could beat the laws of probability and the house percentage—if any soothsayer, crystal ball–gawker, bone-thrower, or prophet on earth could successfully and consistently call the flip of a coin—then, within a few months, that magician would own the world. He'd not only own the world but, my dad told me, never in a million years would he publish a book explaining how he did it.

My own conversations with horses have been a lot more elementary and one-sided. Horses don't talk human. Horses do nearly all of their talking to each other and only rarely will they speak to a human, and then usually only when they want something or their situation requires it. Most horses would rather play with a deer that's jumped into their pasture, or with a dog scampering at their feet, or even with a giant irrigation nozzle going around and around shooting piss-green pond water, than to talk to a human. If you have a small herd of horses in a pasture and you want them to come over to you, then you'd better have something more to offer them than just a bundle of carrots or a bucket of horse candy. If it's springtime and the graze is lush, they won't even lift their noses out of the grass for you. With regards to coming when they're called, horses are a lot closer to house cats than dogs.

Regarding their level of intelligence, nobody on earth is better at being horses than horses. Even before the advent of horse racing or humans, horses had a long track record. But that doesn't mean they can count cards, hire lawyers, fret over estate planning, or speculate on real estate. With tens of millions of years of proven evolutionary success behind them, why would a horse worry over its future? Not even a horse can predict what's coming, and I think as a species they long ago put behind them wondering about how many angels can fit on the head of a pin.

Horses occupy their minds with immediate, tangible things like food and more food and their social positions. In a small herd, horses need to establish to each other who they are and how they fit in. But once the rules have been established and everybody knows their place, at any sign of danger horses will gather together and it will be them against the world. Individual horses can be greedy, courageous, spiteful, cowardly, and jealous, and they can feel a whole bunch of other animal types of emotions, including pride and wounded pride, irrational fears, and temptations. They are very intelligent, in short; very intelligent and very stupid at the same time.

What old Claude the cowboy said about sheep applies to horses and to humans as well: "The larger the herd, the stupider the individual critter."

Now, just because horses can't talk human, that doesn't mean you can't talk to them. In fact, for some reason, everybody talks to the horses and they do seem to like it—the horses, I mean. Whether they glean much information from the chats or are just amused, I can't tell. But certainly sometimes a horse will pay close attention to you, even hang on your every word. Horses can be trained to charge headfirst into artillery fire, to come when called, to get into trap-like horse trailers or starting gates, and even to allow reckless little kids to jerk on their bits or slam car doors behind them. Horses can survive on the seashore, in the mountains, and most everyplace in between. They can smell water in the desert and, if you ever get hopelessly lost, just let go of your reins and your horse will lead you home. And—I always thought this was a neat trick—horses can sleep on their feet.

Whether it's the horse-shoer, a vet making a house call, a groom, rider, trainer, or owner, everybody talks to the horses. I know next to nothing about the maybe ten-thousand-year-long history of horse husbandry, but my guess is that most everywhere on earth people with horses talk their ears off. Like, How are you doing, feeling, been? You want some of this? Let me get that sticker out of your ear, allow me to lift your foot, come on, now, this ain't rocket science—open your mouth wide, you can do it. How am I supposed to file your teeth if you won't open up your mouth? I'm going to walk behind you now and, while I'm switching sides, I'm going to run my fingertips crossways to your coat to give you a little tickle—you like that? Be good and I'll blow gently into your nose. Allow me and I'll take every last itch out of your withers, every last knot out of your mane. Hold still and I'll give you a shower. Stay still and I'll wipe you off with a squeegee—how's that for a treat? Don't you love getting the shivers on your skin one twelve-inch-wide swath at a time and all around?

There's no end to the things a person will say to a horse. But, if you listen carefully, what you'll hear is mostly sweet-talk. That's because in order to gain their confidence, you need to offer horses compliments and reassurances. You want to let them know how much you appreciate them and how proud you are of them and how special they are to you and how you'll always be there for them—how you are their best friend in the world. If you're speaking to a horse, you talk like a parent or a politician. If you want to get something out of horses, you've got to give them something in return. Even if, in human terms, it doesn't amount to much.

$$\bullet \ \bullet \ \bullet$$

Only once can I say I ever had a serious heart-to-heart talk with a horse. There certainly is such a thing as interspecies communication and, in the case of horses and people, it occurs across the shaky bridge of mutual trust. Every horse and every person has their own personality, but so long as a horse acts like a civilized horse, and the person acts like a civilized person, and the two of them have built up a mutually beneficial relationship, then there will be no fear between them. And without fear real communication—not sweet-talk—becomes possible.

So one time I delivered a solo, hot-blooded, feisty young colt to a training facility located up in the cactus country just above the Mexican border. It had been a long haul, the colt had been calm the whole way, and I was looking forward to stretching my legs and grabbing a cup of coffee for my trip back home. It was late afternoon, El Lay's "rush hour" was over, and I was hoping to escape back north via Cajon Pass. I wanted to reach the Mojave Desert in time for the sunset. Smog and vast mountainous horizons make for pretty sunsets.

Well, as soon as I come to a halt in a hollow in the hills just under a mountaintop and in front of the stable, the colt in the trailer goes crazy. He starts kicking and banging and bouncing the truck and sending up a violent, hellacious racket. I look for somebody coming out of the stable to help me—bean counters control the racing industry, too—but even though they'd been expecting me and I was on schedule, nobody was there to help. I searched the nearby hills, saw a collection of crowded, rundown single-wide trailers, and figured most of the hired hands were living way up there, their day's work done. To get help out of any of them I'd have to run up there and, well, I had no time for that.

Since my colt's ruckus was already stirring up the twenty or so horses in the stable, I went ahead and blasted my truck's horn hoping to stir up one or more of the two-legged kind of critter. But nobody appeared in their doorjambs, their necks craning. My colt kept thrashing and, afraid he'd hurt himself, I left the truck to see what I could do.

I slowly opened the side escape hatch of the trailer (escape for people, not for horses) and saw that somehow the colt had fallen and had gotten himself pinned on his back with his hoofs pointing straight up at me. When he saw me peering through the crack in the door, he thrashed all the harder, seemingly trying to kick at me to keep me away. I slammed the door shut knowing I had myself a real problem.

Speaking through the door in a loud (anything above a whisper is loud to a horse) and firm tone of voice, I told the colt to cool it. I scolded him for losing his composure and bothering the other horses. He needed to calm down and hold still so I could have a look at him to see what I needed to do to help get him back up on his feet. Did he want back up on his feet?

And, hearing my voice, the colt finally stopped thrashing, probably more winded than anything else. I slowly reopened the door and he held still and looked at me. I thanked him and made small talk while I ascertained what exactly the problem was. He was tied to the front of the trailer and somehow, while foolishly trying to rear up, he'd gotten his left foreleg up and over the top of the rope and that had caused him to land upside down on his back, trapped in the narrow space that had been allotted for him (feisty horses you usually want to trailer "in a squeeze" (held in place.) The colt had rolled over to his left and now the lead rope was wrapped around his neck and choking him. Since a part of the rope was also pinned against the wall by the back of his neck, he was in danger of strangling.

In a soft, languid tone of voice I told him that I saw the problem and I knew how to fix it. He was to keep still while I went to fetch the hunting knife I kept in the cab of the truck for just such occasions. Was he OK with that? I gently re-shut the door, ran to the truck, and was back in a flash. I slowly reopened the door and the colt was right like I'd left him and still looking at me, except now I could see the whites of his eyes. I showed him both sides of my long knife and I explained to him that I was going to have to stretch out over the top of him to be able to cut the rope from his neck and get him some slack. So I needed him to wait just one more second, to not move a muscle, and certainly to not kick me—I couldn't help him if he kicked me, and I needed to help him. Did he understand?

Since he was holding perfectly still and eyeballing my hunting knife, I took his lack of a response for a "yes." I very slowly reached over him, gently slid the blade of my knife sideways under the rope next to his neck and, after twisting it ninety degrees and giving a couple of slow, gentle saws, the rope snapped in two and the pressure was released. The colt waited for me to back away out of the trailer and, the instant after I silently shut the door, by throwing his weight around and thrashing his legs, even before I'd gotten around to releasing him from the squeeze made by the trailer's divider, he got himself back up on his feet.

Happy to be back to normal and acting like nothing had happened, the colt started whinnying at the stranger horses in the stable. They started whinnying back at him, their various voices combining into a welcoming chorus that echoed in the hills and through the cactus. From the cluster of trailers I saw a middle-aged Mexican fellah coming down the hill toward me, a halter and lead rope looped over his shoulder, and still chewing on a bit of his supper.

"Buenas noches," he called to me, a big smile on his face.

"Sí-mon," I answered.

The colt went like a perfectly well-behaved gentleman into his new stall and, after saying goodbye to him, I gave him a big smooch on the cheek.

WHO I AM AND WHY I WROTE THIS BOOK

I was born in Chicago in 1949. My mom's dad, Joseph(?) Moravic, was a Slovak World War One refugee who arrived in Chicago from Bratislava, the industrial city on the Danube River, in 1920. Until he was killed on the job when my mom was fifteen years old, my granddad worked as a janitor and maintenance man in a skyscraper in the Loop.

My mom's mom, Teresa Amelia (Morachik?), was a mail-order bride brought over from the province of Bratislava in 1922. Illiterate and never able to speak much English, up until she died suddenly of a heart attack when I was ten years old, my grandma mopped floors in the same building in which her husband had been killed (he was crushed in an elevator shaft).

My dad, Charles Edward, was a bastard son of Ireland. His stepdad and my namesake, Bruce Patterson, was a Scotch Irishman who, at the age of eighteen in 1918, came to Chicago from a coal mining town named Florence in southern Colorado. A violent and yet extremely timid and reclusive man who was blessed with artistic brilliance, after World War Two my Grandpa Patterson became a nationally syndicated cartoonist and columnist *(The Cheering Section)* for King's Features.

My dad's mom, Alberta Mildred Rose, a daughter of Ireland, was brought up in a little farming burg in downstate Illinois called Middletown. In 1921, as a seventeen-year-old girl either pregnant or with her baby in arms, she arrived alone in Chicago. Her lover and my dad's father, whom my dad met only once, was an Irish immigrant named Boyd. He got sent up to Joliet Prison for rustling hogs.

Already living in some of Chicago's worst slums (800 North–1,100 West), both sides of my family were hit hard by the Great Crash of 1929. The fact that while growing up my big sister and I would never know hunger, or be rationed, or have anything less than a wide variety of foods available to us at all times was my dad's proudest achievement. The rule in our house was: Take all you want but be sure to eat all you take.

My mom, Amelia Teresa but called "Terry," was Chicago-slums sassy. An excellent card player, shrewd gambler, hard drinker, and party girl, she thought she was as good as anybody. Proud, passionate, and armed with a hairpin temper, after her dad was killed she had to quit school to go to work. As a Grand Avenue hash house waitress, my mom might have broken a plate over your head if you got fresh with her or gave her too much lip. My mom could bluff three men out of a pot in a hand of poker and, if provoked, she could raise her voice loud enough to awaken the angels.

My mom and dad grew up together and my big sister and I were born in the same neighborhood. But by then America was entering its postwar economic boom and, after enjoying some success as a GI Bill–financed service station owner, in 1952 we moved to the Highland Park district of Los Angeles. My mom became a housewife and my dad started his climb up the corporate ladder with Firestone Tire and Rubber.

Much of my mom's life (she was fifty-eight when she died) was spent trying to escape the traumas of her childhood. Add to that an unending series of physical problems and, even though we were now living in paradise (my dad liked calling the four of us "bats out of hell"), my mom started using booze to self-medicate. By the time I was old enough to notice, already she was a drunk, or a "lush," as they said back then. My mom was a drunk on her way to losing her mind. When I landed in Vietnam in November of 1967, my mom had already been "committed" to Camarillo State Mental Hospital.

My dad was my hero. A male, more-violent version of my mom, they made a good pair, a hot-blooded Irishman being not much different than a fierce and excitable Slovak peasant. Except my dad never raised his voice. He'd rather bust your jaw than raise his voice. When I was a little boy he told me—get this—that the only thing worse than a loud man was a loud woman.

I remember, back in 1972, how disgusted my dad was after he saw the movie *The Godfather*. He grew up under the mafia; his mother, who had supported them during the Depression by operating a downstairs beauty shop, had paid protection to the mafia; the street-corner cops were on the Mafia payroll, and when my dad was a young man in desperate need of grub money, he did a few little, nonviolent jobs for them. And the mafioso, my dad wanted me to know, were so loud and foul-mouthed that you'd hear them coming from a block away. And portraying the mafia as deep-thinking businessmen, as strategists? Who were they kidding? The only thing gangsters were good at was killing people, and even then they had to rat pack you or ambush you to get it done.

Listening to my dad go on I began to understand why his whole life he was instinctively repelled by loud people.

When the Japanese bombed Pearl Harbor my dad was twenty-one years old and working in a foundry in Calumet City, Illinois. Like many of his coworkers, my dad enlisted in the army. Expecting to be made into an infantryman, instead he became a bomber pilot, an officer and a gentleman. For the first time in his life my dad was introduced to real law and order, real organization, and—this was crucially important to him—he had a good job, a full belly, health care, and "privileges." Add into the mix the chance to serve his country and my dad nearly fell in love with the military (he "re-upped" one time), though he was never fool enough to fall in love with war.

My dad's military service not only lifted him out of Chicago's slums, it made him fully American—fiercely proud to be an American—and, given what was in store for us as a family, that colored not just his life but mine. When the chips were down my dad was extremely loyal to veterans, and I grew up surrounded by World War Two vets and virtually all of my adult role models had fired weapons.

My dad was my hero until, when I was twelve years old, he left me in my mom's custody while he went off to start a new family. As soon as my big sister turned eighteen she'd gotten married in part to escape our home, which left me alone with my mom, although sometimes my big sister and her new husband, who lived nearby, did allow me to sleep in the little cabin they'd made for me in their basement.

Soon after the divorce my mom and I were living in an apartment next to the Santa Fe railroad tracks just over the York Boulevard Bridge in South Pasadena. Since by then my mom was totally disabled and mostly bedridden, we were living on welfare. We were "living" on welfare but nobody really can or does. By the start of the third week of the month we'd be broke. So, on the fifteenth of every month, my dad would call on the phone to ask my mom how much money we needed to see us through to the first of the month. My sister delivered the cash.

As much as my dad disliked subsidizing my mom's drinking and my pilfering, and as much as he believed in Law and Order, he wasn't about to let his own blood kin go hungry or allow us to sink into the worst and most dangerous slums.

I was a strange little boy. We'd moved West along with a clan of other Irishmen out of the old neighborhood, and even though I grew up in Highland Park, I felt like I was in Chicago. My parents were always battling, sometimes violently, there was often a card game, a party, or a crap game going on and, in our garage, instead of storing our car, my dad kept a pool table. My dad liked teaching and as a boy I learned to add and subtract, figure odds, and read people while playing cards and shooting pool. Booze and violence and violent, reckless talk were so much a part of my upbringing that I thought it was the only natural way to be.

I grew tall quicker than most of the other boys and, because of a tongue-tying stutter, I couldn't speak. Outside of family and a small circle of friends, I rarely opened my mouth in front of anyone. One reason why I always hated going to school was because if a teacher called on me to answer a question in front of class—after a teacher had learned of my affliction I was amazed by how she or he sometimes persisted in the practice—I couldn't answer and I wouldn't even try. If my teacher or anybody else didn't like it, so be it.

Given the truly weird array of sounds I could produce when I tried to verbalize, to find my place on the street I had to learn how to run and how to fight. By the time I left kindergarten I'd already gotten a nail punched into my cheek and I knew how to fight. By the time I entered junior high school the other boys in my neighborhood knew that when it came to my stutter or my muteness, they'd best be watching their own mouths and not mine.

Yet I never did enjoy hurting people. When you whipped somebody's ass in a fistfight you wanted to leave your marks on them, but only twice did my victims have to go to the doctor because of the damage I'd done them—one to get the gouge in his head stitched up and the other to get his broken arm set—and both times it'd been an accident. Also, I should add, a few times I got my own ass kicked.

I always liked girls and some of the more adventurous girls, sensing my "vulnerability" and delighted by my ability to sit and listen, liked me. And because boys out to impress boys are usually jealous of boys out to impress girls, that caused me to get into even more fistfights, especially considering that a couple of my earliest girlfriends were Chicanas.

"What you doing holding hands with that beaner?"

Pow, bam, boom!

Now, I mention my stutter because, I think, my urge to write has its roots in that.

Perhaps the strangest thing about me was that I couldn't foresee the logical consequences of my own actions. Without feeling particularly malicious, I committed burglaries, stole cars for joyrides, committed arson, vandalized, and participated in riot and mayhem, and each time I was caught and handcuffed and sent to the lockup, I was surprised—shocked—that such a thing could happen to me.

If social scientists could ever crack that nut and answer precisely why some juveniles are constitutionally incapable of foreseeing the logical consequences of their own actions, then not only would the problem of youth crime disappear, but war would disappear. You can't get many combat veterans to fight a second war because, outside of a small, hard core of professional killers, one war is more than enough for any one lifetime. And so it is the clueless kids who are sent off to war in order to learn for themselves what their fathers and grandfathers had learned but forgotten.

If my dad hadn't been willing to pay off my victims, or if he hadn't known how to befriend an out-of-town lawyer who was the son-in-law of the judge hearing my case, I'd have gotten sent up out of junior high school. Given the punitive attitude society now takes toward kids like me, no doubt I'd have been shown zero tolerance and tried as an adult.

When I was fifteen years old, in order to keep me out of jail, spring me from my circle of friends, and get me back in school (I'd "quit" school after the tenth grade), my dad regained legal custody of me. For over a year I lived in the suburbs in a new house with my dad, new stepmom, stepbrother, and stepsister. While the move certainly put me higher up on the hog and provided me with new ways to have fun, I never felt comfortable in the suburbs and I snuck back to my old neighborhood any chance I got. Moreover, after three years of living mostly on my own and by my own lights, there was no chance I was going to learn to "straighten up and fly right," as my dad demanded in no uncertain terms. Not for him, not for anybody.

After a series of long and bitter arguments, on my sixteenth birthday my dad signed me out of high school. The same day he bought me a 1959 Chevy, got me a driver's license, insurance, and a job "busting tires" with the Teamsters. Out of every paycheck, I was to repay my dad for the car (he'd spring for the insurance) and pay room and board. Also I was to keep to a curfew, stay out of Highland Park, report my whereabouts, do chores in the yard, mind my manners, show respect, obey household rules, earn my money, and it all sounded like Greek to me.

Unable to hold on to a job, a girlfriend, or my money, again after a long and bitter series of arguments with my dad, in November of 1966, on my seventeenth birthday, I joined the army infantry and volunteered for Vietnam.

I served in Vietnam as a rifleman with the 173rd Airborne Brigade from November of 1967 until I was Medevaced stateside in April of 1968. Because of the Viet Cong's Tet Offensive all of the hospitals in-country were overflowing with casualties and I had a nearly fatal dose of malaria. I woke up out of my delirium in Tripler Armed Forces Hospital outside of Honolulu and, at first thinking I was still in Vietnam, the eventual realization that I wasn't—I saw

Diamond Head out of my hospital room window—hit me like a sledgehammer. I'd escaped combat with my life but, knowingly or not, I'd deserted my partners, my blood brothers.

I'd deserted my partners and yet I knew there was no way I was going back to Vietnam, not after what I'd seen and done, not for them or anybody else. When I learned that what was left of my squad was all but wiped out shortly after I'd left them, with one of my holemates shot dead and the other shot through, I felt intense shame and it became something I'd never live down. As a combat veteran, in that I'm in no way unique.

While I was in Tripler Hospital, for the first time in my life I started writing. In a gush my words spilled onto paper. I wrote trite poems ("In the jungle, men they fight…"), episodes, bits of journal, tirades, long, windy letters—it seemed the words just needed to come out. Metaphorically, I was puking.

I spent over three months in various military hospitals, and during that time I saw a ghoul's gallery of hideous injuries (wouldn't it be nice if we could figure out a way to amputate not just eyes and ears and limbs but also heads and memories?). And patrolling the various wards were young female nurses not much older than me, understaffed and overworked, doing their best to perform their duties while making their rounds, keeping their chins up and never allowing anyone to see how their hearts were breaking, how the joy was getting ripped from their chests. So my scribbling also served to shelter me from the horrors of my environment.

During that time (or was it back in Vietnam?) I lost about nine-tenths of my stutter. Why that was, exactly, I don't know, though I suspect it had something to do with getting it scared out of me. That plus the fact that war has a way of putting personal problems into perspective. Anyway, now eighteen years old, for the first time I could strike up a conversation with a stranger. I could charm a woman with my words, tell jokes to my buddies, verbally respond to insults, hurl insults, explain my opinions, and tell a story. It seemed divinely comical to me that the very fates I wished to cast into hell now saw fit to give me the one thing I'd always wanted most in my life.

But I took my gift and I ran with it.

After I was again fit for duty, I was returned to the 82nd Airborne

Division in Fort Bragg, North Carolina. The outfit was slated to soon arrive in Vietnam as reinforcements, and I and hundreds of other returning vets were being sent there to act as a cadre for the raw recruits. But I'd already gotten a bellyful of war games and stateside esprit de corps, and I no longer had any desire to jump out of airplanes, or to bunk with doomed, scared-shitless "cherries."

So, after a series of long and bitter arguments with my military superiors, I "terminated" my paratrooper status. As punishment I was sent to finish off my enlistment assigned to a janitor company. I wasn't the only "terminated" Vietnam vet in my barracks and, discipline being extremely lax, for the first time in my military career I had some serious GI fun. Booze, drugs, juke joints, dancing, women—I indulged in about every GI vice except violence. Though I hadn't noticed it yet, the violence had gone out of me.

Over the coming months I picked up trash and cigarette butts along Fort Bragg's many highways and byways. I swept PX parking lots, collected trash out of lifer neighborhoods and, while assigned to Womack Army Hospital, I spent my days swinging a mop back and forth over shiny hallway floors. And those sorts of duties helped me reconnect with The World because it brought my Slovak blood, and my Irish blood, full circle.

One day a black dude walked into my barracks and dropped his gear on the bunk next to mine. Having been punitively transferred up from Fort Jackson, South Carolina, he was passing a petition "demanding" that some of his buddies be released from the stockade down there. Soon to be known as the Fort Jackson Eight, his buddies were rotting in the stockade under "pretrial confinement" because, after duty one muggy evening, they'd gathered on the stoop of their barracks and they'd held a bitch session. Since six of the eight prisoners were either black or Puerto Rican, and because Fort Jackson was located in South Carolina, my new friend claimed they were locked up because of racism, and he found that intolerable.

Because up until that point my life had taught me most of all to despise all things chickenshit, and because their imprisonment, whether or not the result of racism, sounded chickenshit to me, I recklessly signed the petition. Soon, as little more than a personal favor to my new friend, I started passing petitions and getting others to do the same.

After a few of us distributed on post thousands of free copies of the American Bill of Rights to our fellow GIs, either sticking the flyers on the windshields of parked cars, or leaving them on empty bunks, in mess halls, servicemen's clubs, dayrooms, or passing them hand to hand, suddenly the brass started treating us as Terrorist Enemies of the State. For doing no more than peacefully exercising the constitutional rights I'd taken a blood oath to uphold, I was busted in rank, forced to forfeit two months' pay, restricted to my company area for two months, and given two months of extra duty. Some of my friends were thrown in the stockade.

The series of arrests made the national news, and some local civil rights attorneys volunteered to organize our defense (my sentence was overturned on appeal). During that time I also started reading unofficial sources on the origins and history of America's war in Vietnam and, the more I read, the more I realized that I, and my countrymen, had been duped.

The die was cast and I'd spend the next four years organizing against the war and for civil rights, first by cofounding GIs United Against the War in Vietnam, Fort Bragg chapter, then by helping to cofound the California Veterans Movement and, later, Vietnam Veterans Against the War, Los Angeles chapter. During those years I wrote and published a fair amount of antiwar material.

In 1972 I worked for the McGovern presidential campaign and, after Nixon was reelected in a landslide, suffering a severe case of job burnout (the war would grind on for another three years) and again single—my first wife, a native of North Carolina and a veteran of the civil rights movement, had left me because of my drinking—I got a chance to strike another match, leave the big city, and I did. I moved to a small farm outside of Fresno and, while trying to remake myself yet again, I sank deeper into alcoholism. For the next couple of years I kicked around as a farm worker.

In the winter of 1973 I moved to a ranch outside of Healdsburg in Sonoma County. A year later, after the barn my friends and I were living in burned to the ground, and having fallen in love with a woman, I moved to Pomo Tierra Ranch outside of Yorkville in

Mendocino County. A rip-roaring hippy commune with a constant flow of visitors and squatters and a continuous party going on, even though I wasn't a hippy or the communal type, for six years the place provided me with safe harbor, cheap rent, and plenty of free entertainment. Living without electricity, television, or a phone steered me toward the books I'd devour (I was fascinated by history), and during that time I also gained a wife and was blessed with the birth of my first son. I also wrote a couple of novels, the first about sixty days in the life of my squad in Vietnam, and the second a novel about hippies. The second work never made it past a first draft, but the Vietnam novel I polished up and got into the hands of a retired but still very well connected Hollywood scriptwriter.

A wily old New York show-business Jew, he was filled with a wondrous collection of stories and a generosity of spirit. He told me that while reading my book he'd been impressed by my talent and deeply affected by my prose but, in its current form at least, my book had, in his professional estimation, no commercial value. My book was too focused, intense, and unrelenting. It needed more back story—anything to get my characters out of the jungle so my readers could get a chance to relax and imagine. I needed to develop more interpersonal conflict and, though he admired my ability to wrest a bit of comedy out of such dreary material, my book needed far more humor.

To be successful as a writer, the old man sagely advised me with an uplifted finger, I needed to learn how to make people laugh.

It was advice well taken but *not* taken. I felt like I'd left my guts on my pages, and maybe that had been the point of the exercise. Was it drink that drove me to write or was it writing that drove me to drink? No matter what the answer, whatever I'd learned in Vietnam wasn't worth the price paid in human blood—that much I knew. Even if I had enough emotional endurance to go back again and rehash my combat experiences, there was no way I could successfully "commercialize" my story. As my old show-business friend knew but was too kind to say, if ever I was going to make any money as a writer, it wouldn't be with that book.

Along with the other piece, my Vietnam novel is sitting in a trunk and I haven't even glanced at it in twenty years. For me, by then having a woman to love, two boys to help raise, a habit to kick, and a need to make a living, writing would be no more than a hobby. After Bruce Anderson took over the newspaper the *Anderson Valley Advertiser* in January 1984, I'd write an occasional piece for him, and sometimes I'd compose a long, windy letter to a friend or family member. But that was about all of the writing I did. I decided that once my boys grew up, moved out, and my dog died, maybe then I'd attempt another book.

Another thing living at Pomo Tierra gave me was a sense of place. My old neighborhood in Highland Park had been the only landscape I'd ever felt a part of, but after the war I never went back home. I could imagine the types of questions my old street-thug buddies would be asking me, and having with me an educated woman who was a feminist, I thought it'd be too embarrassing for me to introduce her to them. Also, seeing how much I'd changed and knowing full well their warrior values, I was too ashamed to show myself. What would be the point?

So, I imagine, most of my childhood friends assumed I'd been killed in Vietnam and, in a sense, I had.

Living at Pomo Tierra was a lot like living in a barracks, what with old people always moving out and new people moving in, whether lovers, squatters, campers, or hitchhikers. Nearly always at Pomo Tierra there were American, European, or Latin American "gypsies" back from Nepal, or Australia, Europe, Siberia, the Middle East, or North Africa. Once, his saddlebags empty, a fellah from Back East rode in on a horse.

I liked meeting wayfaring strangers, hearing their stories, and watching the interplays of people getting to know each other. Both in the janitor company and in the airborne infantry there was more than a fair share of "bloods," as my black partners liked calling themselves, and sometimes at night in the barracks one of them would get up "a big case of the ass." He'd strut the barracks floor like it was city bricks and "rap on" about anything that came into his mind. And if the dude was schooling and his bits struck chords there'd come up a musical wave of human voices, raw and elemental like blues or bluegrass, straight stories like told off a sagging front porch, before electricity and diesel power, and back when, if you wanted music, you made it yourself.

Pomo Tierra was like that. Some truly exquisite musicians often helped provide the entertainment, and conversations were everywhere. But living at Pomo Tierra were some highly educated and multitalented people, and listening to them talking was a whole lot different than listening to some big-city barracks tap rapping or some sad, homesick, illiterate sharecropper boy worrying over all he was missing. The people living at Pomo Tierra were well-read in a wide variety of subjects, and life wasn't nearly so visceral to them. So living with them couldn't help but further my own education.

Beyond the hippies and apple orchards, pioneer redwood barns, cabins, and sheds, beyond the sheep pastures and the invisible ribbon of two-lane blacktop winding up the canyon along the curled toes of the ranch, spread the mountains. Topographically speaking, what surrounds Anderson Valley are the "coastal foothills." But park your car in most any dirt turnout along any Anderson Valley highway or road, set off on foot, and you'll be in mountains. And the mountains breed their own sorts of people, just as the tall grass prairies do, or islands do. In an isolated mountain valley like Anderson, whether native or settler, folks lived by the seasons and they took their livings from the dirt. If they needed something and they couldn't make it themselves with their own hands, they'd find a way to trade for it: a thousand board feet of milled redwood for a horse; two kegs of nails for a roll of sheep wire.

The homesteader economy grew out of the terrain and the homesteaders and their descendents logged the redwoods and hardwoods. They hunted the wilds, fished the creeks and ocean and, if they were good enough shots, they harvested supper out of the sky. They built freehold spreads and they raised sheep and cattle, apples, plums, hops, dry land grapes, corn, barley, berries, and melons. They grew hay, raised horses and pigs, chickens, geese, ducks, and, oftentimes, they raised up and married off a child in the same house they'd been born in and the same house their grandparents, with the help of their neighbors, had built with the materials at hand. And the mountain people were Anderson Valley because what is a locality without a collection of stories rooted in the local terrain, personalities, and lifeways? A real incident becomes a rumor and a rumor becomes folklore. If told through enough generations, or if the initial incident "says" something important, folklore becomes legend.

Needing money, at the age of twenty-four I took my first job logging the big-tree redwoods. Back then among city transplants there was much talk about a movement "back to the land," but none of my friends thought I'd take the notion that far or, as my Irish grandma used to say regarding anything outlandish, that far "beyond the pale." But I did. I'd always loved being outdoors, the money I made working in the woods was real good next to what I was used to and, most of all, the various jobs I did were fun. Because in the woods there was no pecking order, I got to call my own shots and my new tribe became my muse. The woodsmen had their own kind of lingo, their own ways of seeing and doing things, their own code of honor and sense of humor.

Most of all, they seemed to have a limitless number of stories to tell, especially when they'd gather in a saloon after work and one fellah's story would remind another fellah of another story and that would light up a bulb in somebody else's head. Just like when I was a little boy, I'd hear erupting from the midnight poker table torrents of uproarious hillbilly laughter. They'd break into the laughter that springs from a shared reality, shared values, know-hows and done-thats. And what started off as a story about a wily coyote might lead to a dozen stories about grouse and otters, skunks and bobcats.

Though I only worked for logging outfits for seven seasons, I've never left the woods. Before I "retired" to devote myself to writing, I'd spent thirty-two years logging and wood-cutting, ranching and farming in Anderson Valley. My book isn't about how I made my way back home from the war. How I did that, I think, goes without saying. Many other combat veterans have covered that ground quite well and I had no desire to add anything on that count. What I wanted to write was a collection of short stories that amount to a love letter to old Anderson Valley and to some of the old-timers who helped make it what it was and who helped me become who I am.

A GLOSSARY OF LUMBERJACK LINGO

(Author's note: While only seven of the twenty-four stories included here are about logging per se, and though not all of the words and phrases in the glossary below appear in the book, I thought it would be useful and fun to explain some of the lingo.)

ancient redwoods (coastal). Once considered to be the oldest and largest living things on earth, they are neither. Rarely more than one thousand years old, ancient redwoods do at least retain their title as the world's *tallest* living things, some of them topping out at over three hundred seventy feet.

angle of repose. The maximum degree of steepness a particular type of earth can achieve. Clay can stand steeper than sand, and rock can stand steeper than clay.

ass over teakettle. Tumbling head over heels down a canyonside. Often provides rubberneckers with a spectacular sight.

back-cut. The final cut made to fell a tree. See also **face-cut.**

banana peel. A loose flap of redwood bark lying wet side up. Also, a piece of bark that sticks to the spikes of your boots and causes you to tumble **ass over teakettle.**

barber chair. What's left standing after a **timber faller** accidentally causes a standing redwood tree to split up the middle and topple to earth in two pieces.

bar-buckle. Setting a **choker** to a stump or to a standing tree in order to get a **log** to lift, roll, or pivot.

bed. Pushed-up mounds of loose dirt set one behind the other that act as a shock absorber for the trunk of a giant felled redwood impacting the forest floor.

bevel-cut. The second, angled cut of a **face-cut.** Also called the bottom-cut. The cut used to complete the **pie.**

billy goat. A particularly agile and stubborn lumberjack.

the bite. Anyplace that might get you killed.

bonanza. From the Latin word "bonus," meaning "good." In Castilian Spanish, the word means "fair weather" and, by extension, "prosperity." In the redwoods a bonanza is a particularly valuable **bonus, jackpot, pumpkin,** or **windfall.**

bonus. Good fortune. For example, two trunks growing out of one **butt,** two or more **logs** rigged with just one **choker,** a **windfall** tree. When the woods boss provides the crew with an after-work Saturday ice chest full of beer.

boom. A steel-girder tower.

boomer. A modern-day one-donkey, one-blanket prospector. Some boomers are after a **bonanza,** others wish to save enough money to escape the life, and still others just love the rambling ways. "I spent all my money on booze and women," an old washed-up boomer might sorrowfully admit. "The rest I just wasted."

bound up. Getting the bar of your chainsaw stuck in its cut.

branch trail. A **skid trail** forking off from a **trunk trail** and leading into a side canyon. See also **Christmas tree.**

breaking bark. When upon impact a felled giant redwood sheds its bark and covers the canyonside with **banana peels.** Or when, while being skidded, the bark your **choker** is biting into separates from the rest and flies off of the nose of the **log.** Also, banging into a tree, a stump, or a log, as in "barking a shin." To fall off a log.

breaking rigging. Causing a steel cable to snap in two pieces and recoil like a broken thread.

breaking stump. While jacking (see **tree jack**) or **pounding wedges**, shattering the stump instead of lifting the tree.

bridle. Two or more **chokers** connected end to end to make a loop big enough to reach around a giant log.

buck. To slice a tree length into **logs**. Hence, to go up against difficulty or authority.

buckskin. A barkless and decomposing stump, log, or **windfall**. Named for its color.

bull. A lie or a silly idea. Conversely, an earnest proclamation. Also, a particularly strong and stubborn lumberjack.

bullbuck. A boss of timber fallers. More generally, a woods boss.

bulldozer. A big tractor that is equipped with a cutting/digging blade and a forty-ton winch, and is propelled on tracks.

bull-line. In the big trees, an inch-and-a-half-thick, one-hundred-foot-long steel rope equipped with a hook that is spooled in and out of the winch fastened to the rear of a **bulldozer**.

bull-whacker. The drover of draft animals used to skid logs, be they oxen (castrated bulls), mules, or horses.

bumping knots. Using a chainsaw to remove the limbs from a **log**.

butt. Where a tree leaves the ground. The bottom end of a **log**.

caddywhompus. A thing, person, or idea that's bent out of shape.

calks. The spiked boots worn by lumberjacks to gain traction in the bark while walking logs.

carriage. The collection of rollers, gears, and brakes that carries the **haul-back line** up and down the **skyline**.

Cat logging. Using **bulldozers** to **skid logs**.

catskinner. A bulldozer operator. Named for the Caterpillar Corporation's brand of bulldozers. There's more than one way to skin a Cat.

cherry-pick. To rig a choker high up in a standing tree in order to gain enough leverage to pull it away from its **lean.** Also, to **cream.**

choker. A length of steel rope with a loop ("eye") on one end, a steel slug ("nubbin") on the other, and a "sliding bell" in between. Loop the cable around a log, fit the nubbin into the bell like a button into a buttonhole, pull on the eye, and the cable grabs the log by "choking" it.

chokersetter. A log rigger. He who **slings steel,** pulls **bull-line,** and organizes **skids.**

chopping timber. Felling trees.

Christmas tree. A mountain is shaped like a human hand propped up on its thumb and fingertips. The fingers reach to the main creeks and are called sub-ridges, and the spaces between the fingers are called side canyons. The **skid trails** running up and down the tops of the sub-ridges are called **trunk trails.** The skid trails forking off from them and advancing more or less level into the side canyons are called **branch trails.** Seen from across the main canyon, the networks of trails covering the fingers look like stick drawings of Christmas trees.

clear-cut. To fell all of the trees in the forest thicker than a specified diameter. In terms of the production of premium redwood lumber, to destroy a forest for at least one hundred years.

college educated. Somebody who thinks too much. Somebody severely injured or someone who, by escaping injury, has been warned, as in, "If he keeps that up he's gonna get himself a college education in *ah-shit.*"

commotion. What happens when you fell a tree, **skid a log, break rigging,** or when a logger or **bulldozer** tumbles down a canyonside.

corncob. A tree with an extraordinary number of limbs. Named for the corncob-like appearance of its de-limbed **crown.**

cowboy. To lasso a log with one clean movement of the arms.

cream. To take the best and leave the rest.

creamer. A greedy/lazy timber faller or rigger.

crowns. The limby tops of trees.

cut off. To accidentally cut through all of the wood holding a tree erect. To lose control.

dead-centered. A tree that lands exactly where you wanted, hitting the bull's-eye. Getting drilled by a falling tree or by a limb falling out of the **crown**.

dead-tops. Living trees with **snags** balanced on top of them. Sometimes the dead-tops were caused by a lightning strike, but usually they are the result of a prolonged drought. Dead-tops are often surrounded by a number of living **leaders**, fresh trunks grown to replace the dead one, and one ancient redwood can have as many as a dozen tops. Because of their pronounced if sometimes inscrutable **leans**, dead-tops are tricky to fell and, because of the possibility of chunks of deadwood tumbling to earth from their decayed crowns, nobody pounds wedges into a redwood with a dead-top.

decks. **Logs** stockpiled on landings. Lay five logs side by side on the ground and where they come together will be four "saddles." Fill those saddles with logs and then build the next level with three saddles, and so on. Built in the shape of pyramids, log decks are notoriously unstable and nobody on foot spends any time in front of or behind them except **landing chasers**, and then only when they have to.

dog's hair. Tall, skinny baby redwoods that are felled and used to make wood chips or to manufacture third-rate lumber. Also called **pecker poles**.

donkey. Slang for a **yarder**. Back when yarders were driven by steam, they were so weak that you couldn't properly say they had horsepower; they only had "donkey power."

donkey puncher. A **yarder** operator.

duff. The organic litter that carpets a forest floor.

eager beaver. A lumberjack with discipline and ambition.

easy does it. Back off. Find another way to make a living.

face-cut. Made with a **top-cut** and a **bevel-cut**, the wedge of wood removed from the "face" of a tree so that, by giving the trunk a void to fall into, it aims the tree at its **lay**.

goose pen. A redwood that has been hollowed out by successive fires. Named by the pioneers who used the largest of them to corral livestock. Goose pens can be exceedingly easy, or very difficult and dangerous, to fell.

gunning. Using your **face-** and **back-cuts** to aim a tree at a precise point on the compass.

gut-gougers. The spearlike remains of broken limbs still jutting from logs. Also called **stobs**.

guylines. The inch-and-a-half-thick steel cables used to hold a **yarder** upright during **skidding** operations. Extending backward from the machine at five and seven o'clock, the guys are anchored to hopefully "immovable" stumps called **tail hitches**.

guy tower. The tower on a **yarder** from which the **guylines** extend.

gyppo. An owner-operator. An independent contractor. Fairly or not, known for shady practices.

handy. Skillful. Also, something easy to get to or, as often as not, not easy to get to.

haul-back line. The one-thousand-foot-long steel cable that rides in a **carriage** under the **skyline** and is used to fly logs up and out of the canyon and onto the **landing**.

haul-road. A road for logging trucks. Also, in **high-lead logging**, the scuffed-up area beneath the **skyline**.

hay wire. The two-hundred-foot-long spaghetti cables that, hooked end to end, are used to run out a **yarder's skyline**. Also called **pilot lines**.

headache bar. The steel canopy of a **bulldozer** that functions as a roll bar and protects the operator from falling objects. Also, a hardhat.

head-lean. A tree's **lean** relative to the pitch of a canyonside, that is, either uphill or downhill. Because of sliding ground, nearly all trees **lean** at least somewhat down the hill.

heel boom. The "boom" is the steel-girder tower that reels out the **skyline.** "Heel" describes the boom's ability to swing one way or the other in order to deposit logs on the **landing.**

highballer. Somebody getting while the getting is good. Alternatively, somebody who loves his work.

high grade. To harvest only the most mature, crowded, and flawed trees. To practice **sustained yield.**

high-lead logging. Skidding logs under a **skyline.**

Hindu. The connectors used to attach **hay wires** end to end.

hitch. To set a **choker** in a particular way in order to achieve a desired result.

holding wood. The narrow stripe of uncut wood left between the **face-** and **back-cuts.** Holding wood functions as a hinge and guides the tree toward its **lay.**

the hole. The bottom of a canyon. The steep canyonside located below a **yarder.**

hook tender. A **yarder** boss.

jackpot. A **windfall.** A big tree that is easy to fell and **save out.** For a **chokersetter,** a thick **lay** of **logs,** especially one located far away from a **landing** and blessed with afternoon shade.

jackrabbit. Somebody always in a hurry.

jaggers. Steel cables are actually ropes made up of dozens of individual wires woven and re-woven together. This allows them to bend and stretch when put under pressure. As the cables wear out, individual wires break and stick out from the body of the cable like tiny switchblades. Log riggers wear cotton instead of leather gloves so that when they grab and pull on a cable the jaggers snag in the cotton and announce themselves. Even so, getting puncture wounds from jaggers is an inevitable part of the job. When a jagger stabs you in the joint of a knuckle, the pain can last for weeks.

Jill-poke. Any loose-lying limb that causes injury or death. Supposedly named after a particularly ugly lumber camp prostitute named Jill.

kick. Using a **choker** to get a log to go around a stump, a **stander**, or another type of obstruction.

landing. An excavated flat spot used to clean up, sort, and store **logs** until they are loaded aboard trucks.

landing chaser. A chainsaw man who **bucks** and limbs **logs** on landings.

landslide. Ground standing at the exact **angle of repose**.

lay. The precise location on the forest floor where a **timber faller** aims a tree. Also, the often precarious positions logs hold on a canyonside.

lead. A forest's lean, caused by the prevailing winds. Not all trees lean with the lead.

leaders. See **stump shoots, stobs**. Also, limbs that morph into tree trunks.

lean. If left to gravity, the direction in which a tree would fall. Divided into the **head-lean** (uphill or downhill) and the **side-lean** (to the left or right).

lickety-split. Wasting no moves.

limb-locked. Two or more trees whose interlocking limbs prevent one from being felled without simultaneously felling the other or others.

logs. De-limbed lengths of tree trunks usually **bucked** in multiples of eight and ten feet. Common-sized logs are sixteen, twenty, thirty-six, and forty feet long. At the sawmill, to make dimensioned lumber, a forty-foot log can be made into four ten-foot lengths or five eight-foot lengths. Or, if beams and planks are desired, the logs can be kept long. For instance, a thirty-six-footer can be divided to make twenty-foot-long beams and sixteen-foot-long sheets of siding.

lone wolf. A **single-jacking timber faller** who never talks to anyone on the crew. Like an apparition, he disappears into his strip at dawn and, once the afternoon winds turn contrary, he disappears back out of it.

long logs. Logs between twenty and forty feet long. Also, tree lengths or logs that, for reasons of safety or convenience, have been left longer than forty feet.

mule. An extraordinarily strong and stubborn lumberjack.

old growth. A mature stand of trees. Most redwoods achieve their maximum height within two or three hundred years.

old-timers. Pioneer stock. Pre-chainsaw and pre-TV. Yeomen, hillbillies, mountaineers. A type of redneck.

OSHA. The Occupational Safety and Health Administration.

outlaw tree. A giant redwood that cannot be felled without shattering into worthless **toothpicks** and so is left standing. More generally, any tree that is more trouble to fell than it's worth.

pecker poles. See **dog's hair.**

pie. The wedge of wood removed from the "face" of a tree trunk to create a void for the tree to fall into. See also **face-cut.**

pilot lines. Hay wire, straw-lines.

pioneer. What the homesteaders were before they unhitched their wagons and built their spreads. To **punch skid trails** or roads into unmarked canyons.

pistol butts. As the soil of a steep canyonside slips toward the creek, standing trees compensate by bending their trunks skyward. Named for the shape they take when viewed from the **side-hill**, you can walk atop the trunk of a pistol butt. Because of their extreme **leans** and the unpredictable types of **commotion** they cause when they hit the forest floor, most **timber fallers** dread felling them, while others see them as a form of entertainment.

plumb. Something standing perfectly erect, like a tree or a flagpole. Hence, "plumb loco" or "plumb stupid." Also, using a dangling straight edge, like an ax handle, to calculate the precise **lean** of a **stander.**

plumb lucky. Fortunate to be still alive and kicking.

plumb stuck. Getting the bar of your chainsaw hopelessly **bound up** in a tree or a log. Also, getting a **bulldozer** high-centered atop a stump or sunk to its belly pan in mud.

poach. So long as you waste nothing and don't get greedy, taking what is rightfully yours, whether wild game or the logs left behind by the timber companies that are just wasting away.

popping stump. When a tree stump being used as a yarder's **tail hitch** breaks loose from the ground and flies free. In the worst case, popping stumps can cause a **yarder** to topple over into the canyonside.

pounding wedges. Swinging your ax-head to drive plastic wedges into the **back-cut** of a **stander**. In the big trees, a one-inch-tall wedge driven to its head into a back-cut will "swing" the top of the tree a number of feet. Wedges are used to lift trees out of their **leans** and to tip them toward their **lays**.

pumpkin. A giant redwood that is easy to fell.

pumpkin patch. A timber faller's Shangri-La. For a **chokersetter**, a thick lay of logs far from a **landing** and resting in full shade.

punching trail. Using a **bulldozer** to build a **haul-road** or a **skid trail**.

ridge runner. Because working on a ridge top is far easier than working on a steep canyonside, a lazy lumberjack.

roll. To set a choker so that it lifts and twists a log up and over a stump or another type of obstruction.

running hay wire. Monster-stepping the shouldered ends of two **straw-lines** down into the bottom of a canyon (**the hole**).

Russian coupling. A small triangle of **holding wood** left between two logs to keep them from separating and tumbling down the canyon. If done right, Russian couplings are easily broken when one or the other of the joined logs is rigged and tugged on with the winch. If, as is usually the case, the logs are suspended above the earth, Russian couplings done wrong can also break under the weight and vibrations of a chokersetter walking the logs, and so the practice is outlawed. Although for reasons of personal safety log buckers still occasionally make Russian Couplings, it is customary for them to alert the rigging crew as to their precise locations.

saving it out. Felling a giant redwood without breaking it, except for its very top, which, because of the tree's great height, always shatters upon impact. A **timber faller**'s proudest achievement.

a sharp stick in the eye. In terms of gruesome injuries, a logger's second worst nightmare (the first being a sharp stick in the balls).

shotgun. To fell a whole bunch of trees at one time, as in dominoes. Causes a great **commotion.** The world record for the most redwoods ever shotgunned probably rests at about twenty.

show. A logging operation. Named mostly for its entertainment value.

side-hill. Standing at the same elevation as something. Felling trees side-hill means dropping them so they land perpendicular to the slope.

side-lean. The **lean** of a tree to the left or right as measured from directly up or down the hill.

sidewinder. See Jill-poke.

single-jacker. A **timber faller** who works alone.

skid. To move logs from the forest floor to the **landing.** Also, one round-trip made by a Cat or a **haul-back line.**

skid trail. An excavated dirt path cut into a mountainside that is wide enough to support the weight of a **bulldozer.** See also **Christmas tree.**

skyline. The thousand-foot-long cable spooled out from the winch of a **yarder,** threaded through the tower, and run out down the canyonside to a **tail hitch.**

slick as snot. See **banana peel.**

slinging steel. Setting **choker.**

sluff. The loose dirt, rocks, root-wads, and chunks of wood lining the bottom edge of a freshly excavated **skid trail.**

sluff off. To break or peel away. A kind way of telling a fellah to get lost.

snags. Dead, brittle standing trees. Sometimes beautiful to look at, snags are very dangerous to fell or to disturb in any way.

springboards. On steep ground, two-by-six or two-by-eight oak planks notched into the downhill side of a tree, which the timber faller stands on while felling the tree.

standers. Standing trees.

stobs. See **gut-gougers.** Also, **stump shoots** that, denied sun and nutrients, grow no larger than poles and eventually die.

straight hook. To place the hook of the **bull-line** in one location, twist onto it all of the eyes of your set **chokers,** get out of the way, and not have to touch the hook again until the Cat returns from the **landing** for its next **skid.**

straw-lines. See **hay wire.**

strips. Because, to avoid felling trees on people, **timber fallers** need room to operate, a mountain is broken down into sections called "strips," one for each timber faller. Usually four or more tree lengths wide and reaching from the creek to the ridge top or to the **haul-road,** this strip, this territory, is inviolable while a timber faller is working on it. To step foot on any part of a faller's strip while he is working is considered to be extremely bad manners.

stumped. A bulldozer high-centered atop a stump. Getting your saw hopelessly stuck in the **butt** of a **stander.** More generally, not knowing what to do.

stump shoots. Felling redwoods only gives their roots haircuts. Among the most rapidly growing coniferous trees on earth, felled redwoods immediately send up new shoots (**leaders**), some of which become new trees. There are redwood stumps from the 1850s that have regenerated shoots now standing seven feet thick and over two hundred feet tall.

sucker clump. A ring of redwood **stump shoots.** Sucker clumps are often **limb-locked** and the trees always **lean** away from each other. Along with **pistol butts** and **dog's hair,** sucker clumps are considered to be the dregs of the redwood forest.

sucking wedges. When a tree falls over backward in spite of the wedges driven into its **back-cut.**

sustained yield. The practice among wise small-holders of harvesting only the growth of a forest and so keeping their inventory of lumber either constant or increasing. Also, a corporate and Forest Service PR catchphrase.

Swede. Two chokers interlaced to make them twice as strong. A Swede is the only **hitch** that will easily break a **bull-line.**

tail hitch. An "immovable" stump notched to anchor a **skyline** or a **guyline.**

timber faller. Someone who "fells" timber. Called "fallers" because you can't very well call them "timber fellers" without possibly mistaking them for somebody low-down like a **chokersetter** or a **landing chaser.**

tipping point. While pounding wedges, the point where the weight of your tree crosses its center of gravity. You know you have passed the tipping point when your wedges start driving easy. Also, while felling with just a chainsaw, the instant your **stander** is indisputably headed to earth, and the signal for you to run away.

toothpicks. The long, useless shards of improperly felled and shattered redwoods. A fellah who makes too many toothpicks is not long on the job.

top-cut. The first cut made to fell a tree. See also **face-cut** and **pie.**

train. To use three **chokers** to move two **logs** end to end, one trailing the other.

tree jack. A blue-steel-heavy hydraulic jack adapted to lift standing trees. Usually built with the capacity to lift forty tons, they are fit into boxes notched below the **back-cut** and can be used in pairs or in a series.

trunk trail. A **skid trail** running up and down the top of a sub-ridge. See also **Christmas tree.**

virgin redwoods. A nineteenth-century booster's slogan, as in, "Y'all come Out West and make your fortunes in the virgin redwoods."

washing. A felled tree that brushes by a **stander** on its way to the forest floor "washes" it of its limbs. During a **clear-cut** operation, since all of the bigger **standers** are coming down anyway, and because redwood limbs usually break off flush with the trunk, a **timber faller** will often deliberately wash trees to save himself the trouble of having to **bump knots.**

watching out. Keeping your mind on your surroundings and knowing what's around and above you. Not muttering in your head or daydreaming.

widowmaker. A limb falling out of the canopy of a tree that **dead-centers** you.

wild and wooly. A sheep that has left the herd and so has escaped shearing. Hence, somebody reckless and unpredictable; a person who cannot or will not follow orders or the rules of etiquette. Also, a grand adventure.

windfall. A tree knocked over by the wind. Since you don't have to fell the tree in order to get logs out of it, windfalls are considered to be easy money. A **bonus** or **jackpot.**

woods gods. Because even the most seasoned lumberjack occasionally gets killed or maimed, and since there is no such thing as luck, whatever it is that keeps you alive and kicking.

Woody Woodpecker. A combination **billy goat, jackrabbit, bull, mule,** and **eager beaver.** Also, a type of hardhat.

yarder. A machine used for **skidding logs.** Operates like a fishing pole reeling in fish.

young buck. Somebody with more strength, ambition, and appetite than experience and sense.

HEYDAY INSTITUTE

Since its founding in 1974, Heyday Books has occupied a unique niche in the publishing world, specializing in books that foster an understanding of the history, literature, art, environment, social issues, and culture of California and the West. We are a 501(c)(3) nonprofit organization based in Berkeley, California, serving a wide range of people and audiences.

We are grateful for the generous funding we've received for our publications and programs during the past year from foundations and more than three hundred individual donors. Major supporters include:

Anonymous; Audubon California; Judy Avery; Barnes & Noble bookstores; BayTree Fund; B.C.W. Trust III; S. D. Bechtel, Jr. Foundation; Fred & Jean Berensmeier; Book Club of California; Butler Koshland Fund; California State Coastal Conservancy; California State Library; Candelaria Fund; Columbia Foundation; Community Futures Collective; Compton Foundation, Inc.; Malcolm Cravens Foundation; Federated Indians of Graton Rancheria; Fleishhacker Foundation; Wallace Alexander Gerbode Foundation; Richard & Rhoda Goldman Fund; Marion E. Greene; Evelyn & Walter Haas, Jr. Fund: Walter & Elise Haas Fund; James Irvine Foundation; George Frederick Jewett Foundation; Marty & Pamela Krasney; Guy Lampard & Suzanne Badenhoop; LEF Foundation; Dolores Zohrab Liebmann Fund; Michael McCone; National Endowment for the Arts; National Park Service; Philanthropic Ventures Foundation; Alan Rosenus; San Francisco Foundation; William Saroyan Foundation: Seaver Institute; Sandy Cold Shapero; Skirball Foundation; Stanford University; Orin Starn; Swinerton Family Fund; Thendara Foundation; Tom White; and Harold & Alma White Memorial Fund.

For more information about Heyday Institute, our publications and programs, please visit our website at www.heydaybooks.com.

Other BayTree Books

BayTree Books, a project of Heyday Institute, gives voice to a full range of California experience and personal stories.

Archy Lee: A California Fugitive Slave Case (2008)
Rudolph M. Lapp

Where Light Takes Its Color from the Sea: A California Notebook (2008)
James D. Houston

Tree Barking: A Memoir (2008)
Nesta Rovina

Ticket to Exile: A Memoir (2007)
Adam David Miller

Fast Cars and Frybread: Reports from the Rez (2007)
Gordon Johnson

The Oracles: My Filipino Grandparents in America (2006)
Pati Navalta Poblete

BAYTREE